Computerising Work

People, Systems Design and Workplace Relations

LESLIE WILLCOCKS AND
DAVID MASON

Paradigm

Paradigm Publishing
Avenue House
131 Holland Park Avenue
London W11 4UT

© Leslie Willcocks and David Mason, 1987

First published November 1987

British Library Cataloguing in Publication Data

Willcocks, Leslie
  Computerising work : people, systems
  design and workplace relations.
  1. Automation 2. Work
  I. Title II. Mason, David
  306'.36   HD6331

  ISBN 0-948825-65-0

Typeset by Mathematical Composition Setters Ltd, Salisbury.

Printed in Great Britain by Hollen Street Press, Slough

For Doris Louise

Contents

CONTENTS

Abbreviations

CAD	computer-aided design
CAM	computer-aided manufacture
CIM	computer-integrated manufacturing
CNC	computer numerically controlled
CTS	carpal tunnel syndrome
DNC	direct numerical control
EPOS	electronic point of sale
FMS	flexible manufacturing system
HR	human resources
IR	industrial relations
IS	information system
IT	information technology
MIS	management information system
NT	new technology
OA	office automation
OD	organisation development
QWL	quality of work life
RSI	repetitive strain injury
STS	socio-technical systems
VDT	visual display terminal
VDU	visual display unit

Acknowledgements

We are very grateful for the assistance received from many people and institutions. Particular thanks go to John Mingers, Mary Mather and Colin Knapp for reading earlier drafts of chapters; their comments helped to strengthen the book at several points. Discussions with Annabelle Mark, and the further information and contacts she provided, proved very valuable in helping us to clarify our ideas on computer-based health care and medical records systems. As a practitioner himself, Peter O'Hara was particularly helpful on developing computer systems for the social services. Thanks also to Julie Norton for her friendship and support.

Our primary intellectual debts are acknowledged in the text and in the references and guide to further reading at the end of the book. We owe much to countless students, trainees, managers and employees who have attended our courses or lectures, whom we have interviewed, or for whom we have done consultancy or training in introducing computer systems into workplaces. It is not possible to mention them all by name, but they provided valuable information, allowed us to try out our ideas and provided a sometimes very stern testing of these against the 'reality principle' and their own experiences of organisations introducing and using computer technology. Many will see that their comments were not made in vain, but are an important part of the fabric and spirit of the finished book.

We would also like to acknowledge the essential and efficient services provided by the librarians of the Work Research Unit, Polytechnic of the South Bank, City University and North East London Polytechnic. At this point it is usual to thank a typist without peer for her unflagging drafting and redrafting of the several editions of the manuscript as it was being developed to its final form. As a partial sign of the times, perhaps, 'she' was in fact a 'they', and we word-processed it ourselves.

Finally, the authors and publisher are grateful to those cited for permission to reproduce or quote the following material:

> figure from Desanctis G. and Courtney J.—Toward friendly user MIS implementation. *Communications of the ACM*, 1983, **26**, No. 10. reproduced by permission of *Communications of the ACM*.

ACKNOWLEDGEMENTS

Every attempt has been made to trace and acknowledge the original source of material contained in this book. Where the attempt has been unsuccessful, the publishers would be pleased to hear from the author or publisher to rectify the omission.

Introduction

This book addresses a wide audience: practising managers in the private and public sectors; those responsible for, involved in, or affected by computer projects; and students on degree, postgraduate or professional courses covering the subjects of organisational behaviour, systems analysis and design, personnel management, computing, or industrial relations. The audience is as wide as the potentially massive applicability of computer technologies to work organisations. People requiring training for the IT workplace, as well as those already operating in a computerised environment, will find this book relevant and useful.

Our major focus is described by the phrase 'human aspects of computer systems' but it is not restricted to a study of the computer–user interface by which this subject is commonly understood —both in computing courses and the advertising literature and design practice of major computing companies. Throughout we seek to make explicit the abiding importance of 'the human factor' in all aspects of computer system design, implementation and operation. To do so requires a breaking down and reordering of old subject boundaries. This is a proper development if pervasive IT technologies are to be adequately viewed, designed and 'managed in' to effective running. We have given a privileged place in our book to the theme of organisational politics. Chapter 1 provides a detailed overview of a broadened understanding of human aspects of computer-based systems and places the politics of computerisation at its core.

There is a story put around by those who know their computers that by 1990 nearly every garage in the UK will contain a Visual Display Terminal, a great deal of software, and associated equipment and furniture. Those believing in the irresistible rise and efficacy of information technology (IT) are then invited to enquire why this will be so. The explanation goes something like this. In 1988, impressed by advertising and wanting to stay up to date, every British household will buy a computer; 1989 will be spent trying to find a use for them; and by 1990, having found no use, or finding the machines more trouble than they are worth and taking up valuable space, most households will abandon them and put them in the garage.

The prediction is not serious, but it contains a kernel of truth. It forms a useful corrective to the more optimistic noises made about the information technology revolution, and, transferred to what has already happened in many UK work organisations, it goes to the heart of this book. IT has not been an unmitigated success story in the UK in the 1980's, even if it has hardly been a failure. One part of this has been the slow adoption of IT in the UK relative to its major competitors. An authoritative report points to some of the main reasons. These include: fear of new technology amongst non-technical people, poor selling by IT experts who are in the best position to promote the message, a lack of education reflected in the inability of business and IT specialists to work together and understand each others' roles, and lack of UK government effort to provide grants for technical innovation or convince top managers to take IT to their business hearts.[1] British management emerges rather badly from the report, being marked by confusion about the potential of IT and an absence of IT know-how at senior management levels. However these factors reveal only part of the story and a much more detailed analysis is needed—provided in this book by Chapter 2: 'Resistance to Change'.

More central to our focus are the problems experienced in organisations where computer technology is being, or already has been, applied. These difficulties emerge from extensive research and case studies by ourselves and others, as well as our own consultancy and training experiences—all reviewed critically in this book, and used to underpin our points and argument. Two examples to indicate the scale of problems will suffice at this stage.

A 1984 study for the Department of Trade and Industry and Institute of Administrative Management found the IT bill of companies to be £5 billion per annum and rising. Of this an estimated 20% was wasted expenditure.[2] Interestingly the survey found that a major reason for IT expenditure was that companies hoped to cut their workforces rather than increase output.

In the public sector the Comptroller and Auditor General (CAG) has produced several reports highly critical of IT applications in the Inland Revenue, the Social Security System, the National Health Service, and Civil Service generally. In the Inland Revenue, a major computer project was abandoned in 1985, leading to losses of £16.5 millions. The failure was blamed on weaknesses in project management, design and staffing. Particular problems emerged in the management of human resources. Thus the Inland Revenue underestimated the number of staff needed to complete the project successfully. A general shortage of staff with IT skills was also identified. This shortfall was filled by using consultants who on average charged over four times the rate of equivalent Revenue staff, but whose specialist skills were rarely fully utilised.[3] In reviewing the IT performance of government departments generally the CAG found: a critical shortfall of specialist data processing staff of 25%; lack of IT strategy; civil service managers ill-equipped in IT project management skills; lack of IT training for existing staff; underestimation of the difficulties in implementing large-scale IT projects; lack of ways of consulting unions affected; and problems deriving from inter-departmental politics.[4]

We do not argue that all IT applications have largely failed. However, the full potential of IT has too often not been fulfilled in UK organisations. The reasons for this are invariably complex and manifold. But in this book we emphasise the human issues that have raised themselves repeatedly in our experiences of computerisation across organisations large and small, commercial and non-commercial, public and private sector, service and manufacturing based.

These factors, to which we ascribe the phrase 'human aspects of computer systems', have been neglected, or received restricted understanding, in many previous analyses and, more importantly, in actual systems design and implementation practices. One strand of our book analyses through numerous examples how and why this has so often happened. At the core of our finding is that computer-based systems are too frequently designed and implemented with little concern for the social, organisational and political contexts in which they are supposed to operate. The frequent result of this lack of initial and detailed concern is that human problems emerge at later stages when the system becomes operational, and reveal themselves in sub-optimal systems performance. A further strand in our book is positive and partially prescriptive, emphasising human issues and the consequences of their neglect, but also discussing many ways in which this neglect of human aspects in computer projects can be remedied.

This more positive emphasis really begins in Chapter 3 where we point out the importance of human resource planning and of the inclusion of personnel practioners at early stages in computer projects, possibly in redefined roles. Chapter 4 then reviews a range of different systems analysis and design perspectives and methodologies, and argues (though not without reservation) in favour of those approaches that tend to put human beings explicitly in the centre of analysis and design activity rather than its periphery. Chapter 5 extends this approach into job and work organisation design. In chapter 6 we elaborate the important areas with which a phrase like 'human aspects of computing' is more commonly identified, namely the design of VDU screens, dialogue, workstations, and immediate computer environment. In chapter 7 we argue that industrial relations, usually considered a specialist area for managerial activity, is in fact intimately bound up with systems design and implementation practices. Finally in Chapter 8 we bring together the main threads of the book and provide a political–cultural contingencies approach to managing implementation.

The design, introduction and running of computer-based systems in work organisations now has a substantial history. In reviewing critically this history and experience and drawing lessons from them, our aim is to advance the possibility that failures are not doomed to be repeated, and that human aspects of computerising work, as reconsidered here, will receive the more central attention it deserves, not only in training and education for IT but also in systems practice itself.

REFERENCES

1. Griffiths P. (ed.) *The Role of Information Management in Competitive Success* (Pergamon Infotech) April 1987.
2. Bevington T. and Hand M. *The Barriers and Opportunities from Information Technology—A Management Perspective* (A. T. Kearney for DTI and IAM) 1984.
3. *Comptroller and Auditor General—Inland Revenue: Control of Major Developments in Use of Information Technology* (National Audit Office) January 1987.
4. *Information Technology in the Civil Service*; IT series no. 5, HM Treasury (HMSO) March 1984.

CHAPTER I

Systems Design, People and Politics—An Overview

'All systems are go.'—Advertisement for the UK Stock Exchange October 1986.[1]

'From a technical point of view it was a sweet and lovely and beautiful job.'[2]

'The success of the system from the user's viewpoint is *guaranteed—if the system is used.*'—Statement in a computer manual.

INTRODUCTION

On Monday morning, 27 October 1986 the British Stock Exchange launched its new methods of dealing—the so-called Big Bang. Some £80 millions had been spent on the two-year development of the Stock Exchange Automated Quotation (SEAQ) and related computer systems. These were the centrepiece of the new structure, forming the computerised price and dealing information system basic to all transactions in the revolutionised stock market. At 8.29 a.m. an alarm bell rang as the subsidiary information display system—TOPIC—broke down. The entire SEAQ was suspended for over an hour. Breakdowns and suspensions continued intermittently throughout the week and into the next month. All systems were definitely *not* go.

The best publicised technological blunder of the mid-1980s turned out to be the result of a massive underestimation of the volume and timing of computer usage. The existing TOPIC system had been improved to handle a 50% increase in demand. Integrated with SEAQ, it faced a 100% increase on the first morning, and higher than anticipated volumes over the next few weeks, as people switched on merely out of *curiosity* at the new system.

There emerged other aspects of human behaviour that had been neglected in systems design. As TOPIC breakdowns recurred, it became obvious that the possibility of *regular* massive early morning loading had not been considered. But in fact it was quite rational for all market dealers to want to consult, and get their prices on the system as early in the day as possible.

Other facts emerged as Big Bang unfolded throughout November

1986. Speaking at a conference on electronic financial services, one security expert from BIS Applied Systems said that highly paid technicians brought in at short notice to prepare systems for Big Bang could become a liability when their services were no longer required. He had found examples of programmers planting 'logic bombs'—software that would stop the system—as a safeguard against dismissal.[3]

Software design sometimes failed to anticipate user errors or behaviour. Thus the SEAQ system reported one deal of five million shares in Grand Metropolitan—a stock normally trading about three million shares daily. In fact a careless trader had pressed a 'millions' button, instead of the one marked 'thousands', but the system had no way of detecting or correcting this. In another case, Exchange technicians spent a week looking for a quote input problem at two large share-dealing firms. In the end they found the cause related to dealers disconnecting their terminals by switching off at the mains, instead of following a more tedious, but technically required, 'logging off' procedure.

The amazing thing may be that SEAQ worked as well as it did, given the short development period imposed. Michael Newman, the deputy director of information systems at the Stock Exchange, was widely quoted as saying he had needed not two, but four years to build a really rugged and powerful system. But perhaps the human factor intervened here as well, with systems imperfections resulting from low expectations of success amongst designers. As one stockbroker commented in August 1986:

> 'Our computer specialist is really very good. It's just that he refuses to be constrained by what he sees as an artificial deadline like Big Bang'.[4]

These are just a few examples of the often unexpected ways in which human factors intervene in the development and running of computer systems. However, the subject of this book is much larger than this. A central theme is the seriously limited definition of 'human aspects' operating in many computer systems projects. Of related concern is the degree to which the intervention of human factors, and their often detrimental impact on systems effectiveness can go on being regarded as so 'unexpected' and 'surprising'. As will emerge, this does not have to be the case.

The present chapter serves as an introduction to locating computer projects in their proper human and organisational contexts. We argue that traditional systems design approaches have tended to underplay 'people' factors in design. If this neglect has always been inappropriate, it is becoming dangerously so for the computer technologies and applications of the late 1980s. An alternative basis for design philosophy is proposed. 'Technological determinism' is then presented as a very limiting perspective on the possible relationships between people and machines. Thereafter the basis for a political perspective on computerisation is developed. Many problems in computerising work result from failing to take into account the objectives, views and interests of all those with a stake in the outcomes of 'going hi-tech'. Through an illustrative case, we argue that the technical efficiency of a computer-based system does not guarantee its effective use as intended by the designer. Such use will depend heavily on system acceptability to a range of stakeholders. Therefore computer-based systems must be designed and implemented in the light of the organisational, social and political context which pertains, and of which they will be part.

SYSTEMS DESIGN TRADITIONS

In computer projects, systems designers pay much lip service to people being valuable organisational assets with key roles to play in systems development. In practice, far from designing systems with and for people, systems designers then go on to largely ignore them. The roots of this behaviour can be found in systems design traditions, and in the (often mistaken) belief that what worked in the past can still be successfully applied today.

Many computer systems are designed with the intention of automating an existing procedure to make it faster, cheaper and more secure, and to eliminate the human element as much as possible. In this view, humans are unreliable, prone to errors, unreasonably inflexible and, above all, expensive. A good system, on the other hand, is seen as clean, efficient, and reliable. This attitude is summed up in the final statement a systems designer penned to a 1986 list of instructions on how to work his new system:

> 'The success of the system from the user's viewpoint is guaranteed—if the system is used.'

The truth is too often very different. If the system has not been designed from the user's viewpoint, then its success, as far as the *user* defines success, can be far from guaranteed. Moreover, if the system is not found to be usable, then it will fall into disuse.

The following story originated in the early seventies. It is probably apocryphal, but helps to illustrate some of these points. A bemused householder one day received an electricity demand for £0.00. 'Obviously a computer error', he thought, and threw it away. A month passed and a reminder arrived, politely requesting the sum of £0.00.

3

This time the householder returned it with a few humorous remarks, making a mental note to stay well away from computers in the future. The situation changed to annoyance when a final demand arrived, with a peremptory order to pay up at once. The householder took no action and in due course the computer issued a letter informing him that he would be disconnected and face legal action without further notice unless the missing £0.00 was paid forthwith.

The householder thought this was going too far and contacted the electricity company and was assured that it would all be taken care of. To his surprise he was contacted the next day by the company, who asked him to pay them the sum of £0.00, as it appeared that their computer procedures had been arranged with maximum security in mind, and the spurious demand could not be cancelled without an actual payment going through the company's treasury system. The spokesman apologised profusely, but suggested that the only way out of the impasse would be for the householder to write a cheque for £0.00 and let it pass through the system.

The householder duly did as asked and was relieved to receive a confirmation of payment from the computer the following day. His relief was a little shortlived, however: the following day he received a letter from his bank politely explaining that it was with greatest regret that they were bouncing his cheque, but their computer just couldn't handle an amount of £0.00!

Unfortunately there are all too many more serious examples of computer systems whose technical design ignores or overrides the interests and requirements of its users. A 1986 report by Eosys consultancy brings home this point. Called *Top executives and information technology: disappointed expectations*, and backed by the Department of Trade and Industry, it concludes that:

> 'There is considerable disillusionment with the ability of data processing departments to understand and deliver what is wanted reasonably quickly.'[5]

How is it then that computer specialists are not that dependable when it comes to producing a working, usable and acceptable system on time and within budget? Part of the answer lies in the design approaches taken by these specialists, and more importantly, in the basic philosophy underlying their methodologies. In order to appreciate these aspects we need to examine how the early successful systems were developed and implemented.

To obtain a computer system in the 1960s or 1970s, an organisation usually needed to contact a computer manufacturing company with an outline of its needs. The company would respond by sending along a systems analyst. This specialist was normally an employee of the company and fully familiar with that company's products. It was expected that the manufacturer would supply all the hardware and software, would install the system, often program it as well, and remain with the purchasing organisation for as long as was needed.

The analyst went along to the organisation to assess its needs in detail and decide which of the hardware range was most suitable. The analyst would then do a little investigating to discover the data required and processes to install. He (almost invariably 'he') would design the programs needed to transform the data, and supervise the coding. Once installed, the new system was tested and amended repeatedly until it was working reasonably well. The analyst would expect to be in contact with the client company for a long time. Any problems arising, or any changes wanted would be handled by the supplying company.

This sort of system only worked because of the type of applications chosen. When setting out to computerise their procedures, organisations naturally chose applications that were the most simple, the easiest to convert, and gave the most immediate savings. These were jobs such as printing electricity bills or rates demands or invoices. They usually involved handling huge quantities of relatively simple documents, whose processing was fundamentally straightforward. Jobs like these were ideally suited to batch processing and were normally computerised very successfully.

Computer systems seemed simple to implement, made large financial savings, and did away with armies of clerks. These considerations tended to sweep aside possible objections about the adverse effects of change. Moreover, these new systems not only had the benefits of being more accurate and faster, but also avoided many recruitment and training problems as well as large wage bills. Organisations were satisfied, analysts were promoted, and in a period of relatively full employment even displaced staff were not overly concerned—there were other jobs, and standing in the way of progress did not seem a sensible response.

The design and implementation methodologies developed in the 1960s and 1970s became fairly standardised and were applied successfully to more and more systems of the same kind. The only real problems were in establishing precisely which procedures the management wanted automated, and overcoming the perennial problem of over-inflated expectations.

These conditions do not prevail in the late 1980s. Most of the easy system design jobs have already been accomplished. There is no longer a full employment economy. A wide range of hardware is on the market, and software is available as packages, through a bureau, as well as from manufacturers. Client organisations have much higher expectations.

Real-time systems are now as common as batch systems. Communications are an integral part of most systems and even the pattern of work is changing. In short, the whole environment in which systems analysts and designers have to work has been transformed. However, it is by no means certain that systems design practice has altered radically in order to meet the challenge of these changing conditions of the 1980s.

SYSTEMS DESIGN: GOING 'SOFT'

Particularly worrying is the failure of systems design practice to adjust to the increasing centrality of the people factor in many systems. Today's more ambitious projects, like decision support systems, flexible manufacturing systems and office automation, aim to integrate core organisational activities. In doing so they bring more users into direct contact with computer-based systems, and make more people dependent on how a system functions and what its outputs are. But as people become more exposed and dependent upon computer systems, the converse also applies. All this requires fundamental shifts on the part of systems designers in their objectives, tools, methodologies and traditional attitudes to the people side of systems. A particular requirement is to exchange 'hard' approaches for 'soft' systems design practice. More needs to be said on this subject.

Systems investigation of natural systems, and systems design of physical and abstract systems are characterised by, in Checkland's words,[6] 'hard systems thinking' on the part of the analyst. This means that analysts see themselves as dealing with an easily defined system. Moreover, the purpose of the system, the goals and objectives which it is being designed to achieve, are also clear-cut. Systems analysis is relatively easy. What remains is systems design—selecting the most appropriate technology available to achieve the system outputs required.

Traditional analysis and design of computer systems, as described in the previous section, has been greatly influenced by 'hard' systems approaches. These can be successful when 'hard' systems are being designed, for example an oil-refining plant with clear objectives, highly automated equipment needing few people to intervene in its operation, and easily measured, clear performance and control standards. However, where people are increasingly part of the system, then the 'hard' approach needs to be abandoned for 'soft' systems thinking and practice.

'Soft' organisations and businesses may be characterised as associations of people pursuing individual and collective goals that are not necessarily the same, and may even be incompatible. Under such circumstances decision-making can be compromised and risky, objec-

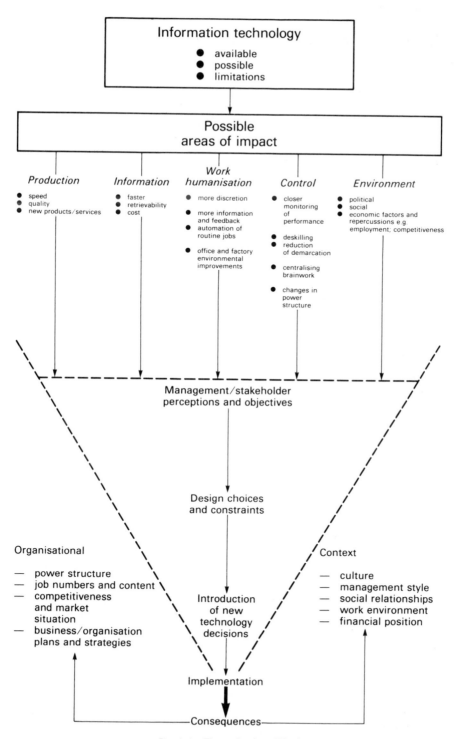

Fig. 1.1 The technology 'filter'

tives are changeable, ill-defined and not always consistent, systems are complex and controls often difficult to establish. An ordinary administrative office about to receive a computer system can be just such a place; and once up and running, the system and the people using it may be usefully characterised as, in Checkland's words, a **human activity system**. Checkland's ideas and 'soft' systems methodologies receive more detailed attention in chapter 4.

The systems analyst can react in several ways to designing computers for human activity systems. One is to adopt a hard systems approach in the belief that it will still produce the best result in the end. A second approach is to design human activity out of the system, or at least to reduce it to the minimum possible, given the technology and finance available. Both these approaches were used in early computer schemes, with some degree of success for the reasons discussed above. A third perspective is to undercharacterise the human being's relationship to the computer as that of an isolated user, subject only to biological limitations. Thus ergonomics and human factors engineering brought into systems design concerns about human limits such as reach, strength, workload capacity, response time, memory and cognitive ability. As shown in chapter 6, these are important, but narrow concerns where computers are used.

A fourth approach, the one followed here, is for those responsible for computer systems projects to integrate much broader human factors into the work of analysis, design and implementation. Figure 1.1 provides an overview of the social and organisational 'filter' through which technology passes into usage. The purpose of the following sections is to deepen understanding of these elements and their interrelationships.

TECHNOLOGY: DETERMINED OR DETERMINING?

Of major concern are people's attitudes toward, and definitions of, technology. It is commonly said, and believed, that computer technology must be accepted, that 'we have no choice'. People must be subjected to the constraints and capabilities of new technology as it becomes available. This approach is aptly conveyed in Robert Taylor's comments[7] on introducing computers in the UK newspaper industry:

> 'The economic logic is a more capital-intensive industry with fewer production workers trained in new automated skills. It looks like a battle royal to convince most print-workers that this must come.'

A further development of this 'technological determinist' view is where the large range of *alternative* designs and consequences possible with computer and microchip technology are seriously underplayed. The technology is designed with technical efficiency the key criterion, and human beings have to fit in with, and act as extensions of, the computer system that results. In fact, microchip technology is very adaptable and can easily be designed to complement human skills and behaviour rather than determine them.

'Technological determinism' also deflects attention toward the 'man–machine' relationship and away from the crucial fact that machine design and utilisation are essentially social products. From Fig. 1.2 it can be seen that, far from there being no choice, a series of choices and compromises are made in the process of selecting, designing and

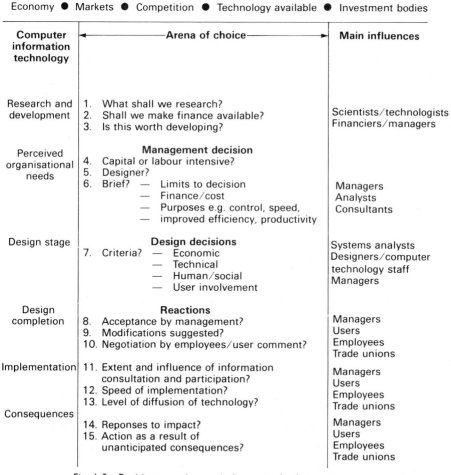

	Constraints	
Economy ● Markets ● Competition ● Technology available ● Investment bodies		

Computer information technology	◄————Arena of choice————►	Main influences
Research and development	1. What shall we research? 2. Shall we make finance available? 3. Is this worth developing?	Scientists/technologists Financiers/managers

Perceived organisational needs	**Management decision**
	4. Capital or labour intensive?
	5. Designer?
	6. Brief? — Limits to decision
	      — Finance/cost
	      — Purposes e.g. control, speed,
	      — improved efficiency, productivity
		Managers
		Analysts
		Consultants

Design stage	**Design decisions**
	7. Criteria? — Economic
	      — Technical
	      — Human/social
	      — User involvement
		Systems analysts
		Designers/computer technology staff
		Managers

Design completion	**Reactions** 8. Acceptance by management? 9. Modifications suggested? 10. Negotiation by employees/user comment?	Managers Users Employees Trade unions
Implementation	11. Extent and influence of information consultation and participation? 12. Speed of implementation? 13. Level of diffusion of technology?	Managers Users Employees Trade unions
Consequences	14. Reponses to impact? 15. Action as a result of unanticipated consequences?	Managers Users Employees Trade unions

Fig. 1.2 Decision areas in a typical systems development programme

introducing new technology. It is usually the case that certain people—for example, managers or designers—have the main say in what will happen, and then hide behind the technology produced—its characteristics—as having determined the decisions taken. This 'technological imperative' argument can be a useful way for the systems analyst to defend a new system, though it sometimes stretches the credulity of affected parties.

There is another way in which the technological determinist view is weak. People not only produce computer systems; they are also an important part of their functioning. Thus technology at work may exercise constraints on human behaviour, and over what is and is not possible. But people working computer equipment also have influence over its utilisation and the ends to which it is applied.

From these understandings a definition of computer systems, as used in this book, can be reached. A technology has three components. These are *equipment* (e.g. machines, instruments, tools), *technique* (skills, routines, methods, procedures; i.e. technical activities devised by people), and *people* (who design, maintain, use, or use the the output from, activated equipment and techniques).

Thus computer-based technologies form complex, interdependent systems of people and equipment, guided by technique, and usually designed by specialists. The equipment will include hardware, software and data; technique means procedures, organisational arrangements and practices for using the equipment; people will include users, managers responsible and systems professionals.

PEOPLE, OBJECTIVES AND INTERESTS

This section looks at the people element in computerisation in closer detail and relates computer-based systems to the organisational contexts in which they will be imbedded. The view is developed that since organisations are political arenas, those responsible for computerising work must inevitably take into account the objectives, viewpoints and interests of a range of people in ways normally ignored in traditional systems design practice. In the authors' experience, a people audit frequently indicates that initial system design and project plans need to be changed quite drastically.

The people audit
Some typical interested parties, or **stakeholders**, that need to be considered during any computerisation are

    — managers
    — users
    — programmers

— analysts/designers
— computer preparation and processing staff
— financiers of the scheme (e.g. shareholders, banks, Government)
— other affected organisational members
— customers
— computer firms and their salesmen.

Whatever designs and changes being proposed, different groups and individuals will have different responses and reactions to them (Fig. 1.3). Thus, in a small office, the introduction of word-processors could mean for some secretaries new skills, higher pay, more interesting jobs with additional responsibilities. For others it might mean redundancy or fears about their ability to cope with 'new' technology. Some managers may fear a centralised word-processor system and the loss of their personal secretaries and the related status. Others may look forward to an improved service and higher-quality finished documents.

People's reactions to specific changes can be predicted to some extent. This then enables these reactions to be planned for and permits the development of systems changes and policies to reduce people's fears and resistance. This theme is developed in chapter 2. One useful device is to examine the cost—benefit analysis that each individual and group is bound to make (albeit not always very consciously or formally) whenever changes affecting them are pending (see Fig. 2.3).

Only when such cost—benefit analyses are properly understood can policies to confront and change perceived losses be developed, and methods to weight such analyses in the direction of benefits be implemented. It is not being suggested here that this can always be accomplished, merely that in the authors' experience this is a useful but rarely

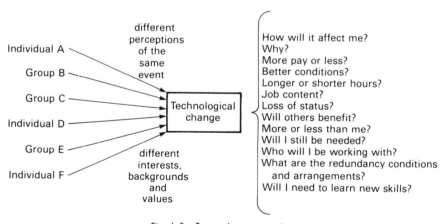

Fig. 1.3 Some change questions

performed exercise during the design and implementation of computer-based systems.

Objectives and politics

As indicated above, an organisation has many stakeholders. They do not necessarily share the same interests, values, beliefs and reasons for being connected with the organisation. In fact, it would be a highly unusual feature of that organisation's life if they did so. It follows that stakeholders will not always pursue and support the same objectives either. For instance, employees may be wanting interesting jobs and higher pay, but both objectives may clash with managers' perceptions of how to achieve their objective of keeping down labour costs. The demand of the sales department to keep high stocks so that orders can be met quickly may be opposed to the Accountancy Department's aim to keep down stockholding costs, or the Production Department's objective to maintain a steady pace of production.

As Cyert and March[8] have indicated, what determines whose objectives are wholly, or partly, pursued is the power that the different interest groups can mobilise, and the allies they can make. The resulting picture of organisational life is of series of conflicts and compromises over objectives that shift as the perceptions or membership of the **dominant coalition** in the organisation changes.

All this points in the direction of 'soft' systems thinking for analysing, designing and implementing computer-based systems. A design process that is more flexible and open to change is necessary, permitting interested parties to influence design. Where this does not happen, and/or design is technically and economically orientated, immense problems can be stored up for the implementation stage, as the authors themselves found in studying the planned computerisation of the Department of Health and Social Security in the UK.[9]

A design has little value if it cannot be implemented. It is not always the case that poor planning or technical problems make implementation an unhappy experience. A clash over objectives among stakeholders may be the crucial stumbling block. Such clashes can be resolved by negotiation at an early stage. More commonly where employees are concerned, such negotiations are left to the implementation stage and are seen to enter the arena identified as the preserve of the industrial relations practitioner. There are problems with such an approach and these are discussed in detail in chapter 7.

Managerial objectives

Since managers have considerable organisational power, their objectives in a computer project can have a crucial bearing on its shape and eventual systems operation. Why then do managements introduce computer technology? In a review of published case studies, Child[10] found four main reasons emerging, with managers wishing to

— reduce operating costs and improve efficiency
— increase flexibility
— raise the quality and consistency of production
— improve control over operations.

In practice many managers only hold one or two of these aims. The authors have conducted surveys of over 200 managers on their IT training courses, and have found these, and additional, objectives espoused. A frequent finding was that individual managers had few, and quite limited, objectives for bringing computer systems into their organisations. Some aims were designed to achieve some of the objectives above; for example

— improve speed of work
— reduce repetitive tasks
— reduce dependency on workforce
— increase control over employees

Others were quite general; for example

— increase annual profits
— increase competitiveness
— ultimate automation

Managers are also being made much more aware of the increasing role computer-based technology plays in changing the basis of competition, and its strategic potential for developing competitive advantage.[11]

Often managers do not state their aims so clearly. Another factor cited in several case studies[12] is that managers at different levels or in different functions within the same organisation will have different, sometimes conflicting, objectives for the introduction of new technology. Frequently managers also have unclear and restricted views of what computer technology can do for them. This makes the tasks of systems suppliers and designers easier in some ways, but more difficult in others. The easy side is that such managers may be more open to the advice and preferences of those possessing computer expertise. This may not always be of ultimate benefit to the organisation or the manager. Some managers have already found out, belatedly, that their suppliers were interested in selling particular systems regardless of organisational need, or that systems designers preferred certain packages or technical solutions, around which the organisation had to fit, rather than vice versa.

The difficult side is that clients' needs and objectives must be clarified and met if the resulting system is to be deemed successful. Again this will mean an open-ended and flexible approach in the analysis and early design stages. It may also require systems professionals to point out bad reasons for incurring expenditure on computer-based systems.

This obviously did not occur in a London-based advertising agency which one of the authors subsequently advised, where nearly £80 000 had been spent on accounting and market data and research systems. It appeared that an influential director with little understanding of information technology had wished to demonstrate that the agency was an up-to-date organisation. In practice the Accounts Department went on using its old, largely manual system, and the market research database was never properly developed. In the author's estimation the systems served no real purpose at all, beyond impressing the occasional client. Computer technology was not used to address the real problems of declining profits and lack of competitiveness. In fact, the misspent capital expenditure probably contributed to the firm being taken over in 1985.

Systems analysts and those providing computer advice also need to point out the full potential of different computer technologies and tie these to managerial and other stakeholder objectives. In fact it is common for managerial objectives to expand with increasing experience and understanding of what information technology systems can achieve. Many computer systems can be observed to develop in stages over time. Typically, at an initial stage, cost-reduction and increased productivity objectives may result in demands for independent, stand-alone equipment such as word-processors in offices. In time, demands for integration of such equipment, the establishment of databases, may emerge as managers see the possibility of achieving objectives involving better quality and faster information. The trend from automating individual activities through to computerising the whole processes and then integrating these with other processes is a common one.

Managers must be made aware that there are advantages in pursuing such a staged, incremental approach to introducing new technology. The slower pace of change may permit easier adjustment to computer-based systems amongst organisational members. However, much time and money may be saved if manager and users are made fully aware of the range of systems of different levels, and their capabilities. This may cause original objectives to undergo considerable modification and expansion. In fact, by their recommendations and influence, computer specialists can cause managers to jump several stages in the organisational development of IT, quickly develop new-technology objectives central to organisational performance, and in this way bypass the more wasteful aspects of incremental IT growth.

POLITICS IN ORGANISATIONS

If work organisations are human activity systems, they are also *political* activity systems. Organisational politics arise where individuals or groups pursue their interests, possibly in association with some stakeholders, but against the interests of others. In practice it is difficult to think of an organisation where this does not happen. From this derives a major premiss which later chapters will provide evidence for and use as a basis: the introduction of computer-based systems into organisations is to be considered as essentially, whether overtly or covertly, a political event.

The main focus here is on power and politics *inside* organisations, though it should be understood that these may be greatly affected, and even determined, by events and processes in the wider environment. To take a computing example, IBM's dominance of its many markets can greatly constrain and influence organisational decision-making on what computer system to have, while its equipment designs can greatly affect the type of work people will do.

Power

Central to the understanding of politics in organisations is the concept of power. Power is the capacity to get decisions and actions taken and situations created which support one's interests and preferred outcomes where their realisation is dependent on the agency of others. Power is the capacity to 'make a difference'.[13]

Power arises in an organisational context that is itself the result of prior political activity. This will have assisted in creating a division of labour, a control structure, a distribution of resources, ways of operation and rules, procedures and goals that will see some people favoured, and others more constrained, in the exercise of power.

The sources of power include

— valued expertise (e.g. in computing)
— control over the provision of information
— interpersonal skills and persuasiveness
— personality and charisma
— control over rewards and punishments
— physical force.

It can be seen that many of these sources arise from the *position* of an individual or group in the organisation. The formal role a person plays in an organisation gives control over information and resources and access to others. It also gives *authority*—the right, ceded by the organisation and inherent in the job, to act in certain ways, instruct people and commandeer resources. A related, but broader, power source is the extent to which people share, or can be induced to share, the values, norms and purposes of the exercise of power and regard it as *legitimate*. Here power comes from the capacity to manage culture, rites, rituals and meanings in an organisation. The importance of culture in the context of computerisation is discussed further in later chapters.

Power is often identified as the capacity to influence decision-making in organisations; for example, on questions like shall we computerise? when? what type of system? But Bachrach and Baratz[14] point to a greater power that lies with *control over the agenda*. This is power to exclude certain items from the decision-making arena, and discussion, altogether. Thus employees at lower levels of an organisational hierarchy are rarely allowed to participate in capital investment decisions on computer systems, though they may be greatly affected by the decision outcomes. Schattschneider[15] describes succinctly this form of control, and the covert conflict it masks:

> 'All forms of political organisation have a bias in favour of the exploitation of some kinds of conflict and the suppression of others because organisation is the mobilisation of bias. Some issues are organised into politics while others are organised out.'

An important point is that the larger opportunities for achieving preferred outcomes and pursuing interests in organisations occur when people operate in groups rather than as individuals. For example, groups are more likely to occupy strategic positions in the organisation relative to those whom they wish to influence. A *negative* power can arise where a group's activities are central to organisational functioning, are not substitutable by others, are immediate in their impact for other people's work, or involve coping with uncertainties on behalf of others. In such circumstances, dependence *on* implies influence *by* that group.[16] As an example, the small number of computer specialists, data entry clerks and maintenance staff responsible for running centralised computer systems in government departments like the Inland Revenue, Health and Social Security and Customs and Excise have considerable bargaining power. If one of these groups stops work, then the whole organisation can become quickly and seriously, affected.

COMPUTERS AND POLITICS: PROMIS IN HEALTH CARE

These considerations on organisational politics and their relevance to computer projects are illuminated by the example of PROMIS. This began life as a research project to remedy three prominent flaws in American medical care: inadequate organisation of medical records and of general medical knowledge, over-reliance on the physician's memory, and flaws in the systems for recording and providing feedback on the progress and appropriateness of patient care. The Problem-Oriented Medical Information System (PROMIS) developed in the 1970s, together with its 1980s commercialised version, form impressive computerised solutions to these and other health care problems.

PROMIS encompasses medical-record, medical-library and administrative functions. At the heart of the system is a complete, on-line computerised medical record for each patient. This can be accessed using a password and via a touch-screen terminal. It can be consulted and updated from any terminal within the medical institution. Users can also access a medical knowledge database just for reference or while interacting with a patient's medical record. The database includes information on medical symptoms, diagnoses and procedures that can be carried out, such as laboratory tests and drug prescriptions. The system can also handle most administrative functions, including patient admissions and discharges, an internal mailing system permitting automatic ordering of treatment by other staff (e.g. X-ray, drugs, tests), collection of charges for billing private patients, a warning system where a treatment is overdue, and data presentations for ward management (e.g. to check for bed availability, or create worklists in patient or health-care-provider order).

Given the technical exellence of PROMIS, what remains remarkable is the slowness with which it has been adopted in both the USA and UK. Some reasons emerged from tests runs in a Vermont hospital in the USA in 1976–7.[17]

An underlying tenet of the PROMIS philosophy is a health care team approach, with more equal participation in health care problems by all team members. At the Vermont hospital, nurses welcomed the system as providing more patient information, and expanding their professional discretion and ability to intervene without physician permission or approval. The pharmacists' traditional role of dispensing drugs to doctor prescription was also expanded and more use was made of their professional knowledge. The system provided full patient records to pharmacists, who could now check prescribed drug and quantity for correctness against patient symptoms and history. Radiologists responsible for X-ray work found opportunities for involvement in diagnosis greatly enhanced by the complete, up-to-date and easily accessed patient record provided by PROMIS. Hospital physicians were the one major group to register negative responses to PROMIS. They argued that PROMIS was more time-consuming than manual systems, compromised patient care and disrupted existing staff relations.

The real problem seemed to lie with the extent to which PROMIS impinged on the sovereignty of the doctors and exposed their work to public gaze, questioning and alteration. Furthermore, in operation, PROMIS ceded some of their decision-making and discretion to act to other team members traditionally perceived as less knowledgeable subordinates. In short, PROMIS threatens the sources of power, the legitimacy of action and the strong political positions of most doctors in hierarchically organised hospitals.

The significant feature is the amount of control doctors have over the selection and use of systems that, like PROMIS, seem to threaten their interests. As Child[18] indicates, this comes from several sources. Doctors occupy senior formal positions in hospitals and in the institutional decision processes relating to computer technology. Their expert knowledge means that their compliance is required in the development of software. Medical knowledge is continually expanding and is difficult to codify as a database; and it is doctors who can cope with, and have a hold over, this uncertain knowledge base. Doctors also gain power in their direct responsibility for patients undergoing high personal risk. Furthermore, doctors have a strong occupational organisation and through bodies like the British Medical Association they exercise considerable control over workplace and market conditions.

These factors provide some explanation for the slow reception of PROMIS into UK hospitals. In fact, in 1980 some eminent doctors serving on a Health Department computer research and development committee championed the introduction of PROMIS into a large London hospital. This project was at the relatively cheap price of £2.5 million payable over eight years. Though the committee was given a £3 million annual budget, of which it rarely spent half, its proposal was rejected by the Department of Health. The Department suggested that such expenditure was too great in a time of financial stringency.[19] This decision caused four members to resign from the committee, thus marking a temporary end to pressure for PROMIS.

Behind the scenes the real problems seemed to have been political ones. In particular, PROMIS created considerable resistance and antagonism amongst other members of the medical profession. The Health Department, though conceding that it was the best available, probably doubted whether the PROMIS system could be 'managed in' successfully. Others developing health care software may have learnt from such experiences. One doctor has worked for many years on GLADYS, a computer program for diagnosing people with chronic stomach-ache. The *Observer* newspaper commented:

'He and others working on computers for medical diagnosis stress the importance of designing packages only for conditions that present real problems for doctors. Otherwise they will see it as a gimmick.'[20]

It may be, however, that PROMIS is merely struggling to find its political level. Its acceptability seems to be low in hospitals and clinics which are hierarchically structured, with fairly rigid job demarcations, and traditional relationships between doctors, nurses, and ancillary and other professional staff. PROMIS presupposes the existence or the creation of a health care team that is problem- and patient-oriented, less concerned with maintaining traditional roles, and dependent on shared expertise and information easily accessed by every member. There is an increasing trend in the UK for training health care practitioners, including doctors, in this task-centred approach; and PROMIS tends to have much more support amongst groups already funtioning in hospitals along these lines.

CONCLUSIONS

This chapter has introduced the main strands in a broadened 'human aspects' perspective on designing, introducing and using computer-based systems in work organisations. A 'soft' systems approach may have to replace 'hard' systems perspectives and methodologies in the processes of systems analysis and design. This is more fully considered in chapter 4. The 'technological imperative' argument derives from a lack of awareness of the immense flexibility and potential of computer technologies. Alternatively, it is used as an ideological device by some stakeholders in support of their own interests. 'Technology', usually narrowly defined as equipment and technique, in fact cannot be seen as separate from its designers or users.

The organisational context into which a computer system is introduced has a crucial bearing on its acceptability and subsequent effectiveness. Particularly important are its likely impact on the power and control structure, and the outcomes of political activity surrounding its design, selection, introduction and use. It is to develop this theme that chapter 2 addresses the human issue most commonly raised with regard to computer-based technology, namely the probability of 'resistance to change.'

CHAPTER 2
Resistance to Change

'To a large extent, one's whole perspective on implementation is reflected in one's view of resistance and how to handle it.'[1]
'To find out how an organisation really works, try changing it.'[2]

INTRODUCTION

In one office, a word-processor operator occasionally sabotages the machine with a paper clip to break up the monotony, isolation and intensity of work. In another, an insurance broking clerk types fictional client data into the terminal to complete the electronic work quota for the day. A trade union develops the practice of requiring a specific new technology agreement for each local government computerisation scheme, no matter how small. At the headquarters of a medium-sized cosmetics company, the new Decision Support System is bypassed by managers because 'it's too complicated' and they 'prefer to talk to real people'. In these real life examples, found as by-products of other research by the authors, a variety of workers, for their own reasons, are seen to be 'resisting' computer technology.

Such behaviour feeds the nightmare on the far side of technology managers' hopes for the automated workplace. One manager states the fear succinctly:

'Employee resistance to new technology could become the "Achilles' heel" of the long-awaited Information Age.'[3]

Despite such fears, in fact contributing to them, the phenomenon of resistance to change is all too frequently the subject of limited analysis, definition and understanding.

One of the unfortunate attitudes sometimes encountered amongst technical staff and those managing a system implementation is that resistance to change and protection of vested interests are faults. Emotively 'resistance' suggests that those doing the resisting are in the wrong and acting against desirable norms of behaviour. It follows that 'resistance' should be suppressed, ignored or overridden.

A slightly less damaging response would be to get the 'experts'—for example, the personnel department or organisation development con-

20

sultants—to handle the 'people' problems. This merely passes on the responsibility, though possibly to safer hands. In fact, the requirement is for a more detailed analysis of the nature of that 'resistance'— here placed in quotation marks to emphasise its status not as fact but as an attribution; that is, a value judgement on the attitudes, motives and behaviour of other people. From the analysis can be determined whether something, and if so what, can be done about it. This chapter provides that analysis in the context of technological change.

PERSPECTIVES ON TECHNOLOGICAL CHANGE

There are as many perspectives on change as people in the organisation affected. However, Figure 2.1 summarises the major views most frequently found. As Fox[4] notes, managers often have a **unitarist** perspective on the organisation. They see the organisation as a team with shared interests and goals. Management's proper place is leading that team and making the rational decisions to ensure computer technology is efficiently employed to achieve organisational objectives. There is no room for conflict or resistance to systems implementation in such a view. Such

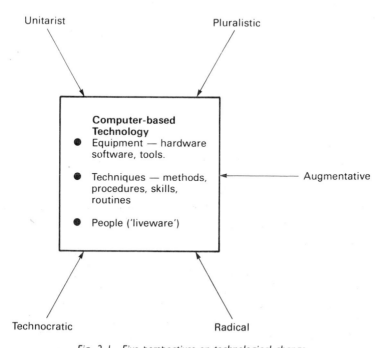

Fig. 2.1 Five perspectives on technological change

21

phenomena are aberrant, the work of people who are misinformed, have personality defects or are born troublemakers. It is common for such managers to relate resistance to change to specific individuals, who may be dubbed as 'troublemakers'. Group resistance to new technology may then be explained away by the undue influence of such individuals.

A **technocratic** perspective is frequently held by systems analysts, programmers, technology managers, systems professionals and those highly skilled in the use of computer-based systems. Here the focus is on the virtues and inevitability of the new technology and the need to optimise its utilisation to safeguard the health of the organisation. 'Resistance' comes from misunderstanding, ignorance, reactionary attitudes and perhaps a fear of the unknown.

A variant on these two perspectives is where technically minded managers identify resistance as due to systems factors such as lack of user-friendliness, poor human factors, inadequate design. Even so, a unitarist perspective would cause them to stress that the systems purposes and design are consistent with managerial objectives and therefore should be accepted by all interested parties. Markus[5] calls this a system-determined theory of resistance.

A more fruitful way of looking at systems implementation is from a **pluralistic** perspective. Here, those responsible for introducing new technology would recognise conflict and resistance to change as normal rather than unusual features of organisational life. These result from individuals, groups and coalitions pursuing their particular interest with—but often against—each other. As a result, where compliance and co-operation exist, these are products of more or less temporary alliances between stakeholders to pursue specific interests. Organisational stability and mutual co-operation are thus revealed as negotiated, rather than natural, order.

A **radical** perspective takes this analysis further. Pluralism sees organisational life as a struggle between a number of interest groups of a similar power. In a radical view, power resources are unequally distributed in organisations and there are only two main interest groups. In fact, the power balance is seen to favour strongly owners and managers in their conflicts with employees. At the heart of these conflicts is a fundamental divergence in interests. Owners and managers want subordinates to work harder for less reward, while employees demand more reward for less work. The latter group will continually struggle for more control and reward against unequal odds. In the radical view, order and co-operation are only temporary features of organisations. The truce is bound to be broken sooner or later, and a computerisation scheme could easily be the trigger.

A further refinement of the radical view is the **augmentative** perspective. This sees computer-based systems being used to perpetuate and reinforce the existing patterns of organisational power relationships, whatever these may be. In so far as power and influence are reallocated through computerisation, this is done in a way that is likely to increase, rather than diminish, existing inequalities. The view here is that organisational members are influenced in direct and indirect ways to anticipate the requirements, and serve the interests, of the organisationally powerful. Here 'resistance' would be seen as any attempt to undermine the use of computers to augment organisational capability to support the interest of those who control the organisation.

These perspectives are put forward as possible ways in which organisational participants view technological change and resistance. In fact, in specific circumstances each could be a fairly accurate picture of an organisational reality; for example, a unitarist view in companies like computer giant IBM, car manufacturer Nissan, or Wang in computing, or an augmentative view of computerisation in US local governments.[6] However, Fox[4] suggests that the radical (as opposed to the unitarist or pluralist) view is most accurate for the majority of UK organisations in the 1970s and 1980s.

Whether this is true or not, the general tenor of his argument cannot be disputed. In the context of technological change, this means that the nature and reasons for resistance need to be understood as a basis for handling design and implementation. To achieve this, those responsible for computerisation need to become aware of other people's perspectives, but also need to adopt an appropriate perspective on technological change, the one most closely approximating to the pattern of power relations and how the specific organisation functions.

A further point needs to be made. There is often a close, though not a necessary, relationship between people's perceptions, values and interests. This touches on the politics of computerisation. The perspectives outlined above can be used as ideological support for the pursuit of specific interests during computerisation. The managerial rationalism of the unitarist view can support managerial initiatives and decision-making that will see computing used to enhance managerial objectives and position. The technocratic imperative can be voiced to maintain and enhance the role of a computer-based technocracy. A pluralist perspective may be voiced by those wishing to portray as legitimate their opposition to some elements of computerisation. A radical view will justify continuing resistance by lower-level users after a computer system has been made operational. Clearly, the perspectives discussed in this section can operate as descriptions of reality, value and belief systems, but also as political weapons in the pursuit of vested interests. In specific computerisation projects these different uses need to be carefully analysed if a proper understanding of any 'resistance' to change is to be reached.

OVERVIEW

This chapter will look at individual, group, coalition and organisational behaviour in conditions of technological change. A premiss emerging from the argument so far underlies what follows: the human activities and reactions to be reviewed must be considered as fundamentally conditioned by stakeholders' different perceptions and beliefs about, as well as their vested interests in, the computerisation process.

It is vital to avoid the easy mistake of viewing resistance to change solely as an individual and psychological response. Figure 2.2 indicates the other possible variables. These interact to produce often complicated patterns of resistance that need to be analysed carefully before and during the implementation of computer systems.

Resistance should not be seen merely as a problem to be solved so that the original system can then be installed as intended. Resistance can be used more positively in systems design. In fact, resistance is a good clue as to what is going wrong and what can be done about it. The narrow determination to see a certain system design up and working will inhibit useful analysis of resistance. Instead, resistance needs to be viewed in relation to the general results and outcomes required from a computer

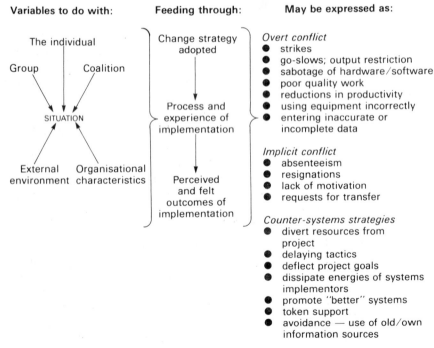

Fig. 2.2   Resistance to systems implementation—a model

system. There then tends to be much more discretion and freedom as to how the system should be designed and implemented.

COMPUTERPHOBIA, INDIVIDUALS AND RESISTANCE

There is much contradictory evidence on the extent to which people fear, and so resist, technological change. One approach has been to elevate computer anxiety to the level of an illness called computer- or cyber-phobia. Rout,[7] Paul[8] and Coli[9] independently report high incidences of computer anxiety, accompanied by physical phobic symptoms such as cold sweats and stomach cramps. Computerphobia is also said to be manifested in a reluctance to utilise computer equipment or computerised information, stress when asked to use the computer or related technology, avoidance of, or delays in, undertaking training, and minimisation of the importance of computers to the organisation.

However, in a detailed study of managers, Howard and Smith[10] found very few cases of computer anxiety. Virtually all cases derived from type of education, or lack of knowledge of, or lack of experience with, computers. The solutions were to be found in more directed, appropriate induction and training for automation. The probability is that computerphobia is a very real phenomenon, but neither as widespread as once thought, nor as severe in its impact on the individual concerned.

This is not to say that people do not have genuine fears about computers and their effects on working life. Figure 2.3 indicates the type of issues that arise when people find themselves involved in change. As Thompson[11] points out in reviewing a number of case studies, computer technology in particular tends to create fears of personal cost that precede its introduction, due to the forbidding reputation for job loss, skill obsolescence, changes in job content, need for new skills, and health and safety dangers. It follows that even more care is needed with computerisation than with other types of change.

The key considerations in planning for automation are increasingly understood to be not technological, but behavioural. If that is so, then people's fears need to be addressed, but so do the reasons for those fears and for 'resistant' behaviour.

For Galitz,[12] the main reasons for individuals resisting automation are feelings of inadequacy, fear of failure or of the unknown, disturbance of social relationships or of psychological work habits related to established rules, policies and procedures, lack of understanding of the purposes of change, and lack of identification with changes which they had not promoted. Moreover, computer systems are commonly (not always incorrectly!) identified with a loss of control over what goes on in the work environment.

Perceived losses

1. *Fears on economic grounds*
   - more work for the same or reduced pay
   - fewer skills required means less pay in the long term
   - loss of overtime

2. *Fears about personal inconvenience*
   - less pleasant working conditions (environment, hours, location, travel)
   - more difficult work requires more effort

3. *Concerns over decreased job satisfaction*
   - less interesting and challenging
   - less (or more) responsibility
   - reduced authority
   - more (or less) supervision
   - less important job

4. *Social fears*
   - isolation
   - loss of status
   - establishing precedents that others might not support
   - a job for me means redundancy for others?
   - my trade union will be against it

5. *Personal insecurity*
   - can I learn these new IT skills?
   - new standards might be harder to meet
   - IT makes people redundant Will it be me?

6. *Dissatisfaction at handling of change*
   - no one asked me!
   - it's being pushed through too quickly. There's no time to think
   - no information about why and how. Expect the worst!
   - why are they picking on me?
   - I see no reason for these changes
   - they're obviously doing it wrong, but if they don't ask I'm not going out of my way to help

Perceived gains

1. *Anticipated economic gains*
   - earn more money
   - more opportunities for advancement
   - new skills will enhance pay and career prospects

2. *Hopes of more personal convenience*
   - cleaner, easier VDT work
   - more pleasant work environment
   - better location and work hours
   - less effort required

3. *Anticipated job satisfaction*
   - more interest and challenge
   - more discretion and responsibility
   - more (or less) pressure
   - I'll be able to deal with a whole product now

4. *Social gains*
   - enhanced status
   - more social contacts while working
   - group work suits me
   - a good manager to work for!

5. *More security because:*
   - more skilled work
   - more important post
   - company's competitiveness has increased through it

6. *Satisfaction at how change is handled*
   - consultation and participation. They took notice of my views. I was influential in the process
   - kept informed from the very beginning

Fig. 2.3   Anticipating resistance to change

Any or all these explanations may well apply. However, it is important not to assume, but to analyse, their applicability in specific circumstances. The rest of this section deals with other possible explanations. In particular, the focus is on technical issues, redistribution of information resources, participation, communication and managerial interests as possible sources of opposition to computer systems at the level of the individual.

Resistance may be engendered by technical issues. If there is not a perceived need for the system amongst users and senior management, the system is almost bound to fail. Its reception and use by staff will not be helped either where the system is seen, then experienced, as difficult to work, unreliable, slow in response, not available when needed and/or containing inaccurate and incomplete data. A common experience is that the system will fall into disuse if such factors persist for any length of time after start-up. Information workers will find ways around the system, rather than working through it.

Another point, that will receive more lengthy treatment below, is that the introduction of computer systems invariably results in a redistribution of resources, authority, status, rewards and control. But the major resource that a computer system may be responsible for redistributing amongst organisational members is **information**. This is significant because:

'Communication systems are carriers of power'[13]

In looking at decision-making in a large manufacturing company, Pettigrew[13] found information access and control to be power resources. The point here is that in the process of computerisation, each organisational member will make some attempt to get a hold on such resources, or prevent others from doing so. Keen[14] summarises the situation succinctly:

'The systems designer needs to ask

(1) Who owns the data?

(2) Who will share it?

(3) What will be the perceived impact on

    (a) evaluation
    (b) influence and authority
    (c) communication?

He or she should then get ready to deal with counter-implementation' [i.e. resistance].[14]

Kanter[15] finds additional reasons for people's resistance to change. They do not like surprises, even when the change may be positive; they resist loss of face or the extra work related to bringing in change; past resentments may cause people to resist change if its source is a person or organisation about which they have a grievance. Finally, people may be right to resist change because it really will threaten them. Her advice here is to involve people:

> 'You can mitigate some of the pain by giving people different options for how to handle the pain.'[15]

However, there is some evidence that the participative approach to systems design and implementation may not always be such a good idea.[16] The participation process means higher interaction, which can act to heighten and make more obvious the differences between people, rather than strengthen co-operation. The question then is whether or not the greater differences in opinion, and increased, more overt conflicts can be turned to constructive ends rather than damage system implementation.

One must also be cautious about finding the panacea in communicating with those affected by the new system. A major myth in management circles is that all differences between organisational members can be eliminated by their communicating properly with each other. One review of the evidence finds that complete information and knowledge make each party's self-interests fully visible and reveal any and all inequities. In this way, resistance against change is created in those who, with imperfect knowledge, might have gone along with the new computer system.[17]

A final point here relates to status and interests. Littler and Salaman[18] find that most managers strongly resist having to use a keyboard. Even in the USA, where they are taught to type, they find it demeaning. In practice, managers may wish to retain traditional manager—subordinate, manager—secretary relationships. In looking at the introduction of numerically controlled machines in West Germany and Britain, Swords-Isherwood and Senker[19] found evidence of managerial resistance due to perceived unreliability of the machines, but also worries about the consequences of reorganisation. Shaiken[20] also found computer technology resisted by operating managers fearing inroads into their authority and greater control over them by higher management.

Northcott et al.[21] also document for the 1980s that *managerial* resistance to new technology has been as noteworthy as the general pattern of *acceptance* by workforces and unions. Littler and Salaman[18] suggest that such managerial resistance could have an interesting consequence:

> 'It may yet turn out to be the case that managerial resistance to office automation prevents the worst consequences of the office revolution in terms of both employment and depersonalised work.'

Where people assess their gains as outweighing their losses as a function of computerisation, then resistance and conflict in some form or other can be anticipated. The need here is firstly for those fears and perceptions to be understood; they then need to be addressed. However, these factors may be operating not just at the level of the individual, but amongst collectivities of people within the organisation. Therefore it is to an analysis of resistance at this level that we now turn.

GROUPS, COALITIONS AND RESISTANCE

A group is formed where two or more individuals come together, are interdependent and interact to achieve particular objectives. Distinctions can be made between a work group, an interest group and a coalition. A work group will have special assignments or tasks (for example, the staff of a computer services department), or belong to a particular hierarchical level (for example, supervisors), such features distinguishing them from other groups. An interest group has members with common motivations established on a base broader than the fulfilment of particular jobs or duties: a trade union like the EETPU, attempting to recruit a range of managerial and skilled workers, may be an interest group. A coalition is one or more interest groups that may have diverging interests but see it in their interests to act together as a front.

There is a vast literature on group characteristics and their impact on individual members' behaviour. For our purposes, the main findings from the classic studies by Mayo, Rothlisberger and Dickson,[22] Asch,[23] Sherif,[24] Milgram[25] and Sayles[26] are as follows.

Groups establish norms and values and can become cohesive, especially under an external threat such as an impending change perceived as against the group's interests. Groups tend to resist disruptions to those norms and settled patterns of working. Many cases show how individual members tend to conform to group norms in their attitudes, judgement and behaviour, though such conformity depends upon the cohesiveness of the group, the extent to which an individual believes in the norms and values, how far the individual's interests are served by the group, and the penalties the group can bring to bear on non-conformist behaviour.

The NGA (National Graphical Association), a union operating in the UK newspaper and print industry, provides a highly publicised example of a cohesive group that has for many years successfully resisted the full introduction of computerised photocomposition technology and the 'single keystroke'. Computerisation would make its members traditional typesetting skills obsolete and create mass redundancies amongst NGA members. Martin[27] suggests that new technology could be used to increase managerial control over NGA members in more subtle ways.

The design would require more co-ordination, a unified composing room and the merging of jobs. NGA labour and traditional skills would become more easily substituted and a wider recruitment area of unskilled workers could be drawn upon to fill jobs. This would end traditional NGA control over recruitment sources. A dissolution of job demarcations would end the factional bargaining and differentials disputes generated by the print unions to boost earnings. As an aside, one should note that the new technology can have differential affects on various interest groups. Thus, in Fleet Street, electricians had their position enhanced with the strategic need for computer maintenance and 24 hours a day breakdown cover.

NGA resistance over several years has ranged from strikes and disruptive unofficial action, through long drawn out negotiations over the terms of the introduction of new technology, to insisting on long training periods for workers to adapt to VDU terminal and keyboard work. In Times Newspapers in 1980, after a nine-month lockout, the NGA agreed to the new technology provided its members retained control over typesetting and were made responsible for typing into the computer all the news stories. However, introduction was further delayed because many members selected by the NGA for computer training proved to be quite difficult to train. Such tactics contributed to the selling of TNL by the Thompson Organisation to News International in 1980–81.[28]

Markus[5] provides an illuminating example of a professional group resisting technical change. She studied the introduction of a computerised financial information system into a large US corporation in the late 1970s. Markus found that head office corporate accountants supported the system, whereas divisional accountants resisted its installation and subsequent use. The new system collected all financial data into a single database controlled by corporate accountants. Divisional accountants entered the data and the system automatically generated summaries of divisional performances. Moreover, corporate accountants could now look into the database at will and check up on divisional financial records.

All this meant a major gain over information control by the corporate accountants. Previously, divisional accountants retained divisional data and exercised considerable discretion over what went into the financial summaries sent to corporate head office and divisional general managers. The problems experienced with the new financial information system may be characteristic of human responses to the introduction of computers into large organisations. People's working processes become too explicit, easily checked and thus inflexible. In Crozier's words:[29]

'The benefits of human social systems are that they are

imperfect and always evolving, thus capable of learning from experience. The computer, on the other hand, might fit too well with the exhaustive controls idolized by bureaucracies which ignore these benefits.'

Here, the divisional accountants lost power, were more accountable. They resisted the financial information system by running parallel systems, entering incomplete and inaccurate data into the database, writing angry memos, and publicly supporting a replacement system.

Coalitions can develop against the introduction of new technology. They may be quite temporary, depending on the specific interests of the different interest groups composing the coalition. Thus, in the 1985–86 dispute between News International and the unions at Wapping, temporary coalitions formed on the union side between the NGA, SOGAT (Society of Graphical & Allied Trades) and the NUJ (National Union of Journalists). However, many journalists found it in their interests to settle with management and work at the Wapping site following the dismissal of several thousand NGA and SOGAT members from their jobs for going on strike.

Much resistance can be related to poor implementation planning and procedures; that is, how the change is managed, and how people experience the process of implementation (Fig. 2.2). In looking at a British clearing bank, Child and Tarbuck[30] found personnel specialists commenting on their senior managers' unthinking attitude toward the personnel aspects of introducing technological change. There was a notable absence of systematic studies into employee reactions to new technologies, into how consistent these technologies were with staff competences, and into the consequences of changes for job satisfaction. This neglect of the motivational foundations of staff performance created a lack of enthusiasm amongst staff that contributed to the failure of the bank's experiment with counter terminals.

In researching the introduction of a computer-based management information system into the US Post Office in the 1970s, Dickson and his colleagues[31] found numerous examples of dysfunctional behaviour. Many of the high number of transaction errors made in the first months of systems operation were made by postal workers on purpose. There were threats, union resistance and sabotage. Co-workers also grumbled about the system and managers never responded positively to questions about the system's usefulness. However, the researchers concluded that the major reasons for such reactions were poor planning and implementation procedures.

In looking at supervisors and new technology in a wide range of companies and industries, Rothwell[32] found that successful implementation related mainly to the extent which management foresaw, planned and managed the changes. Managers tended to get too involved in system technicalities or concerned only with schedule slippage and getting the system running. As a result, supervisors were left to cope and adjust to change as best they could. Some experienced the ambiguities and insecurities of their position intensely, and in fact withdrew from involvement and commitment.

> 'By the time management realised this, certain patterns of resistance to change, or, at the least, cynicism about its benefits might well have set in and spread to others.'[32]

A final point here is related not just to the introduction of new technology, but to any managerial attempt to rationalise work; for example, by conducting work study or job evaluation exercises. In the process of developing a computer system, much analysis of work processes and procedures and the way work is organised needs to be carried out. This makes work practices more transparent and gives management much more information about what is going on lower down in the organisation. Such studies may be perceived as, and actually be, threatening to individual and group interests and, by themselves, will promote resistant behaviour of various kinds.

ORGANISATIONAL RESISTANCE TO CHANGE

We have established that technological change can often mean an attack on power, prestige or security of vested interests in an organisation, or violation of decision-making prerogatives or territorial rights that have been established and accepted over time. Where a significant power bloc or senior people with influence experience new technology as such a threat, then there may arise what amounts to organisational resistance to technological change.

Additionally, a variety of organisational characteristics may hinder the reception of new technology, or create conflicts as a result of it. These commonly include the reward systems, the custom and practice and machinery of collective bargaining, the appraisal system and the criteria used for assessing performance that prevail in the organisation.

One illustrative example emerges from conflicts over the pay system at Austin Rover in September 1986. A five-tier pay structure had been introduced in 1980. This had received little support from the shopfloor unions, but their antagonism was reinforced by the redrawing of job boundaries occasioned by subsequent introduction of robots and computers. 'We are stuck with a 1980 pay structure in a company using 1986 new technology', one trade union leader claimed.

Electricians retrained to identify and repair robot and computer faults wanted upgrading from top skilled to technician level. However, other electricians in the skilled grade also wanted upgrading, while existing white collar technicians resisted both these developments. Lower down the existing pay scales, Amalgamated Engineering Union (AEU) members would also claim new skills and status as a result of working with computer-numerically-controlled machines. Production workers in the Transport and General Workers Union (TGWU) claimed new technology meant greater responsibility, increased stress and more maintenance work. Meanwhile, white collar members in the Association of Scientific, Technical & Managerial Staff (ASTMS) claimed higher pay because new technology blurred the line between technicians and supervisors, requiring the latter to develop greater technical skills in addition to their supervisory responsibilities.

Clearly, the existing trade union, grading, job description and pay structures, and the pervasive impact of computer-based systems had created a multiplicity of conflicts within the company. The question then raised was whether the existing collective bargaining system could handle changing the pay differentials of some 30 000 workers. Much of the explosive industrial relations potential of these issues could have been avoided had the necessary changes been introduced with, or before, the new technology.

Culture

Culture is another important feature that can assist in explaining resistance to change. Organisation culture is the set of shared norms, values, attitudes, myths and beliefs that evolve in, or within parts of, an organisation over a period of time.

Dickson and Simmons[33] suggest that the culture of an organisation can be a crucial factor in how technological change is received and processed. If top management has established a culture of high trust throughout the organisation—for example, if it deals with grievances, maintains open communications, rewards performance and provides job security–there is less likely to be resistance to new computer systems. However, if top management remain isolated or aloof, if class antagonisms are perpetuated at work, or if the organisational culture actively supports inflexible, conservative or 'safe' behaviour, then effective implementation of computer-based technology may be hindered. Interestingly, a number of writers on the subject[34] suggest that UK work life has been characterised mainly by low trust relations, from which may stem some of the problems associated with employee resistance to change.

All organisational cultures are products of human investment in time, activity and precedent. They will also support a range of present activities and interest groups. Organisational members imbued in a culture may represent considerable obstacles to technological change, especially if that change process also necessitates the development of modified or new cultures. However, we need to enrich this picture.

Handy[35] distinguishes between four types of culture in organisations, namely:

power (central power source, few rules and procedures, precedent and whim important)

task (project-oriented, flexible)

role (rules, roles, procedures and predictability important)

person (individual specialism more important than organisation goals).

Such cultures can span the organisation or might be specific to a department or even a group. Power and task cultures are probably more suitable for receiving and operating rapidly changing technologies, or one-off or batch production. Role cultures fit with technologies' running routine, programmable operations or mass-production.

Given the immense potential and flexibility of computer-based technologies, they can be used in any of these ways, the important thing being to develop the appropriate organisational culture. However, what is important for our purposes is to suggest that task cultures tend to be much more receptive to technological change, while the receptivity of power cultures tends to depend on the preferences and self-perceived interests of the power-holders at the centre. Role cultures (typical of bureaucracies) tend to resist change, though this is probably less true where the computer technology's potential for standardisation and using rules and procedures is used to enhance bureaucratic functioning.[36-38] A relevant point here is made by Peters and Waterman.[38] They researched 43 'excellently managed' companies, many of them in high-tech industries. They conclude that strong cultures that are focussed externally (i.e. centred on service to the customer), rather than internally, are more sensitive to environmental changes and more willing and more quickly able to adapt to them. As a matter of experience, organisations with a high-tech culture also tend to be more receptive to computer-based technology than organisations with limited exposure to computers and computerisation.

Organisation structure
Cultures tie in closely with organisation structures, which also can enable, or be unsupportive of, the introduction of computer systems.

Many organisations are still bureaucracies or include bureaucratic elements. Bureaucracies persist for good, and sometimes not so good, reasons. However, they are designed, as computers are often programed, to reliably perform a narrowly prescribed assortment of functions. To ensure reliability of the prescribed operations, bureaucratic structures tend to be inward-looking and have strong, inbuilt defences against change. As Child[39] says:

'There is always tension in the design of organisations between preserving control and encouraging flexibility, and bureaucracy comes down heavily in favour of the former.'

Crozier[40] found that bureaucracies do adjust to change but in peculiar ways:

'Change in a bureaucratic organisation must come from the top down and must be universalistic i.e. encompass the whole organisation *en bloc*. It will wait until a serious question pertaining to an important dysfunction can be raised. Then it will be argued about and decided upon at the higher level and applied to the whole organisation even to the areas where dysfunctions are not seriously felt ... crisis is a distinctive and necessary element of the bureaucratic system. It provides the only means of making the necessary adjustments.'

Hage and Aiken[41] and Bonoma and Zaltman[42] have looked at the structure–change relationship in a range of organisational structures, and their findings are consistent with related research in the published literature. For considering the implementation of computer systems, the interesting points made are that the greater the degree of commitment a change requires, and the more formalised the organisation, the longer is the decision-making period, and the less likely is full adoption. The less divisible and the less reversible the change, and the broader its impact, the more important and efficient are highly centralised structures. Changes that require strong and widespread commitment if they are to be effective are more likely to be successful with decentralised decision-making.

The published research supports the notion that less bureaucratic structures tend to be more receptive to change. But in practice any structure, be it a matrix, functional, conglomerate form or whatever, will tend to impede the introduction of computer systems where redesign is, or is felt to be, needed to ensure 'fit' with the process and consequences of computerisation.

This is an important point when one considers some of the predictions made about organisational forms and modes of working in the computer age. Tynan[43] discusses the example of Fanuc—part of Fujitsu, a multinational electrical company. Fanuc operated an FMS (flexible manufacturing system) and was designed with a matching diamond-shaped structure. As Tynan points out, most organisations are hierarchical pyramids:

> 'Information technology will mean that they become more fluid inside ... organisations will become a diamond-shaped amorphous mass quaking with its own agitated movement.'[43]

In *The future of work*, Handy[44] suggests that the new technology makes possible the dispersed organisation. The tendencies will be toward decentralisation, not wages but fees and self-employment, the federal organisation highly automated to enhance communication and co-ordination, with a professional core but most tasks subcontracted out to semi-independent small businesses. Another possibility, given the communication and control potential of computer technology, is reductions in the numbers of middle management and supervisors, and the move toward the 'hour-glass' structure.

The critical problem then becomes how to move from one structural form to another under the impact, and even while introducing, computer systems. To an extent this formulation of the problem downplays the mobilisation of power and influence by interested parties during conditions of change. Resistance by interest groups may be sufficient to perpetuate existing organisational shapes, and indeed to cause the new technology to be implemented in ways that reinforce the status quo and existing power structures in organisations. This is by no means a necessary result, however. Thus Rank Xerox in the UK identified a need to reduce central overheads in 1982, but successfully used computer technology to establish a federalised organisation based on a 'Xanadu' support network.[45] Former employees developed independent units that retained contact through terminals with each other and central office. Their services could be contracted to Rank Xerox or other businesses as demanded.

THE ENVIRONMENT OF TECHNOLOGICAL CHANGE

So far the main focus has been on finding explanations inside an organisation for 'resistance' to computer technology. But this may be confusing the reasons for resistance with its **manifestation** as an internal organisational event. The problem here is separating out causes from effects.

As an example, in one small company investigated by the authors the discontent of computer staff manifested itself in demands for longer rest breaks, high absenteeism, high labour turnover and demands for more pay. One major grievance was isolated as the poor ergonomic design of the workstations resulting from internal design team decisions. But on a wider canvas it emerged that the company was in a highly competitive industry. A fight for survival made new technology more necessary, but the desperate financial position of the firm restricted capital expenditure. Furthermore, the equipment manufacturer and supplier offered generous terms, dominated the hardware and software markets, and were under little market pressure to change existing design criteria, especially for such a small company. Clearly, in this case environmental factors circumscribed significantly the possible organisational choices about new technology.

Each organisation operates in a **task** environment consisting of suppliers, customers and competitors, and a **general** environment consisting of the political, social, legal, technological and economic factors in the wider society. All these factors can have a bearing on whether, and, if so, how, technological change will take place in a specific organisation. They might also explain organisational effects that take the form of conflicts and 'resistances'.

Thus, the relatively slow adoption of IT in the United Kingdom has been related to an inappropriate education system developing an anti-industrial culture.[44] Additionally, government and industry-wide initiatives in IT training seem to have had little impact, creating a gloomy picture of skills shortages.[46] The UK trade union movement has commonly been accused of resisting technological change, though most of the available evidence points to this not being a general pattern at all in the 1980s (see Chapter 7). The failure of competitors to invest in IT could reduce the need for an organisation do so. On the other hand, technology 'champions' may find in the experience of other organisations, or their own failure to adopt IT, evidence for the attractiveness and competitive advantage derived from utilising computer technologies.

A more generally applicable explanation for the slow adoption of IT may lie in the traditional low-wage, low-productivity character of the UK economy. Historically this has tended to push employer preferences in the direction of labour-intensive rather than capital-intensive new technology options for generating profits and performance. This preference may well have been reinforced in the 1980s in the face of recession cutting back on the need for, and the ability to make, large capital outlays. The labour-intensive option is also encouraged by the relative docility of the workforce (indicated by the lowest strike figures for decades), and by rising unemployment exerting downward pressure on wages.

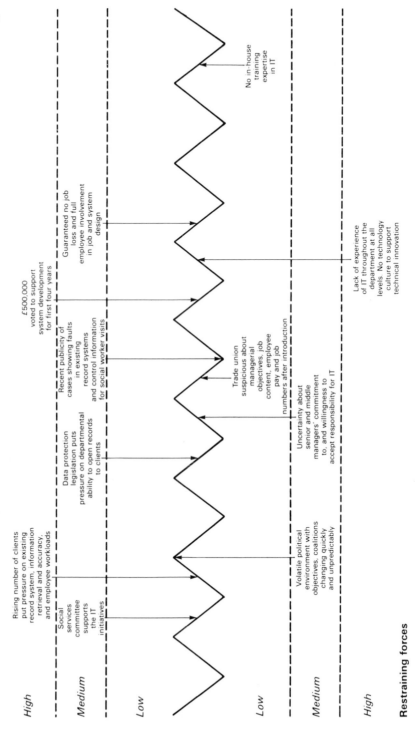

Forces for change

High

Medium — Rising number of clients put pressure on existing record system, information retrieval and accuracy, and employee workloads

Social services committee supports the IT initiatives

Data protection legislation puts pressure on departmental ability to open records to clients

£500,000 voted to support system development for first four years

Recent publicity of cases showing faults in existing record systems and control information for social worker visits

Guaranteed no job loss and full employee involvement in job and system design

No in-house training expertise in IT

Low

Low

Medium — Volatile political environment with objectives, coalitions changing quickly and unpredictably

Trade union suspicious about managerial objectives, job content, employee pay and job numbers after introduction

Uncertainty about senior and middle managers' commitment to, and willingness to accept responsibility for IT

High — Lack of experience of IT throughout the department at all levels. No technology culture to support technical innovation

Restraining forces

Fig. 2.4 Force-field analysis: introducing computer technology into a borough social services department

As a final twist, these labour market characteristics partially explain why many foreign firms and multinationals have developed offices and factories in the UK in the 1980s. However, these bring with them the financial investment, greenfield site opportunities, managerial culture, labour practices and competitiveness that form not a resistant but a receptive organisational context for new technologies.

CAN 'RESISTANCE' BE MANAGED?

While the question, 'Can "resistance" be managed?', is always posed at some stage in a computerisation project, its very phrasing limits the extent of analysis and of proposed remedial action. 'Resistance' is seen as a managerial problem. There is little room here for seeing that new technology may present a very real but possibly different set of problems for other participants. But even if those problems are recognised, to the extent that they fail to coincide with managerial or technical requirements their legitimacy is open to question.

Perspectives on new technology often reflect interests and muddy the analysis of the problem field. The need to step inside other people's perceptions is an essential prerequisite in handling computer projects (see Fig. 2.3). Another practical tool useful for preliminary analysis is shown in Figure 2.4. This is necessarily simplified, but illustrates the authors' own analysis of the forces for and against change in a project researched in 1986. It is important to see conflicts, problems and opposition as possible in a computer project from conception and throughout design, implementation and subsequent operation (see Fig. 2.2). This means that the analysis shown in Figure 2.4 must be regularly updated and enriched. In the example, the project manager found this to be quite crucial, given the volatile political environment, the importance of internal politics, the clash of cultures within the organisation and the massive impact these factors could have on the success of the computer project.

The need to cast over a very wide range for possible factors influencing the path of change has been a theme of this chapter. Equally, signs of opposition may take a variety of forms easily missed in analysis. Figure 2.2 indicates how conflicts may take overt and covert forms.

People may employ a variety of tactics in pursuing interests, and these may even rise to the level of counter-implementation strategies. Bardach[47] indicates a range of methods for diverting resources from a project, diverting its goals, or dissipating energies. In the latter, a possible strategy is to be seen to support the implementation but insist that it is really done properly. This could result in much expenditure in time and energy, such that those involved in the project run out of staying power. Keen[14] suggests that typical counter-implementation ploys are to lie low, rely on inertia, keep the project complex and hard to define and co-ordinate, minimise the implementers' legitimacy and influence and play on their lack of insider knowledge.

Clearly, people are capable of political and even strategic action against computer projects. However, it is difficult to agree with Bardach and Keen that counter-implementation can be looked upon as an organisational 'game'. This may be true sometimes, but people rarely commit themselves to well thought out, long-term strategies, requiring investments in time and energy, without serious interests being at issue. Again, the importance of detailed analysis arises.

A preliminary analysis of the human forces for and against change is essential, but is invariably skimped. This tendency to short-circuit a full analysis is reinforced by the relative ease of (and the established techniques available for) examining technical matters, as opposed to the messy reality of human behaviour in organisations. This is why all to often computer projects fail through behavioural rather than technical factors. But the full analysis embracing human factors suggested by this chapter has the benefit not only of forming the basis for more appropriate design and implementation approaches; it also serves to indicate what is possible and not possible, what can be controlled by managers and computer project leaders, and what *cannot* be managed, what has to be muddled through, and what needs to be left alone.

It does not advance the cause of new technology management to suggest that the solutions to human problems in technical change are all to be found in a kit bag of psychological tools, the managerial task being to administer these to recalcitrant individuals and eliminate their 'resistance'. The complex situations arising from technological change can be, but rarely are, manageable in these terms. The service to technology managers is perhaps to suggest what the wiser ones know already, that the assumption of managerial omnipotence can be a dangerous dream fed by inadequate analyses of the reasons for 'resistance' to change, rather than a material reality. The final irony is that this dream itself may come to harm and hinder rather than further the technological change project.

CONCLUSIONS

'Resistance' is an attribution often delivered from the perspective of those organisational members powerful enough to set the technological agenda against those who are not. It is more useful to substitute the idea of 'conflicts over' rather than 'resistance to' computer-based technologies. Such conflicts are expressed in diverse ways, and the relationship between cause and symptom is not always easy to discern.

For this reason, all projects require a preliminary behavioural analysis that operates on group, coalition, organisational and environmental levels, as well as at the level of the individual employee. The interrelationship of these factors contributes to the problem situation. This will change throughout the course of a project and so will require regular reassessment as a basis for guiding future activity. Such behavioural analyses are invariably skimped because of a lack of expertise within the project team, preferences for more clear, clean technical problems, and an over-reliance on simplified models of human behaviour. But the messy, complex reality of human aspects of computer projects demands more, not less, detailed analysis. When this is not forthcoming, it is not surprising to find computer systems failing for behavioural rather than technical reasons.

This chapter may seem overloaded in the direction of human 'problems' with and 'resistances' to computers. In fact, as indicated briefly above, any situational analysis also needs to look carefully at those human factors which may support the introduction of the computer system. Beyond this, much can be done to make human factors work with, rather than against, computer projects. This theme receives detailed attention in the chapters that follow.

CHAPTER 3
Human Resource Planning for IT

'Too often what companies talk of as their employment policy is in reality a set of free-floating personnel policies, often developed in the 60's and 70's, which continue regardless, unconnected with each other or the business plan.'[1]

INTRODUCTION

Sound human resource planning is necessary for the introduction of computer systems. The objectives are twofold. Firstly, human resource planning operates as an insurance policy on the computerisation project itself, focussing on the necessity for appropriately skilled staff to be available when required and the avoidance of implementation bottlenecks. Secondly, the relationship between the computer system and its future development and the workforce as a totality needs to be explored and delineated carefully.

So much seems obvious. However, much case study and survey evidence supports the contention that the tasks following on from these objectives, particularly the latter, are frequently not carried out properly, if at all. As a working explanation for where this is an organisational reality, three factors can be mentioned. Firstly, it is a remarkable feature of most UK organisations how much they have lacked detailed strategic as opposed to operational planning—and organisations without clearly defined strategic goals can rarely have coherent IT strategies, or direct accurately their technological investment.

Secondly, and partially as a knock-on effect, UK organisations often lack employment policies and a strategic focus on human resource management before IT is introduced. In reviewing some 950 employing organisations, a 1985 study of IT manpower into the 1990s remarks, almost casually:

'Future IT demand trends indicate a continuing growth in IT skill requirements. Expectations of employers ... were difficult to quantify because of the general lack of detailed manpower plans in companies. The focus for many was on meeting short-term objectives.'[2].

Thus IT often finds its way into organisations through inadequate personnel machinery, procedures and perspectives, along with failure to consider, or at least an underplaying of, the likely short and long term *human* impacts of IT.

Thirdly, personnel managers, supposedly *the* people specialists, have all too often operated in low-status, advisory roles removed from positions of power such as Boards of Directors, and absent from strategic decision-making, even where the implications of such decisions for the workforce may be immense.

While these tendencies may not be true for *every* organisation, nevertheless they appear to apply widely enough in the UK to merit detailed attention and some consideration of alternative approaches. Planning may not be the panacea many make it out to be: planning needs to be detailed and realistic, but also the resources, power and authority to make plans operational need to be available and utilised. However lack of human resource planning will show up when systems become imperfectly operational. For computerisation, as for any other organisational change, the law of the six p's applies: proper planning prevents pathetically poor performance.

A ROLE FOR PERSONNEL?

Personnel managers specialise in dealing with the problems emerging from the fact that organisations employ human beings. A primary group of tasks concentrates on supplying and maintaining staff— through recruitment and selection, training, performance monitoring, appraisal, health, safety and welfare, payment, redundancy and related policies. At a deeper level, personnel management is concerned with managing conflicts and tensions that result from trying to use the efforts of human beings who all wish to make their own use of the organis- ations they join. Since microtechnological change tends to cut across all these activities, one might expect to find personnel practioners in key roles during computerisation projects. Much evidence points to a different picture.

As one example, Rothwell[3] looked at the introduction of new technology in some 23 public and private sector organisations between 1981 and 1983. She points to the reality and, by implication, the possible roles for Personnel:

> 'There was little evidence of serious consideration of employ-
> ment policies until close to the implementation stage ...
> company personnel managers seemed to play a surprisingly
> small part in most of the implementation process, apart from

handling union negotiations ... the role of the personnel function was still reactive rather than proactive, concerned more with implementing redundancy or providing training facilities than planning ahead, and setting employment policy criteria, which those responsible for designing and installing new systems would have to take into account'.[3]

A 1984 survey of over 2000 workplaces adds to this picture. Daniel[4] found that personnel management involvement occurred in only half the cases where microelectronic technology was introduced, and was frequently only at the later stages of implementation. This contrasted sharply with frequent Personnel involvement where more conventional organisational changes were proposed; for example, in work reorganisation or changes in working practices alone. The explanation seems to lie with perceptions by other managers of personnel specialists as mainly trouble-shooters, to be brought in only where resistance and negotiations are likely. In fact, Daniel found that, unlike other organisational changes, advanced technical change was rarely resisted by manual workers or their representatives, and rarely the subject of collective bargaining. As a result, computerisation was still often seen as a technical matter, with no established role or function for personnel management.

There have been many attempts to explain the low status and lack of strategic influence of personnel specialists in UK organisations generally.[5] The personnel function is shot through with ambiguities: is its role a caring or controlling one? Does it represent primarily the employer or employee? How can the effectiveness of personnel work be demonstrated and in what does it lie? How does its advisory role impinge on line managers who are also responsible for their subordinates' performance? A major problem lies with the lack of line authority to influence events and policies. Some commentators point out that personnel work attracts people who are reluctant to make decisions or side wholeheartedly with the employer. One 1980s survey suggests a continuing 'pervasive amateurism' with much personnel work done by line managers anyway and not professional personnel staff.[6]

In the 1970s and 1980s, personnel specialisms have developed in response to changing organisational requirements, particularly in handling employment legislation, industrial relations, and more recently redundancies. However, a personnel specialism in the handling of advanced technological change has not yet developed nor generally been perceived as necessary, although there are signs that the experience of computerisation may be changing this in some organisations. Daniel[4] found that foreign-owned firms and those making most use of advanced technology were most likely to employ professional personnel managers. There is also reason to believe that foreign-owned firms are more likely to be using advanced technology. Certainly a 1986 survey found this to be the case in the engineering industry in South Wales. This discrepancy in favour of foreign-owned firms was even more marked when future investment plans for adopting new technology were compared.[7] Futhermore, according to Daniel's 1984 survey, personnel managers were substantially more likely to report an increase in their influence in workplaces that were making most use of advanced technology and where there had been recent technical change.

Some tentative remarks may be made at this stage. Personnel specialists, where they exist, have only a modest role in the early stages of most systems implementations. However, when new technology introduction brings in its train the more obvious 'people' problems, no doubt partly stemming from poor human resource planning, it seems that personnel managers are called in, and this enhances their subsequent influence over system running and modification. One result may be that, in organisations where Personnel is not present or has low status, 'people' problems experienced with computerisation may lead to serious consideration for the first time of the employment of, and expanded role for, personnel professionals.

Some feel for how the personnel function and people are forgotten in technological change is given by Clegg and Kemp's study[8] of 20 companies introducing flexible manufacturing systems (FMS) and computer-numerically-controlled machinery. Thus one electronics company spent millions of pounds on FMSs but generated for itself rows between different departments, management–union arguments over demarcation and inter-union conflicts. In particular, a failure to consider work organisation and people at the FMS design stage led to subsequent long-drawn-out disputes between engineers, machine operators and programmers over responsibility for routine edits of program tapes. Such problems could be traced back to the FMS project team being totally controlled by technical specialists. Line managers, industrial relations and personnel specialists, shopfloor supervisors and shop stewards had virtually no input. Decision-making was almost wholly devoted to technical design, while 'human' issues like training and operator responsibilities were considered only after the system was up and running.

The lessons of the many cases in new technology implementation reviewed for the Institute of Personnel Management by Evans and Wilkinson[9] would seem to be that:

'A senior member of the personnel function should be involved from the start in the planning and decision-making process ... human aspects should be considered alongside technical, financial and other considerations as an integral part of the planning process.'[9]

This is a correct but limited analysis from a personnel practioner viewpoint. The phenomenon of technological convergence has immense implications in the organisational sphere. Fully applied, IT can break down organisational boundaries and transform the nature of work, roles and relationships. One development could see systems analysts no longer cut off from the human aspects of the systems they design. On the contrary, they would be as fully involved in the human resource planning areas as users and personnel practioners are in the design and implementation of computer-based systems. It may be that the division of labour at managerial level has held back UK organisational performance even more than the more publicised 'restrictive practices' amongst lower level staff. IT could force a new concentration on the need for integration and co-ordination of tasks and roles. It is in such a context that the personnel role in the process and timing of technical change needs to be assessed.

PLANNING FOR IT: AN OVERVIEW

The human resource planning discussed here needs to be placed within the larger framework of 'strategic human resource management'. For Hendry and Pettigrew, [10] this means for an organisation:

— use of planning
— personnel systems designed and managed coherently in the light of an employment policy and manpower strategy, and underpinned by a 'philosophy'
— matching human resource activities to some explicit business strategy
— seeing the people of the organisation as a 'strategic resource' for achieving 'competitive advantage'.

Ironically, computers themselves can be powerful tools for 'strategic human resource management'. In particular, they can provide much more sensitive and useful human resource planning systems able to cope with planning in and for unpredictable internal and external organisational environments. They can also provide personnel managers with greater expertise, more organisational influence, and so greater opportunities for promoting human resource policies in IT projects. But all too frequently, where personnel functions have adopted computerised systems, these have seldom been exploited beyond their capacity as electronic card indexes.

In a 1984 sample of 350 different establishments, Hall and Torrington[11] found 68% using computers for personnel work. However, computers were much more frequently being used in organisations of more than 1000 employees, simply because record storage and routine clerical tasks there were much more burdensome. Throughout the sample, the computer was less generally seen as a tool to enhance managerial activity such as personnel planning, control and forecasting. Major problems seemed to be the lack of expertise in, and conviction about, computer use amongst personnel managers. Many lacked hands-on experience; software was mostly disappointing, but its full potential was rarely exploited anyway.

As early as 1978, Legge[12] identified the need for personnel practioners to acquire expertise in computer-based processing and information systems. This would be one part of a strategy to improve their organisational power and status. From this improved power base, personnel managers could ensure that human resource issues featured more largely in higher-level planning and decision-making. In the late 1980s, and with human resource issues in IT projects receiving little detailed attention, this advice has become even more pertinent. For a range of reasons, then, personnel specialists need to develop IT skills just as much as systems specialists need to be inducted into the human implications of their work.

Human resource planning needs to be detailed and continuously updated and cannot proceed successfully unless it is closely related to organisational missions and various linked strategies, particularly in the areas of finance, IT investments, marketing and production. The introduction of computer-based technology into the British coal industry illustrates the difficulties.

Between 1983 and 1986, some 63000 miners were made redundant through pit closures and new technology. The objectives were to increase productivity and produce cheaper coal. Union resistance to the programme collapsed with the failure of the 1983–84 miners' strike. In 1986, productivity increased by 23% mostly due to more concentrated coalface working with high-technology heavy-duty equipment, and secondly to more intensive working among coalface teams with the reintroduction of high bonus payments. However, such record productivity levels through new technology produced coal stocks far higher than could be justified by normal economic considerations. This implied an unplanned-for speed-up of redundancies in 1987, to be paid for at the rate of £700 for each year of service for miners over 30 years old; it also implied that new technology would need to be under-utilised.

Clearly, human resource planning on redundancy, labour productivity and payment systems were poorly related to the timing and volume of new technology implementation. Moreover, neither were formulated in the light of marketing and sales strategies based on realistic assessments of market demand for coal. Ironically, the success of the industrial relations plan to break union resistance to closures and new technology had converted *increased* productivity into a problem.

Figure 3.1 focuses particularly on the crucial links between human resource policies, IT plans, and systems development and implementation. Note that human resource planning for the whole workforce and for running the computerisation project occurs *before* and *during* systems development, rather than reactively, as problems arise, or merely at the systems implementation stage.

The rest of this section looks at the issues raised under two headings.

Integrated personnel policies

A primary need is to develop integrated long-term personnel policies in the light of proposed computer usage. As a working definition, Rothwell[1] sees the need to develop:

> 'An overall employment strategy which integrates the organisation's various personnel policies and manpower plans. It should enable it to meet and absorb the changing requirements of technology and markets in the foreseeable future.'

Strategy here implies anticipation and flexibility. These features become crucial because existing personnel policies and practices can be quickly outgrown through new technology impacts; their maintenance can prove organisationally embarrassing.

As one example, banking, building societies and insurance companies are labour- and information-intensive and lend themselves particularly well to automation. New technology means further undermining of traditional employment arrangements based on job security, managerial paternalism, incremental salaries tied to loyalty, age and length of service, and apolitical, non-militant employee representation.

As such firms take to IT they increasingly need to develop phased redundancy packages but also to prepare for new jobs and skills. More routine decisions can be pushed down into the hierarchy, thus bringing middle management jobs into question. Managerial work requires new technical and informative skills to fully utilise IT and its information product. The new information specialists who service senior management (e.g. programmers, systems analysts) find career paths blocked by traditional promotion patterns. Traditional grading structures and job evaluation schemes creak in the face of new skills and jobs, while pay needs to be more performance- and market-oriented to attract in scarce IT specialists.

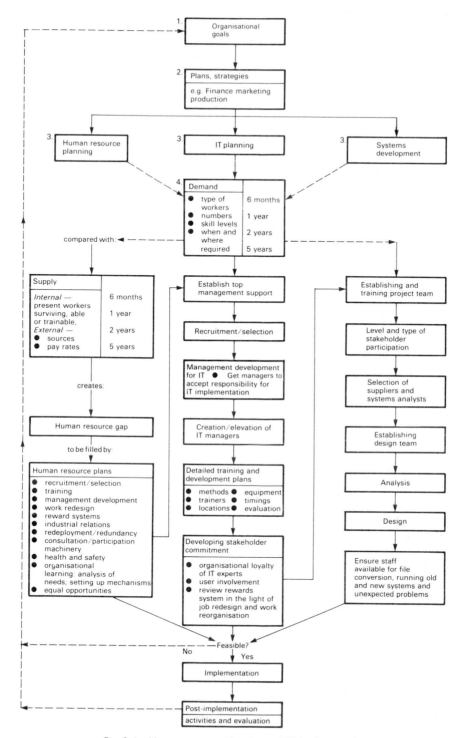

1. Organisational goals

2. Plans, strategies

e.g. Finance marketing production

3. Human resource planning

3. IT planning

3. Systems development

4. Demand
- type of workers — 6 months
- numbers — 1 year
- skill levels — 2 years
- when and where required — 5 years

compared with:

Supply

Internal — present workers surviving, able or trainable, — 6 months / 1 year

External —
- sources — 2 years
- pay rates — 5 years

creates:

Human resource gap

to be filled by:

Human resource plans
- recruitment/selection
- training
- management development
- work redesign
- reward systems
- industrial relations
- redeployment/redundancy
- consultation/participation machinery
- health and safety
- organisational learning: analysis of needs; setting up mechanisms
- equal opportunities

Establish top management support

Recruitment/selection

Management development for IT ● Get managers to accept responsibility for IT implementation

Creation/elevation of IT managers

Detailed training and development plans
- methods ● equipment
- trainers ● timings
- locations ● evaluation

Developing stakeholder commitment
- organisational loyalty of IT experts
- user involvement
- review rewards system in the light of job redesign and work reorganisation

Establishing and training project team

Level and type of stakeholder participation

Selection of suppliers and systems analysts

Establishing design team

Analysis

Design

Ensure staff available for file conversion, running old and new systems and unexpected problems

Feasible? No   Yes

Implementation

Post-implementation activities and evaluation

Fig. 3.1   Human resource planning and IT implementation

New technology implies systematic training which many financial firms are not yet geared up to provide. The drastic reductions in numbers employed, and changes in job content and working conditions implied by IT will attract employees into trade unions like ASTMS, BIFU and CBU, only too anxious to recruit in the computer-based industries of the future. Computerisation thus means long term personnel planning and integration of employment policies. As Hepburn and Handy[13] state:

> 'Consideration urgently needs to be given to job and organisation design, to recruitment and selection, to rewards (financial and non-financial), to job evaluation, management development and communication, if new technology-induced change is to be introduced effectively to the full benefit of the business.'

The importance of *integrated* personnel policies cannot be overstressed. Thus if, like BAT Industries, an organisation possesses a policy of employee involvement, developing teamwork and encouraging employee creativity, it is important that systems specialists embody such objectives in computer system design and its implications for job content and how work will be organised. A policy to maximise labour flexibility, as at Nabisco, the US food group, must be accompanied by a commitment to proper training.

Organisations seem to have particular problems formulating coherent policies on pay, training and development when introducing new technology. The difficulties experienced in this area by the Austin Rover and Vauxhall car firms are discussed in detail in chapter 7. These were avoided at Courage's new brewery at Reading in the early 1980s. Automated production resulted in extensive job restructuring. To cope with this and to build in flexibility to facilitate further technical changes, new job evaluation and grading schemes were introduced. The key criterion for evaluating jobs became 'responsibility', and a simple four-grade structure was drawn up, with opportunities for progression in each grade and between grades dependent on training and performance. This encouraged training, flexibility in attitudes and skill deployment amongst employees, and a receptivity toward future technological change.

As job boundaries are broken down to optimise new technology usage, more employers are seeing advantages in the simplification and harmonisation of pay, benefits and conditions; for example, for white collar and manual, direct and maintenance, managerial and specialist workers. In some borough councils the opposite has occurred. Thus in 1985, faced with shortages of computer specialists, Lambeth had to offer 'scarcity' allowances of up to £2500 a year to bring salaries nearer the 'going rate' in London. Other boroughs have had to make 'technology' supplements to retain computer staff and those acquiring technical competencies through training. Unfortunately these measures complicate existing reward structures, lead to regrading and pay claims from other workers and can create industrial relations problems.

A broader perspective on the organisational and human impacts of new technology can be taken. An organisation development (OD) approach would ask the following questions. What sort of jobs, teamwork, organisation structure, human relationships and work organisation do we need to facilitate the business we are in? What personnel policies do we wish to pursue? How can computer technology help us to get there? In this view, an intended computer-based system becomes an enabling rather than a determining technology, its design and use planned to further organisational objectives and preferred personnel policies from the start. Few organisations take such a broad view, and considerable political skills are required to push through the organisational transformations frequently embodied in OD schemes.

Personnel policies and system development
Common problems experienced with the introduction of computer technology flow from its novelty and the uncertainties surrounding its implementation and use. Thus, even where formulated, redundancy and training plans may be thrown out of phase where technology implementation has to be some 6–8 months later than originally planned due to a problem with system design, program bugs, or supplier delivery. In the same way employee relations issues—such as extended disputes over information disclosure, negotiations over future pay and conditions, unions insisting on a 'buy-out' of jobs displaced by computers—can hit system implementation. It is frequently difficult to ensure that properly skilled staff in the right numbers are available when required at different stages in system development and implementation. This may be due to a lack of training resources, or more often to shortages in specialist computer staff. Where key data processing, information or system design personnel leave a project part of the way through, or even after implementation, delays of months may result. Such staff prove difficult to replace, and then continuity is broken as their successors need time to read themselves into the project. These delays can have unanticipated knock-on effects. For these reasons it is vital to ensure co-ordination and mutual feedback between strategies being pursued, and contingency planning for the worst possible scenarios. This enables adjustments to be made on an ongoing basis instead of too late in the day, if at all.

The timings of personnel policies and systems development need careful consideration. The relationships become difficult to secure given the long lead times typically needed for systems development and equipment delivery. Thus in 1971, British Rail invested £13 million in a computerised Total Operations Processing System (TOPS) to control freight movements. It required a four-year implementation programme. Some 150 locations throughout the UK were linked to a central computer in London. Each location required 24-hour clerical staffing to make computer inputs, while manual staff in marshalling yards needed to be able to make use of output computer information. A major staff training and education programme was required. The solution lay in a two-year staged TOPS implementation, bringing local areas into the system gradually. How was training kept phase with system implementation?

> 'By using condemned railway coaches as travelling classrooms, it was possible for the trainers to continue as implementors at each location and thereby see the staff through the entire process of their 'conversion' to the new system.'[14]

But in the 15 cases they studied, Rothwell and Davidson[15] found such good planning atypical. Especially where there were technical problems, manpower issues tended to be put off until they became of pressing importance. This often created further delays through human resource problems, even where the technical hitches had been sorted out.

Thus, in one medical care products company, a Computer Inventory Data Control system was to be installed to control raw materials. However, programming difficulties caused delays. At senior managers' insistence, and against agreed plans, the system was implemented piecemeal, as programs became ready, in order to generate some payback from the system. This threw training plans out of phase and these slipped to the provision of basic keyboard skills. Thereafter, for three months, poorly trained staff had to run a chaotic dual manual and computer system. When programming was finally completed, the continuing imbalance between manpower and technical developments meant a further six months were needed to stabilise the computer-assisted work system. Clearly, senior managers should have delayed implementation for three months to attain a better technical/manpower balance and a smoother direct changeover from manual to computer system, as originally planned.

Many of the issues touched on in this section, particularly participation in systems design, industrial relations, job redesign, work reorganisation and design of the work station and environment, receive detailed treatment in later chapters. The rest of this chapter brings into focus a number of important human resource areas unjustifiably neglected, or where problems are frequently experienced, when introducing computer-based systems.

RECRUITMENT AND SELECTION

One area for concern may be poor recruitment and selection practice with regard to computer specialist and general user staff. Recruitment is the attracting of suitable applicants, selection the discrimination between applicants, on determined criteria, to secure appropriate staff.

There may be a lack of clear goals on selection, a failure to lay down a logical systematised selection process, a failure to utilise all the available or appropriate sources of recruitment, a failure to specify clearly job or person requirements, weaknesses in test methods and interviewing techniques, and weaknesses in how decisions are made on who to appoint. Organisations may not devote enough time or resources to selection, or, embittered by past experience, selectors may have given up on the possibility of getting suitable applicants.

Figure 3.2 gives an overview of the recruitment and selection stages for both the computer specialist and general staff implied by new technology investments. Stages 1–3 are particularly crucial; they must be dynamic and result in regular updating of job and person specifications to maintain their accuracy. In stage 4, tests must be appropriate. For example, a test of keyboard skills and speed reveals little about a person's ability to utilise different programs. If there is likely to be a shortage of computer-related skills amongst applicants, trainability tests may prove useful. These assess applicant ability to develop the required computer usage skills through the organisation's training scheme.

Staff shortages during system development and implementation can result from the seeming paradox of high unemployment coupled with serious shortages in skilled computer staff in the UK economy. Even a firm as profitable and well run as Barclays Bank experiences difficulties, according to one of its general managers.

> 'The problems we have recruiting skilled computer specialists is inhibiting our ability to expand our product range particularly to corporate customers. Last year we had 12 advertising campaigns. We managed to recruit 100 computer specialists. In the course of the year we lost 97 of them to other companies.'[16]

Facing budgetary restrictions, public sector organisations such as the Civil Service, Department of Social Security and the Inland Revenue have additional recruitment problems in not being able to pay the 'going rate' for skilled computer workers in short supply. Thus a 1986

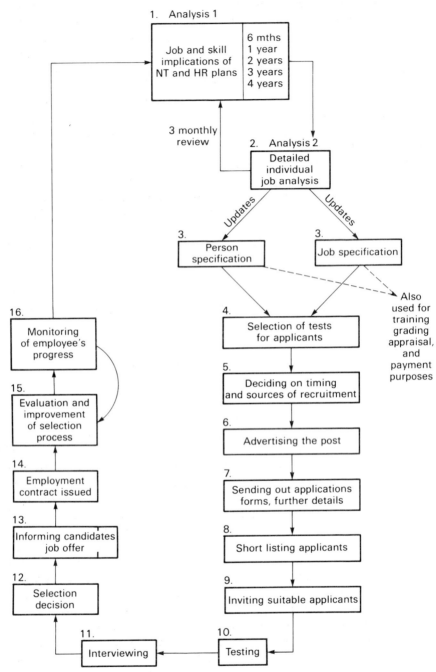

Fig. 3.2 Recruitment and selection for IT—a staged approach

management consultancy report found a national 15% vacancy level for systems development staff in the National Health Service. It rejected privatisation of the entire computer function as impracticable, and recommended a new merit-based pay structure with 30% salary increases needed to attract senior experienced staff of high calibre. According to the SCPS union, throughout 1986 departmental managers in the Civil Service were deliberately preventing staff from answering internal recruitment drives for computer workers. Desperate to keep their staff, managers were failing to circulate recruitment material, vetoing applications, or just failing to forward them.

Such organisations sometimes attempt to get round recruitment problems and staff shortages by contracting out computer-related work. However, failure to recruit, and the bypassing of the existing in-house staff can create industrial-relations problems. Thus in 1985 the Department of Health and Social Security planned to bring in eleven programmers from the software house CAP, to work at the Reading computer centre on the Local Office Microcomputer Project. This was prevented when the SCPS union, representing in-house programmers, threatened strike action. A union spokesman blamed staff shortages on low wages and poaching by neighbouring companies like ICL, British Telecom and Digital Equipment:

'You can get a £2–3000 pay rise just by walking 30 yards across the road'.

Faced with such shortages in computerate and specialist staff, selectors may be induced into reducing the person specification criteria to minimum requirements or less. However, one consequence of the use of less competent labour may be problems in systems analysis, programming, and implementation, and imperfect running of the computer system. The short term savings resulting from poor recruitment or selection practice may be heavily outweighed by the long term costs of their impact on the computerisation project as a whole.

Skimping on stages 1 and 5 (Fig. 3.2) can result in the underestimation of staffing requirements at systems implementation stage; for example, due to an undercalculation of data loads for file conversion, or a failure to embark on the internal training and development and redeployment programmes early enough. Temporary workers then have to be drafted in and they may lack the relevant skills, the organisational and system experience and the commitment to make a good job of implementation. An often observed symptom of poor implementation practice is a large number of temporary and part-time computer workers, whose presence to all intents and purposes turns into a permanence as implementation drifts on from one bad experience to the next.

Experienced interviewers at stage 11 are crucial. They must be fully knowledgeable about the job requirements, having observed performance of the job, or ideally worked in similar posts themselves. One common practice is to abandon selection to the 'people specialists' in the personnel department. In fact they may have little idea what makes up a competent systems analyst, for example, let alone being able to discriminate between different candidates for such a job.

Selection is particularly difficult in information technology appointments. Skills tend to be specific to machines or programming languages, for example, and not that easily transferable. One author recalls involvement in the appointment of a data processing manager with twelve years computer experience to implement a computerised accounting system in the small London branch of an American oil company. It was only after seven months and no implementation that it was discovered that though this present highly paid job required programming skills, the last programming the appointee had done was some eight years before, and then in another language. His subsequent job in a large data-processing department had involved overseeing a range of work. Other staff were relied upon to accomplish skilled tasks like programming. Such an example indicates the importance of recruitment and selection. The seven month delay was estimated to cost the company over £80 000.

MANAGEMENT DEVELOPMENT AND IT

Where IT will be used to transform work and organisational modes of operation, it is vital for development of the competencies to manage IT to occur *before* the IT is implemented. Indeed, this is one main theme of recent work in the Brunel University MANDIT project.[17] Fonda provides a useful five-fold classification of management development approaches observed in practice, each more or less appropriate in different circumstances.

The first approach is 'Sink or swim'. Here, managers are left to their own devices. No training assistance is given unless asked for. This is useful where managers already have a sound grasp of IT and their learning needs are small, as a deliberate attempt to put managers in charge and learn to manage IT situations, or where the system is small and does not impinge on core business operations.

The second approach is 'Management training'. Managers are given formal 'top-up' courses to provide the knowledge and skills they will need to carry out new responsibilities resulting from IT. This approach is most typically used where computer and system staff exist to deal with the major burdens of IT development and operation.

The third approach is 'hands-on with support'. Managers spend off-the-job time using IT equipment to develop work-related projects under trainer guidance. This problem-based approach develops managerial competencies not only in IT equipment skills, but also in managing IT situations.

The fourth approach is 'management education'. This long-term approach integrates development programmes for general management competencies with management development for IT. Unlike the three approaches above, 'management education' will begin well in advance of any technology decisions being taken. It utilises a broad range of training methods and techniques and covers topics like organisational design, scanning the environment, and management of change and technology. It provides a valuable springboard for subsequent application of other approaches.

The fifth approach is 'management culture'. This is a long-term approach particularly applicable where an organisation sees significant changes in future operations, tasks and organisation structure, and where IT will play a vital role in continued success. The OD approach described earlier in the chapter (under integrated personnel policies) is an example of its practice. To achieve a transformation in managerial culture, this approach may use some or all of the other four approaches, but takes a 'whole organisation' view. Thus jobs, roles, career paths, assignments and appraisal schemes are closely related to training programmes in order to develop managerial track records in handling IT competently.

Some comment on these approaches is necessary. Far from being a policy for management development, 'sink or swim' can degenerate into its abandonment. Also, the organisation must be prepared to absorb the cost of likely managerial errors on IT.

'Management training' is a common approach where managers have limited uses for IT and need only to follow rules and procedures drawn up by systems specialists. However, keeping management largely in ignorance of IT may enhance the status and influence of systems professionals, but does little for realising the full potential of the computer system. Futhermore, this approach may be part of the managerial willingness to largely abandon IT strategy and use, seeing it as a chore to be delegated to the systems department. One unfortunate result of such dependence, strongly emerging from two large-scale surveys in 1986,[18,19] is subsequent top management dissatisfaction with their systems departments, including widespread complaints of late delivery of information, and lack of responsiveness to user needs.

'Management education' can prove expensive. It also provides no obvious short term benefits. As a result, the long term commitment of participants and senior management may be difficult to sustain. Similar problems can be encountered with 'management culture', while the political activity engendered by the processes involved and the changes implied may derail its success.

Underlying all these approaches is the need to identify required management competencies for using IT, and the existing training gaps in this area. From research work in a very wide range of organisations using IT, MANDIT establishes some 28 possible managerial competencies for fulfilling ten key responsibilities in managing information technology. Competencies include 'know-how'—for example, understanding the impact of IT on the business, ability to work with management concepts, user skills, and awareness of the availability of programs, systems and facilities suitable for managerial tasks. Other competencies are in the areas of strategy formulation for business, IT training, IT implementation, decision-making (e.g. selecting appropriate technology), managing processes and systems (e.g. supporting use of new systems) and managing IT users, specialists, and organisational learning processes.

A key point is that many organisations expect managers to carry out instructions but not to take initiatives unless given specific authority. However, fulfilling IT potential depends critically on its users and those who manage its use. It follows that

> 'management development policy for *all* managers may need to be directed towards developing the competence to 'manage situations' [i.e. take initiatives, take charge, go outside the rulebook where procedures are incomplete, cope effectively]... if the organisation is to obtain maximum benefits from the use of IT.'[20]

TRAINING PROBLEMS

Training for IT can be conceived as the systematic development in an individual of the skills, knowledge, commitment and receptivity to change necessary to perform competently a given job involving IT user tasks. An overview of how the training process may be accomplished is shown in Fig. 3.3.

A common reason for the failure of computer systems to attain their full potential once installed is earlier omissions in investing the time,

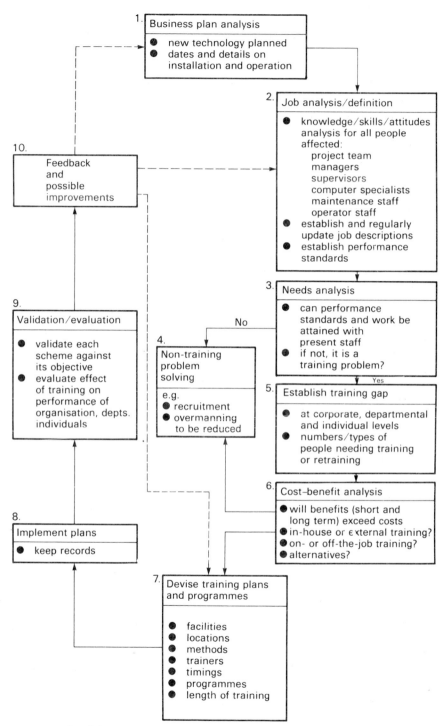

1. Business plan analysis
- new technology planned
- dates and details on installation and operation

2. Job analysis/definition
- knowledge/skills/attitudes analysis for all people affected:
  project team
  managers
  supervisors
  computer specialists
  maintenance staff
  operator staff
- establish and regularly update job descriptions
- establish performance standards

10. Feedback and possible improvements

3. Needs analysis
- can performance standards and work be attained with present staff
- if not, it is a training problem?

No

Yes

9. Validation/evaluation
- validate each scheme against its objective
- evaluate effect of training on performance of organisation, depts. individuals

4. Non-training problem solving
e.g.
- recruitment
- overmanning to be reduced

5. Establish training gap
- at corporate, departmental and individual levels
- numbers/types of people needing training or retraining

6. Cost–benefit analysis
- will benefits (short and long term) exceed costs
- in-house or external training?
- on- or off-the-job training?
- alternatives?

8. Implement plans
- keep records

7. Devise training plans and programmes
- facilities
- locations
- methods
- trainers
- timings
- programmes
- length of training

Fig. 3.3 Training and development for computer-based technology

finance and effort in planning and carrying out appropriate types and levels of training for staff. Strassman[21] puts it succinctly:

> 'If information technology-use is not learned adequately, the technology itself has only the negligible value of its materials.'

Yet many senior managers fail to see the crucial link between training investment and organisational performance, even though it has been proven. Two examples suffice. A 1985 Manpower Services Commission survey, *Adult training in Britain*, shows high-performing companies having 8.9 days training per employee per year, while low performers show only 2.8 days. Furthermore, in the previous five years, high performers showed a 25% increase, low performers a 20% decrease in training activity. A 1986 Technical Change Centre study into the introduction of advanced packaging systems into three food companies found effective training reducing one firm's labour costs per unit of output to one fifth those of its two competitors.[22] How was this achieved? As one example, the firm trained machine operators to anticipate and handle routine faults. This resulted in significantly fewer and shorter breakdowns, 60% fewer maintenance and 50% fewer direct workers, and a 30% faster production system compared with its rivals.

Even so, organisations fail to make the appropriate investments. In fact, UK organisations historically have a poor record on training and development generally, and this seems to knock on into underfunding of training for the introduction of computer systems. A 1986 Coopers and Lybrand study of 60 large companies[23] found most chief executives not knowing their firm's training activities, and training viewed as merely a reaction to other corporate decisions, and regarded as an overhead and cost to be reduced when times were hard. The links between training efficiency and profitability were rarely recognised. One training manager asked the inquiry team not to bring training to his Board's notice, because it might remind them to cut his budget again.

The general UK attitude at the level of the organisation has too often been that training is not our responsibility, and that we can always buy in more labour when required. For example a 1986 Policy Studies Institute study, *Microelectronics in industry*, surveyed 1200 manufacturing establishments using microchips in products or processes. Managers cited shortages in key skills as by far the greatest organisational problem. By far the most crucial shortage was amongst microelectronics engineers. Even so, half the factories had not sent any engineers on special computer courses in the past two years; more than two thirds did not plan to do so between 1986 and 1988. According to the study, the average number of other technical people sent on special training courses was about half the number of engineers sent.

Small organisations in particular tend to do little formal training and rely much more on the labour market. Many firms fear poaching of their computer staff once trained. For Hoskyns, a London computer group, this became such a problem in 1985 that they seriously considered ending their policy of recruiting 50–70 new graduates a year. These received high-cost training at the firm's expense, only to be attracted away by higher salaries a year later. Organisations respond in different ways to such a situation. In a 1985 Institute of Manpower Studies survey of 900 manufacturing and distribution companies, Rajan found that:

'Rather than choosing the technology they need to compete and then training their workers to use it, many companies are only introducing new equipment which they can quickly and cheaply train their existing workforces to operate ... There is a tendency to muddle through with limited in-house training facilities without recourse to external sources. Opportunities to upgrade work skills and realize the potential benefits of innovations are being missed.'[24]

However, the advent of computer technology makes such attitudes and approaches more counter-productive than ever before. Staff training and development is needed to ensure the safe reception of radical technological change into an organisation. Furthermore, training and development need to be ongoing throughout workers' lives if the full potential of present and developing technologies is to be fully utilised. One firm which understands this is IBM, with 5% of its employees undergoing training at any given time.

New technology implies training for all employees, not just shopfloor operatives. Thus the 1986 perception of R. Shepherd, training director at Ford UK:

'The new pressures on skills are not from individual changes in the production process, like the introduction of a robot. It comes from the automation and computerisation of the process as a whole. We are moving into an era where the control and organisation of the system will change and that requires new skills throughout the company.'[25]

Higher-levels skills for operatives, multi-skilled maintenance staff, supervisors as facilitators rather than overseers, the continual need to update engineering and design skills of professional grades and managers with more strategic leadership and general management skills—all these are implied by how new technology is being introduced at workplaces like Ford, Hitachi, Nissan and Barclays bank; and all have immense training and development implications.

The trend in more dynamic organisations is toward manpower flexibility. This means developing internal training programmes in organisation-specific but varied and updatable skills for core workers. This internal labour market in permanent employees could be developed by personnel policies permitting career development, interesting work, employment security and high rewards. High levels of organisational commitment and receptivity to technological change would be expected as the payoff on the training and development that all this entails. As Atkinson[26] has pointed out, other less interesting and skilled work will be done by various types of peripheral workers, who will be trained in the specific low-level skills required by the organisation.

Accepting its necessity, what, then, is good practice in training for computer technology? A major point emerging from a number of studies is a lack of awareness of available external training. UK organisations also need to match other countries in co-ordinating the training efforts of government, educational institutions, trade unions and industry. They also need to take their own responsibilities for training more seriously.

Figure 3.3 illustrates the central importance of detailed, pre-emptive planning. A manager in a hi-tech firm once told one of the authors that his company did not have time to train people: 'We need people who can do the job now, not in 18 months' time.' This rather begged the question about the extent of training initiatives in the previous two years.

Organisations differ in their size, their goods or services, their market and the nature of their industry. Not surprisingly, training objectives and programmes also differ, though Fig. 3.3 provides a generalised systematic framework for training operations. Its application can be illustrated by some examples of training schemes for the development of computer skills.

In the 1980s, Gallaghers, a major cigarette, cigar and tobacco manufacturer, embarked on major investment in highly automated production machinery. In June 1983, faced with inadequate production training programmes, a team consisting of the training manager, a factory manager and an independent consultant were commissioned to carry out an in-depth audit of training needs. They found the new technology generating new skills not covered by the existing training arrangements. The engineering department controlled the buying and installation of the new equipment; minimal contact with other departments meant no ongoing analysis of changing training needs. The suppliers provided standard training courses not tailored to Gallagher's needs; there were large variations in trainer competence; machinery on the production line was used in unsuitable conditions for training. Supervisors were expected to pass on what they had learnt to operatives; they did not have the time to do so. Furthermore, training left important gaps in their basic understanding of how microprocessors performed their role in production.

The solutions lay in giving the training department direct control over supplier courses. Suppliers are given early warning about specific training needs, and tailor courses to suit. Each course is attended on site by employees with similar learning requirements. Thus supervisors may receive appreciation training, while repair and maintenance courses operate for technicians and craftsmen. The role of supervisors in the operation of the new technology is considered paramount. They would be responsible for passing on training to subordinates. A team of consultants joined with the training department to devise a series of courses to develop core supervisory skills. Each supervisor is scheduled to pass through the four-year programme, with refresher courses also built in. The training programmes are continually evaluated by participants and trainers, leading to improvements in design and content.

Trade unions have also branched out into training. The Electrical, Electronic Communications and Plumbing Union (EETPU) provides three main electronic courses at different levels, and modified to customer requirements. In fact over 200 companies have utilised the EETPU training facilities at Cudham Hall. Thus Hotpoint send newly recruited electricians there for foundation courses, without which most of the subsequent supplier courses would prove too difficult.

At Austin Rover, much of the work done by electronic specialists in 1981 was by 1986 being handled by first-line electricians. This resulted from the introduction of five-day electronics updating courses. These themselves were updated regularly to develop required knowledge and skills prior to any major investment in new production technology.

A variety of methods and techniques are applicable in training for IT. Thus Austin Rover invested heavily in an open learning centre. This is open all day, all employees may use its equipment, and courses are available in work time with line management permission. Gallagher recognised the uses of computer-based training. Their evaluation found the system more effective than traditional methods because it was individualised, more interactive with the trainee, self-paced and performance-based. Computer-based training could also take place periodically and in-house on an individual basis with minimum disruption to production. A National Computing Centre market analysis estimates that spending on computer-based training is likely to increase from £60 million in 1986 to some £230 million in 1990.

Even in such a brief review, it becomes clear that, where training for IT is concerned, the best training programmes pay attention to advanced planning and detailed analysis of trainee needs, go beyond mere technical skills like keyboarding, and permit hands-on experience with trainee-paced learning. The best organisations also take responsibility for IT training, see training as investment not cost, co-ordinate with external training providers, and continuously review and update training needs, courses and methods in order to optimise returns from future systems developments.

EQUAL OPPORTUNITIES

Organisational representatives frequently suggest that their computer systems designs are non-discriminatory and that IT jobs are open to all. However, the general pattern of **outcomes** across the UK economy reveals that IT is being applied to work in ways that amount to systematic discrimination against certain employees and groups.

A major influence on this process is the prevailing framework of discrimination and interests in work organisations. Thus, taking the case of women, the Department of Employment *New earning survey* (1984) found few amongst professional groups; on the other hand, women accounted for 98% of secretaries, 81% of cleaners, 77% of personal service workers, and 70% of clerks. Furthermore, in all industries and services, women and ethnic minorities are concentrated in lower-graded and lower-paid jobs with restricted career opportunities. As one example, 76% of clerical assistants in the Civil Service are women, whereas, at higher grades, 96% of Deputy Secretaries are men. Furthermore, women and ethnic minorities predominate in areas less protected by employment legislation: 80% of part-time workers and most homeworkers are women. Despite the belief that the widespread application of electronic engineering and computers would take the 'dirt' out of work and make such job segregation unnecessary (where it ever was), this has not generally happened. In Zimmerman's words:[27]

> 'Without a whisper of conspiracy each new generation appears to recreate a technological infrastructure that miraculously maintains existing class, race and gender divisions thus adding support to the illusion that these divisions are an immutable consequence of nature.'

In fact, the pattern of computer technology usage and outcomes is more complex than this, but there is evidence to support Zimmerman's view, mainly from studies of women and microelectronics. Strangely, but perhaps significantly, there is a dearth of published research on the relationship between computerisation and other disadvantaged groups, including the disabled and ethnic minorities, at work.

Cockburn[28,29] studied occupational segregation and technological change in the clothing, mail order and print industries, and the case of radiographers in medical care. In print, men dominated the 'skilled', maintenance and technical jobs, and held on to these when computers arrived. Women mainly occupied the low-level clerical and administrative posts surrounding the computer system. In the clothing industry, CAD/CAM systems were found to reinforce the processes of feminisation and routinisation of lower paid work in pattern and cutting rooms. It brought new jobs for women, but not more technical training and competence. In mail order warehouses, new computerised stock files and mechanical goods-handling systems still maintained order-filling as low paid, unskilled 'women's work'.

A major point, endorsed by more general studies,[30-32] is that women are found occupying operator, push-button jobs in computer technology. Jobs involving intervening in the mechanism itself—maintenance workers, technicians, engineers and systems managers, the highly paid, skilled jobs of the future—were dominated by men. In fact, the new technology jobs in which women are predominantly found are those most vulnerable to displacement by further automation.

All these studies find women ill-placed (and only partly through lack of technical education) to fill the more skilled jobs created by the spread of microelectronics. Indeed, the outlook for women in growth areas like programming, electronic engineering, data management and systems analysis are not encouraging. For example, in the USA, where automation is more advanced, in 1980 90% of computer specialist occupations and 80% of technician posts were filled by men, with women concentrated in the lower end of the skills spectrum.

There is evidence pointing to a more complicated picture. Cockburn found that the introduction of computed tomography (CT) scanners into hospital X-ray departments avoided deskilling and maximised the learning potential for radiographers. This resulted from the pre-existing high degree of professional autonomy and control over work operated by this mainly female occupation. Webster[33] found word-processing systems in small organisations having little effect on existing work organisation, and in some cases increasing rather than displacing skill levels of female secretaries. Women are increasingly found as programmers. However, there is irony here. Originally done by women, programming became men's work when redefined as creative and important. However, in the 1970s, with an increased division of labour, standardisation and deskilling, women re-entered the field of programming.

Organisations designing or using computer systems, and faced with severe shortages in specialist computer skills, are increasingly realising how discrimination may be highly wasteful of valuable human resources. Thus banks like the Midland, Barclays and National Westminster, and computer systems firms like F International, are willing to adapt personnel and training policies to attract, develop and retain skilled female computer staff. Examples include special training courses for women only, re-entry schemes for staff leaving temporarily for domestic reasons, and part-time or job-share at higher levels of work. Rank Xerox recognises the strict economic sense in operating equal opportunities for potential computer specialist staff. Moreover, its distributed computer network scheme was primarily designed to reduce high administrative overheads, but has attracted some women into continuing a career through computer home-working.

While much discrimination is determined by events in the wider society, an individual organisation can still act positively to develop equality of opportunity at work. The best schemes see equal opportunities as not another, but an integral part of every, personnel policy and practice. There is the need to declare an equal opportunity policy. This is followed by an analysis of the workforce to discover where and how discrimination is occurring. Job descriptions, person specifications, the processes of recruitment and selection of staff, and the content of employment contracts need to be examined for discriminatory practices.

New computer technology renders training and retraining practices particularly crucial. Thus, in 1985, the Greater London Council found data preparation officers and word processor operators disadvantaged through lack of training and short career ladders. A series of courses was created covering new technology training, assertiveness, office skills, and group, supervisory and interviewing skills. One product of a positive action project at Thames Television was a basic science and technology course aimed at women.

New policies may need to be developed, covering areas like part-time workers, job-sharing, employees with disabilities, employees with parental responsibilities, racial and sexual harassment and pension rights. Finally, monitoring of the whole programme and its results is needed, with written records. Despite all this effort, however, equal opportunities may prove difficult to achieve with regard to IT and its impacts without substantial input by disadvantaged groups into the computer systems design process itself.

REDUNDANCIES

Virtually all studies find job loss occurring with the introduction of computer systems. However, it has been difficult in the 1980s to distinguish between demanning resulting directly from the application of microelectronics, and job loss as a result of other organisational changes or economic recession. Either way, redundancy policies need to be planned, and integrated with manpower forecasts, and other policies such as recruitment, training and redeployment.

The employer has certain minimum legal obligations where redundancies are impending. However, the better employer will go beyond minimum legal requirements. This is because the way redundancies and dismissals are handled at times of technological change can determine future staff commitment and union attitudes to system running and further automation. Moreover, redundancy may be wasteful of existing staff resources; thus retraining rather than recruitment of new or temporary computer staff may be a better long term option.

One more positive response by some organisations to the peak levels of redundancies in 1980 and 1981, and the higher redundancy levels in the 1980s compared with the 1970s, has been the development of 'job security' policies. Although essentially concerned with the possibility of job loss at a time of technological or other change, these present a more positive approach to human resource planning than traditional reactive redundancy agreements, or the total lack of redundancy procedures.

In the context of technological change, their major objective is to encourage employee commitment and sense of security in the face of likely major concerns about job change and redundancy. Their major features are

— forward planning and regular consultation with employee representatives on human resource issues
— automatic and regular disclosure and discussion of information on a range of pre-agreed subjects
— earliest possible notification of and consultation on possible redundancies
— lists of measures to be taken to minimise job loss.

(Typically, measures taken to minimise job loss include reduction in temporary staff, reduction of overtime, redeployment, retraining, early retirement, temporary short-time working, reducing subcontract work, and voluntary retirement.)

If redundancies are agreed as necessary, a number of steps can still be taken to reduce their impact on employees affected. The timings of redundancies can be staggered over an agreed period, enabling employer and employees to adjust to the changing work position. The implications for those made redundant might be immense—for older workers it may mean the end of their working lives. Government agencies will provide courses for people needing different skills to get a new job. Organisations can assist this process by offering paid time off for such training. In fact, employees to be made redundant are entitled to time off for job search. Organisations sometimes go beyond this by offering job counselling, retraining assistance, and active help to find people new jobs. In fact, an effective redundancy scheme might be defined by management's achievement in not only reducing the workforce, but also ensuring that dismissed employees can secure alternative employment.

The major mistakes organisations can make where job loss is likely during technological change include failure to consider alternatives to compulsory redundancies, and failure to consider the impact of how redundancies are handled on the co-operation, commitment and feelings of security of the employees who remain.

DEVELOPING COMMITMENT

A key problem in computer projects is getting user managers to accept responsibility for, and actively participate in, IT implementation. A common avoidance strategy adopted in the face of IT is the passing of responsibility for action to 'the experts'. This may mean the data-processing department staff, external computer consultants or suppliers, or systems analysts. Such parties may be all too willing to pick up that responsibility. However, in the long-term this may not benefit the organisation or its staff, or the effectiveness of the computer system. Such assistance may also have a large price-tag attached to it.

Another avoidance method is to delegate to subordinates the responsibility for introducing IT. All too often the project is then seen to lack higher-level support and loses credibility. This may be reinforced where subordinates have not been delegated the authority and the command over resources commensurate with their responsibility for making IT a success.

It is important to secure the organisational commitment of technical staff in IT projects. Programmers, systems analysts, data-processing managers tend to be 'cosmopolitans' rather than 'locals'—their loyalties lie with their technical know-how and a sense of profession rather than being tied to the health of the organisation to which there is a career commitment. However, these are key staff in any computer project. Given the typically long lead times in practice for systems development and implementation (a 1983 NEDO report examined 15 companies and found lead times as long as five years[34]), retention of key staff becomes crucial. Planning for staff departures is necessary, but replacement can work out expensive in terms of money, more importantly in terms of lost project time. Departing staff members take with them experience accumulated on the project. New staff take time to acquire this. Their work may suffer; likewise the project. Indeed, early bad experiences may induce the replacement to leave, thus redoubling the original problem.

Thus, technical staff need to be valued and their careers linked to the health of the organisation. They need training to be put in the organisational picture—how their work relates to organisational success, business training, understanding the products or services, links with other functions and other customers. This commitment can be developed by ensuring that technical staff also include line managers who have been trained for, and moved into, IT management. In looking at 44 organisations Earl[35] concludes that:

> 'The importance of fostering a coalition between user managers, general management and information management may well argue that IT managers should have general and line management experience. This has been found beneficial in conventional DP management ... and in 50% of the survey organisations the top DP manager had line management experience.'

Following on from this, what tends to be crucial for the success of computer project implementation is a history and culture of IT developing as an integral part of organisational functioning. Typically this means that IT executives have senior positions in the organisation (e.g. a seat on the Board of a limited company); that they have broad business/organisational experience and that they and their staff have regular—not necessarily formal, but real—contact with other staff and general managers as part of their day-to-day work.

CONCLUSIONS

Human resource planning needs to be long term, to be integrated with, and frequently to drive systems development, if IT investments are to be fulfilled. Where they exist, personnel professionals have proved useful but under-utilised in IT projects. They need to gain greater influence, with new roles and skills, not just in the delivery but also in the planning and design stages of computerisation.

This chapter has pointed out the need to work at the frequently neglected areas of proper recruitment and selection, management development, training, equal opportunities, and redundancies in the context of technological change. Human resource policies are particularly important for their influence upon the commitment and co-operation of future computer users in the organisation. Systems design philosophy and practice also have key roles to play here, and should operate as an integral part and extension of the organisation's personnel policies. They are the focus of the next chapter.

CHAPTER 4

Design and the Systems Analyst

'The person who only has a hammer, tends to treat everything like a nail'.[1]

INTRODUCTION

The modern systems analyst is expected to be competent in three essential tasks. These are, firstly, the analysis of the information requirements of an organisation; secondly, the design of computer-based information systems to achieve organisational objectives; and thirdly, systems implementation. How did this role develop? Do the actual analysis and design practices of the vast majority of today's systems analysts really work? Are there alternative approaches? What are these and how successful can they be? These are the major issues addressed in this chapter.

One major cause of systems failure is the neglect of human factors in dominant systems analysis and design practices. This is sometimes difficult to substantiate, not least because designers and organisations are less than anxious to publicise their computer disasters, let alone the reasons for them. Furthermore, organisations rarely possess accounting and costing systems that can fully show the true costs of neglecting human factors in computer-based system building and subsequent operation.

However, the neglect of human factors exists, has had serious consequences in numerous organisations, and may contribute to a growing crisis in the IT field. One of the seeming contradictions of computer-based technology is that it can displace human activity but also it must increasingly be designed with human beings in mind. Why is this?

Declining hardware costs make computer acquisition attractive to, and possible for, more organisations than ever before. As relative costs go down and availability and choice in equipment improve, more organisations use computers. Software and programming language developments make systems more accessible to workers who would not consider themselves computer professionals. The applicability and capability of computerised solutions are accelerating and, though computer appreciation amongst potential users does not keep pace, nevertheless computerisation is increasingly seen as both acceptable and necessary for increased efficiency and to maintain competitiveness.

Furthermore, within organisations, over time, the 'Heineken' factor operates. A characteristic of computer-based technology is its potential pervasiveness. It is a technology that can get to parts of the organisation previous technologies could never reach because of their limited applicability. In its most developed form, in hi-tech companies like Rank Xerox or in Wang UK head office, IT leaves no job untouched. All this means that the systems analyst is practising skills in increasingly human activity systems. This in turn creates dilemmas for traditional systems analysis and design practices.

Additionally, as different types of organisation develop, and increased reliance on a wider range of users is required to fully utilise the potential of modern computer-based technology, the thorny problem of participation arises. Given the high capital investment in IT, the need to optimise its operation, and the vulnerability of computer-based technologies to employee misuse, it may become highly pragmatic to develop participative planning and design to secure the active co-operation of users in running computer systems.

There are a range of partial developing responses to this situation. They all question not just *what* is designed, but also *how* design should be conducted. Too often the latter question has been answered by the adoption of traditional approaches. But, in fact, the way design proceeds has immense implications for *what* is designed, its acceptability and effectiveness in use. This necessary link has been underplayed in the past. Here the balance is redressed and the importance of human factors in systems design is given the emphasis it deserves.

TOOLS, TECHNIQUES AND PRACTICES—THE INHERITANCE

The role of the systems analyst has developed historically. Firstly, new computer-based technologies could be exploited with little concern for the organisational and social implications. The key computer specialist was the programmer. Over time, some organisations began to utilise large batch-processing systems which tended to be separated from the rest of the organisation and run by an enclosed and developing group of computer professionals. Again, such systems had limited impact in organisations (e.g. they might be limited to an accounting or a payroll application) and were rarely designed with other than technical efficiency criteria in mind.

In time, the computer professionals developed their own internal divisions of labour. Systems analysis became separated from programming, and software development from system operation and system maintenance. New jobs became separated out or created, along with improvements in technology or increases in organisational information requirements. Examples of such jobs are database administrators and programmers and telecommunication specialists.

Thus there has come to be in place accepted, well defined groupings of computer professionals whose basic tasks involve the analysis, design, introduction and running of modern computer-based systems.

The first point to make from a human aspects point of view is that, like lawyers, accountants and other professionals, computer specialists frequently share interests, values and perspectives over and above other groupings in an organisation. They also have a power base in the mystique and the reality of technological expertise. Furthermore, this expertise is difficult to substitute. It also creates dependence in other organisational members who rely on computers but who have little control over how they work. Computer professionals are one of those groupings bearing out the thesis of Hickson *et al.*:[2] they gain power to the extent that their work is important to the organisation and reduces uncertainties that affect other workers in the organisation.

It is rarely commented upon but it is not surprising, from a political perspective, to find that such computer professionals not only utilise that power, but frequently do so for their own reasons and to pursue their own interests and objectives, even where these may be different from the interests of other stakeholders and indeed of the declared goals of the organisation. This forms a small but significant part of what might be called the politics of computerisation, for the power and perspectives of systems professionals tend to predominate in, and so have immense implications for, computerisation projects.

What, then, are the perspectives and preferences of systems analysts that feed into their work, and in what directions do they tend to push the analysis and design process? Markus[3] has reviewed extensive research evidence. She finds systems professionals needing social interaction much less than other computer users. They also have different thinking and problem-solving styles from other users. However, in traditional systems design, computer systems are too often built on the implicit assumption that users have the same cognitive styles and needs as the programmers and analysts responsible for design. One research project concludes that the differences in cognitive styles between user and analyst are in fact the major explanation for later difficulties in system implementation.[4] Systems professionals also make assumptions about employee work needs and practices. These tend to be inaccurate, but nevertheless are reflected in designs that push jobs into being well defined and structured, with carefully set targets and close supervision.

Computer professionals also tend to identify with their occupation more strongly than with their employing organisation. For example, this may cause them to advocate actions not in the best interests of the organisation. They tend to prefer building software in-house and play up the disadvantages of using standardised packages or external consultants (The Not-Invented-Here syndrome—if it's not invented here, we do not want it). They emphasise the need for the latest hardware and software, even where no clear benefits are likely to arise from their acquisition. One explanation for these phenomena may be the desire of systems professionals to retain up-to-date marketable skills that are not organisation-specific. This enables them to escape the short career ladders in organisations. It also pushes up their market price. None of this influences systems analysts to design systems that are necessarily in the interests of managers or other users.

The traditional systems development life cycle (Fig. 4.1) and the 'hard' systems paradigm are also essential parts of the inheritance. In practice, they impose serious limitations on the effectiveness of a computer system design. They imply the existence of a well identified

Traditional

1. *Problem definition*

2. *Choice of objectives*

3. *Systems analysis*
   a) data collection
   b) fact recording
   c) analysis of recorded
      facts

4. *Generation of*
   possible solutions

5. *Selection of best*
   design solution in
   the light of financial
   constraints

6. *Client approval*
7. *System design*
   output, input files,
   processes, controls, program
   design and testing

8. *Implementation*

'Soft'

1. *Data collection* (quantitative and qualitative)
   a) what is the situation?
   b) what are people's perceptions of
      what are problems in this situation?

2. *Situation analysis*
   a) rich picture of situation (from 1)
   b) idenfity issues in the situation
   c) identify primary tasks and
      essential activities
   d) establish relevant systems
      from b) and c)

is
it
logical?

3. *Root definition*
   precise description in words of
   relevant systems

4. *Conceptual model*
   model of activities which relevant systems
   logically perform

5. *Compare abstract model*
   with rich picture and reality
   a) does the logical model happen in
      real life? Why not?
   b) construct agenda of possible changes

6. *Debate possible changes with*
   client, problem-owners and
   problem-solvers
   a) what is systemically desirable?
   b) what is culturally feasible?

7. *Implementation of agreed*
   changes

Fig. 4.1   Traditional and 'soft' systems methodology compared

system ready for analysis, thus blinding the analyst to relevant events outside the very restricted definition given to 'information' and 'system'. In fact, traditional analysis rarely looks at the whole organisation as a system with interactions, but simply takes a subsystem as it exists and attempts to convert it to computerised form in isolation. Even then, traditional analysis tends to emphasise the components and their functioning rather than treating the system as a whole. Analysts are distracted from problem identification and problem-solving into utilising techniques. This has the further disadvantage of making the analyst 'expert' in a technical sense, thus reducing the ability and desire of others to participate. But in practice the systems analyst undertakes a very restricted form of analysis. Despite the name, traditionally the analyst's main role is design, not analysis. Thus the analyst's main concern becomes for the efficiency, not the effectiveness, of the computer system being designed.

Hard systems thinking has dominated systems development. This means common agreement amongst analysts that reality is *systemic*; that is, made up of systems that can be identified and examined. The problem here is that reality is reduced to one populated by systems. This can be a helpful view but it has limitations. In organisation theory, systems thinking is identified with seeing consensus, co-ordination and regulation in organisations. Where conflict, disruption and lack of system exist, these are viewed as deviations from the norm, dysfunctional abnormalities that need to be eliminated. But in practice these may be normal facts about any organisation based on human activity. In such an organisation, systemic thinking can impose limitations on analysis and subsequent design. A stark example of such an imposition of professional thinking and perspectives on reality with disastrous results is that of the TV cameraman in South America who, while covering a riot, filmed himself being shot dead by a policeman. He became so concerned with seeing reality from a limited, professional viewpoint that he could not fully accept the reality with which he was dealing and of which he was a part.

Hard systems thinking assumes a clear-cut system that has obvious objectives. In practice, it means imposing a clear-cut problem definition on what is all too often a messy organisational reality and a fuzzy system. It also means the adoption of systematic, orderly, rational procedures that restrict research and design in what is all too often a very complex organisational reality. A further implication is an overriding concern for technical design and the bypassing of the organisational context in which the system is to operate and the social implications of the system. In a way this is a *lack* of systemic thinking; the technical and economic subsystems are considered but the social and political subsystems are omitted. Furthermore, the hard systems paradigm goes for full specification of the system on the drawing-board, leaving little or no leeway for alterations and improvements in the light of experience and further knowledge. Finally, it leaves the computer professionals to decide the extent to which user participation is useful and permissible. The result has been little user involvement in design, let alone in the process of systems analysis.

In summary, the traditional approach discussed here pays little attention to organisational and social facts, regarding them as marginal to the successful technical design of an information system. As a result, little organisational theory is employed in the analysis and design processes. Where the organisation intrudes, it is mainly easily identified, formal elements that are considered. Furthermore, once the system has been planned, any difference between it and the organisation means that the latter, not the former, must be changed.

Traditional approaches also tend to separate the user from the technology, allow computer professionals to take responsibility for systems development, and fail to analyse user needs, or discriminate adequately between different users other than at the simplified level of formal role, tasks, functions and relations. The result is a lack of end-user and worker involvement in research and development, in setting objectives, and in analysis and design of the proposed computer system. Such involvement usually occurs only at the implementation stage.

The limitations of hard systems thinking and traditional analysis and design practice are becoming more widely known. However, though these approaches are only appropriate for certain types of systems—and probably not for computer-based human activity systems—they still predominate and are the highly influential inheritance for modern systems analysis and design practice.

However, several approaches can be utilised to take analysis and design beyond the limitations imposed by relying upon superior technical design and the systems analyst's technical expertise alone as guarantors of successful computerisation.

'SOFT' SYSTEMS AND THE CHECKLAND METHODOLOGY

The hard systems approach is particularly appropriate for the analysis, design and implementation of machine-based and hardware-dominated systems. By contrast, 'soft' systems perspectives and methodologies evolved as tools for organisational development in human activity systems. How are they relevant to the analysis and design of computerised information systems? Checkland[5] provides an answer:

'In some cases, of course, especially at a low level of

operational activity, such as paying wages or processing incoming orders, it may be the case that all actors will be ready to conceptualise the activity in the same way. The IS is then a system to be engineered to achieve its (unproblematical) objectives, and hard systems engineering methodology can be helpful in that process. In general though, at higher levels of activity, there will be multiple perceptions, multiple meanings attributed to real world activity, and the relevant systems thinking will be the soft variety.'

There are several 'soft' systems methodologies, but here the focus is on Checkland's work. This is because it has a record of practical use. Also, though complex, it is the most formalised and understandable of the methodologies so far published. This section is intended as no more than an introduction to the usefulness of the Checkland approach.

It can be seen from Fig. 4.1 alone that soft systems methodology has little to say about physical design. But it does clearly indicate the importance of involving clients, managers, end users, in fact all the important stakeholders, in the *processes* of analysing what are the existing system(s) and problems therein and agreeing, if possible, the required changes.

The advantages of including elements of soft system methodology in the analysis/design of possible computer systems are as follows. Firstly (at stage 1 in Fig. 4.1), problems are not taken as obvious and given. Indeed, not even the situation and existing systems are accepted as easy to define. The analyst can arrive at some definition of what might be considered to be the main systems and activities in the organisation, but only after involving many stakeholders in the data collection stage in order to create a *rich picture* of what these problems and systems might be.

Secondly, there is a new emphasis on, and consideration of, the role of different people's perceptions, interests, values and beliefs in suggesting what the problems and possible solutions are. The increased participation in these areas may improve the quantity and quality of data collected and the quality of problem definition. It can also increase people's acceptance of the solutions/changes that are proposed to remedy the problems they agree exist.

Thirdly, the methodology places new weight on the importance of qualitative, subjective information for systems analysis. Previous methodologies have tended to play these down in favour of reliance upon 'hard', quantitative data.

Fourthly, it is accepted that the analyst cannot be detached from the situation, but also has perceptions, interests, beliefs, a way of seeing which influence what are put forward as problems and solutions. The methodology allows other interested parties to participate not just in design, but also in the early analysis stage, and thus builds in checks on over-reliance on the analyst's judgement.

Fifthly, after data collection, analysts arrive at definitions of what they believe the main systems and tasks to be. A logical model of each of these systems is then prepared. This practice is similar to that of the traditional approach called structured systems analysis. These models of what should be are then compared with what is, and an agenda of possible desired changes is drawn up by the analyst. At this point, the methodology improves upon the traditional one in opening up this agenda to considerable discussion, debate and alteration by a variety of stakeholders, and not just management or whoever is the immediate client. The new assumption here is that it is not only problems that are difficult to define and agree upon; solutions even to agreed problems may also be a matter of considerable disagreement, negotiation and compromise.

Sixthly (at stage 6 in Fig. 4.1), the methodology insists that what are considered desirable changes by the analyst in terms of the logical design embodied in the 'conceptual model' are measured against what is culturally feasible; that is, acceptable to those who would be responsible for implementing and living with the proposed changes. Here again (this time on completion of the logical design stage), the human factor is given much more emphasis than in more hard systems methodologies.

The Checkland approach cannot pass without some comment on its limitations, however. This methodology still relies heavily on the analyst to formulate suitable alternative 'relevant systems'. The analyst's background, assumptions and skill are also depended on for 'growing' a 'conceptual model' out of a 'root definition'. The methodology also has little to say about the methods of investigation that need to be adopted to secure an adequate analysis. Qualitative information is considered important, but how is it to be gathered?

More crucial limitations emerge when Checkland's treatment of conflict and power in organisations is examined. Interestingly, the Checkland methodology addresses the likelihood of conflict in organisations at the level of perceptions and ideas, but not at the level of economic and material interests. But several commentators would argue that the latter types of conflict are a basic feature of organisational life, and much more difficult to resolve than conflicts over ideas.[6] This makes agreement in stages 5 and 6 of the methodology much less likely than Checkland supposes.

Where agreement does occur, it may well be a false consensus arising from the managerial orientation of the project and inequalities of power amongst its participants. As Rosenhead[7] puts it, for workers at low levels in an organisation:

'There is no point in articulating demands which are evidently out of keeping with what is attainable'.

Naughton[8] sees as inherent in the use of soft systems methodology so far:

'A strong orientation towards the power structures and influential actors in organisations'.

In some respects, then, the Checkland methodology may seem to offer widespread user participation in analysis and design, but in practice it can end up serving the objectives of the more powerful interests in the organisation, permitting only those changes and designs that reinforce the existing power structure.

Soft systems methodology, as discussed here, says little about making the system 'physical' and operable, or about how the process of implementation can be managed. However, in involving so many people other than the analyst in the design stages, it does force consideration of implementation problems all the time.

Traditionally the analyst proceeds linearly through the various analysis planning and design stages and only thereafter confronts the problems of implementation. The systems analyst is also largely buffered from end-user opinions on the physical design, and on the relevance and accuracy of the analysis and logical design. All this has often resulted not only in serious technical hitches at the implementation stage but also in considerable human resistance to change. Soft systems methodology does offer an approach that can confront and provide a degree of remedy for such problems. More accurately, and in its own language, it seeks to appreciate and improve such problem situations.

USER INVOLVEMENT IN SYSTEMS DESIGN

The Checkland approach is particularly important for the great emphasis it places on stakeholder involvement in the *analysis* of information systems. But other approaches help to focus on the human aspect by stressing the need for user participation in systems *design*. The major participation questions here are why, who, in what and how?

Participation as an issue in a computer systems project may arise as a demand from organisational members who wish to protect their interests. It may also be sponsored by managements for a range of reasons. Such reasons might be to utilise staff skills and understanding of the existing system; to provide familiarity with and training in the new systems; to secure staff commitment to change and working the computer system; to pursue 'fairness' in personnel policy; and because it seems the most cost-effective way of achieving a system that is efficient and meets the needs of those working in it and those it serves. Proponents of user involvement stress that these aims are frequently mutually supporting.

One problem is that different people have different understandings of the word 'user'. A computer system will have many stakeholders. These are people who will be affected in a significant way by, or have material interests in the nature and running of the new computerised system. For our purposes, 'user' means a stakeholder who relates actively and/or is part of the computer-based system. Users can be classified as follows:

> — **primary**—analysts, programmers, and systems maintenance and operations staff: systems professionals dealing directly with and able to modify the system and its technology
> — **secondary**—user department managers, clerks, secretaries, supervisors; provide input, receive output, interact with technology but as part of another job
> — **tertiary**—senior managers with little direct system contact except receipt of some output; responsibilities may include terms of reference for design and overall objectives, or providing finance
> — **user type 4**—customers, clients, claimants, and people with information about them held in system data files; no direct contact with technology, but affected by the system.

Traditional design techniques tend to identify the 'user' with primary and tertiary users only. Secondary users have a restricted role as sources of information about the existing system.

As systems become more pervasive and interactive, and figure more largely in users' work roles, and as smaller organisations increasingly computerise, the relevance of this classification breaks down. The involvement in the design process of all four types of user then grows in importance. The problem here is that the newer types of system, with which more users are drawn into direct daily contact, are still being brought in using traditional non-participative design techniques.

What will the users be involved in, and *how* will they participate? Land[9] makes a useful distinction. Firstly, there can be involvement in *decision-making* about design matters. The sorts of issue that may concern users, together with methods of involvement, are shown in Fig. 4.2.

Traditional approaches have tended to be quite restrictive in the

| Type of involvement | Typical decision points |

- *Responsible*
  Full authority to make decisions
  and involve specialists and advisers

- *Democratic*
  Each user has equal vote in
  decisions

- *Negotiated*
  Users bargain with each
  other until consensus or
  compromise is reached

- *Consultative*
  Users questioned and interviewed
  evidence considered when others
  make decision

- *Information*
  Users provided with details of
  decision, evidence on which
  it is based, and details of
  why alternatives were
  rejected

- Terms of reference for
  whole project
- Project managers
- 'Expert' assistance
- Finance
- Terms of reference
  for local subsystem
- Suppliers
- Equipment and software
- Which solution/design from
  alternatives produced
- Stop/go
  decisions in project
  life-cycle
- Low level decisions on
  job design, preferred
  workstation, screen layout,
  program design

Fig. 4.2 Involvement in decision-making about the design process

amount of information provided to most users about the nature of change, despite a large number of studies showing that information to users in advance can smooth rather than disrupt the change process. Consultation permits various degrees of discussion and exchange of ideas and opinions, as well as of factual information, but leaves most of the decisions about systems design to the traditional systems design group. With negotiated, democratic or responsible types of involvement, users are allowed to directly participate in various decisions about the design and implementation of the proposed computer system.

Land's second category is the more intense, committed, 'lived' participation in *the design process itself*. A particularly influential analysis of mechanisms for, and types of, such participation is provided by Land[9] and Mumford,[10] and summarised in Fig. 4.3.

Participation is perhaps best judged by the extent to which a person feels he or she has been party to decisions about, has taken part in, and has influenced in a preferred direction, the processes of design and implementation. It is important to stress that even supporters of user participation in computer systems design in fact propose very restricted forms of participation. User involvement is most frequently on very few of the issues cited in Figs. 4.2 and 4.3, while the mechanisms permitting full participation are rarely used. This can pose problems.

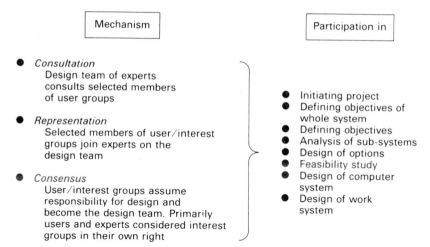

Fig. 4.3 *Participation in the design process (based on Land[9] and Mumford)[10]*

Mumford's work is a particularly instructive example. Reading her case studies carefully, one finds that 'consensus' participation is practicable only where the total number of users is small. The other aspect that emerges is that, in practice, she operates a hierarchy of participation, whereby consensus participation is permitted only in low-level decision-making about job design and work organisation that affect the user immediately. More indirect, less involving, 'consultative' forms of participation will be applied the more strategically important the decisions become. One can question how seriously users will regard the limited influence such a hierarchy of participation permits in practice.

Wainwright and Francis[11] have indicated three alternatives to the traditional design approach, taking cases of office automation in a nationalised industry, a college of further education, an international insurance broker and a financial service company. In their classification, centralised non-participative design (the traditional approach) means design by technical specialists from the central data-processing department. This simplifies the design task and retains central control, but has many weaknesses, not least of which are its inability to deal with complex computer applications and its failure to seriously consider user needs.

Centralised participative design permits a body of user representatives to take part in a central steering group and influence the decisions taken throughout the design stage. This may increase user commitment to the emergent system and follows a socio-technical systems (STS) design philosophy (see chapter 5), but difficulties may arise in representing users properly, and in terms of users' ability to contribute on more technical matters.

Decentralised non-participative design puts computer specialists in to deal directly with user needs at a branch, office or department. This can give the analyst greater awareness of local and user needs, and greater local control, but does not permit design decisions by users.

Decentralised participative design requires much less involvement by the specialist, follows STS design philosophy, and generates much user commitment where this might be vital to the success of the system, but it does depend on user training, expertise and ability to fulfil the design function.

This is only an outline of their discussion and findings. However, two major points emerge. Firstly, there is no one best design approach. Secondly the question 'Which design approach?' is a crucial one to answer, because each approach is more usefully applied in some situations than others. Of course, these four approaches do not exhaust the possibilities for mechanisms and levels of participation that might be found appropriate.

Mumford, in a number of publications, has tended to favour a centralised participative design approach, with a design group established consisting of computer specialists and analysts and representatives for all users. These representatives are appointed by management or elected by users. However, she supports as much user participation as possible in the design process.

An influential participative design approach has been developed by Mumford and Weir.[12] It is based on the assumption that computer technology in particular is flexible enough to allow for systems design to take into account employee needs for satisfying work. Called ETHICS (Effective Technical and Human Implementation of Computer-based Systems), this is a seven-stage approach:

1. (a) Diagnose human and social needs. Issue questionnaire to all employees to establish level of job satisfaction and what employee needs the new system should be designed to meet. Discuss results in detail with employee groups.

   (b) Specify technical requirements and constraints (e.g. product quality and quantity, time factors). This is most likely done by management and systems analysts.

2. Specify social objectives. Specify technical objectives.

3. Set out possible technical solutions. Evaluate against ability to fulfil technical objectives. Establish possible social solutions and evaluate the ability of each to fulfil the specified social objectives.

4. Compare social and technical solutions. Assess the compatibility of

each social solution with each technical solution. The result should be a series of feasible 'socio-technical' solutions.

5. Rank socio-technical solutions by evaluating each against social needs and technical objectives in 1 and 2.

6. Prepare detailed work design to assess type of jobs that will result.

7. Accept best possible socio-technical solution.

This approach does provide a strong emphasis on the human side of system design, and relies on user participation throughout to generate the type of jobs that will produce job satisfaction together with required productivity. It assumes that all interested parties are represented on the steering group throughout the design process and that as much user participation in design is permitted as is financially and practically feasible.

There are many published examples of the successful application of this, and similar, methodologies. Mumford cites the case of the introduction of a word-processing service in ICI Management Services Department, where a small group of secretaries designed an efficient, new and satisfying work system for themselves. In this example, it was a system with no dedicated word-processor operators, but with all secretaries retaining general duties and capable of using the processors. Tetley Walker, a trading company of Allied Breweries, also found benefits from user involvement and the ETHICS methodology, when designing and introducing a computerised personnel information system. [13]

However, there are a number of problems with approaches that stress user involvement in system design. Firstly, user understanding of the technical objectives, proposals and solutions may be very limited, at least initially. Does the design process halt while they gain a better grasp of technical matters? If not, who does make the decisions?

Secondly, the idea of assessing social and technical solutions for the best possible fit is not unproblematic. The question, 'Best possible fit for whom?' must be asked. The process will inevitably create conflicts. These may be large and time-consuming, and will have to be managed.

Thirdly, who makes the decisions about the degree of participation, and who should participate? And how much of a voice should users be allowed? There is an existing power and control structure which may ensure that where user needs and objectives clash with ideas of managers and computer specialists, the latter two groups will get their way. If this happens, the supposed benefits of participation may well be lost. On the other hand, increased user participation and influence may eat into the prerogative of management and specialists and create much resistance and resentment amongst them.

Fourthly, how representative can the members of a design group remain?

PARTICIPATIVE AND EVOLUTIONARY SYSTEMS DEVELOPMENT

The many problems experienced both with approaches of traditional technology-led 'one-shot' design and with approaches of user participation in systems design have led the HUSAT (Human Sciences and Advanced Technology) Research Group at Loughborough University of Technology to develop a further design strategy for introducing computerised systems.

This design approach begins with a commitment to the value of user participation in the design process. But a problem with user involvement in design is that most users invariably require a learning period before they fully comprehend the organisational and work ramifications of computer technology. That learning rarely keeps pace with the rate at which design decisions are made. However, as each such decision is made, the degree of freedom, the openness of the design to alteration and improvement, is reduced. The result all too frequently is that design is left to the technologists, with the technological choices then constraining decisions about job design, work organisation and which user needs can and cannot be met. Thus, in practice, participative design methodologies often create a problem typical of more traditional approaches to design, namely over-specification.

Many system designers come to rely upon a single model of future requirements. They then design the computer system to optimise efficiency on the basis of those requirements. But what if that assumed set of circumstances changes; for example, the system needs to serve new purposes, or users find that the system is not 'user-friendly', jobs are not satisfying, or there are easier ways of doing the work than going through the computer? The over-specified design will close off the possibility of refinements, let alone radical change. The system will become degraded.

This can be avoided by the adoption of the principle of **minimum critical specification**. The initial design specifies what is essential, but nothing that is non-essential. The process of design does not then stop with implementation, but continues throughout the life of the system and enables it to grow and change. As design and system usage progress, so will the learning and adaption of users. Their experience and deepening understanding of the system and its potential can then be fed into the design process to further system capabilities and effectiveness. In this approach, the system will grow and change along with the need of the organisation and its members. Crucially, this approach requires technologies that are flexible and can be developed to serve quite different purposes over time. Eason[14] rightly sees modern microcomputer and telecommunications technologies as having those very characteristics.

In the HUSAT view, a design group including user representatives would be responsible for introducing a limited computer system initially, but as organisational learning and needs developed and informed the design process, the computer system would become increasingly sophisticated and its potential would be increasingly related to user needs and organisational effectiveness (Fig. 4.4.).

Clearly, all this needs mechanisms to provide for effective user involvement in an evolutionary design process that remains flexible and always open to change.

To enable people to make informed decisions, Eason suggests that cheap pilot mini- or microcomputer systems should be implemented to facilitate tests, experiments and learning. Also important are the provision of institutionalised feedback loops from users to managers and designers. Such loops facilitate system modification in the light of

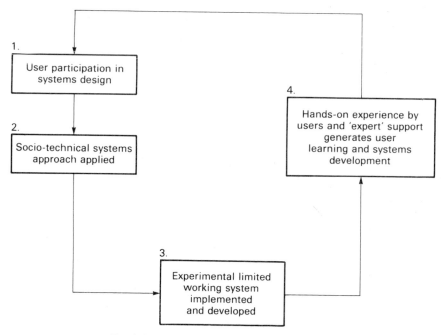

Fig. 4.4 Evolutionary systems development cycle

emergent user needs and problems. A further point is the need to develop a social system committed to the use and development of the technical system. Unlike in more traditional approaches, the system design team would continue in existence to maintain and develop the computer system. Additionally, support staff (e.g. trainers) would promote user learning and exploitation of the system and convey details of inadequacies and possible improvements to the design team.

In attempting to operationalise evolutionary systems development, Eason has found that users tend to exploit only a small part of the technical capability of the increasingly powerful and flexible systems with which they are provided. His research evidence shows that, for further systems development, users require not only continuous technical assistance, but also support from people who understand both the technical system and the application context of the user.[15] Interestingly, the people best able to provide this informal, pragmatic social support system are those users who were principally involved in the original design process, who thus gained more expertise and knowledge than their colleagues.

Such informal social support roles may become increasingly encouraged and formally recognised in future systems design approaches. However, this needs to be done with care. In several systems projects witnessed by the authors, users were promoted to project teams, gained technical expertise, and could never be reintroduced into the user community. Their new skills set them apart. In the case of one large pharmaceuticals company, these 'techno-users' became a separate 'business analyst' group, adding yet another layer in the organisational hierarchy. The practical effect of this development was to severely restrict, rather than enhance, liaison between users and systems analyst.

While the HUSAT Research Group has not yet provided a complete methodology for systems design, they have gone some way in the direction of combining a proper stress on the importance of human factors and user involvement in system design with the exploitation of the immense flexibility and potential of modern technologies to further organisational learning, organisational members' objectives and organisational effectiveness.

SYSTEMS PROTOTYPING

The workability of a systems design is the most important consideration for the end user. The traditional approach—getting the complete technical system design right first, making some attempt to add on 'user-friendliness' then implementing it, all too often does not achieve the results desired. Critical and expensive problems can result from not getting the design right.

One solution is to involve the user in the design process. But the user's lack of technical expertise can make this a time-consuming and sometimes self-defeating exercise. A modern solution to these perennial problems is prototyping.

Prototyping depends on very powerful computer hardware and fourth-generation software only developed in the 1980s. These permit a systems designer to produce a working model of an application. Users and the designer can then work together to improve the model's ability to meet users' needs and the organisation's information processing requirements (Fig. 4.5). The major advantages are as follows.

Firstly, users gain experience and technical know-how as systems design proceeds.

Secondly, prototyping is a very efficient technique for fact-finding.

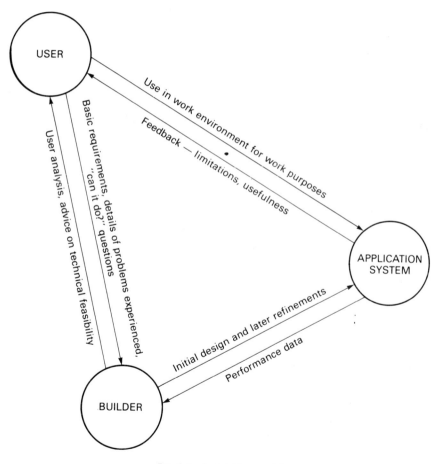

Fig. 4.5 Prototyping model

Thirdly, user participation contributes to the usefulness of the design, while generating high commitment to the final working system. The high interaction between builder and user can also generate co-operation and the feeling of being a team.

Fourthly, training occurs during system development rather than after its completion. This gives much better insight and understanding of the systems's characteristics and uses.

Fifthly, development time can be cut significantly and merged with implementation time.

Sixthly, the design approach is flexible enough to allow for users' expanding requirements.

Seventhly, prototyping can break down the traditional specialisms and barriers between systems analyst/designer, systems programmer, computer department staff and end users. The mutual learning process can generate confidence in each other and about the aims of the system and its operation.

Prototypes can be developed and applied quickly as up-and-running working systems. In the more advanced forms of prototyping, development would not end there but would occur continuously over the usable life of the system. The major problem with prototyping is resource requirements. These include very high level languages, generalised input and output software and interactive and database management systems. At the time of writing, these each have high cost implications.

DEVELOPMENTS: TOWARDS AN INTEGRATED APPROACH

This chapter has reviewed a range of developments in 'soft' approaches to systems design. Can these methodologies learn from one another? Can their various strengths be combined in a more integrated approach?

One promising development in this direction is Multiview (see Fig. 4.6). This attempts to utilise Checkland's methodology for analysing and modelling the human activity system. More 'traditional' charting techniques (e.g. functional charts, data flow diagrams) are then used for information modelling. Mumford's ETHICS is next employed to integrate the computer system into people's work. The fourth stage is focussing on human—computer interaction; in particular, creating user-friendly dialogues (see chapter 6 for a discussion of this topic). Finally, the technical subsystem is designed using a database, and utilising packages and prototyping where feasible.

The common thread in Multiview is using more traditional, 'hard' system tools and techniques with 'soft' methodologies to achieve, through a human focus, an effectively operating information system.

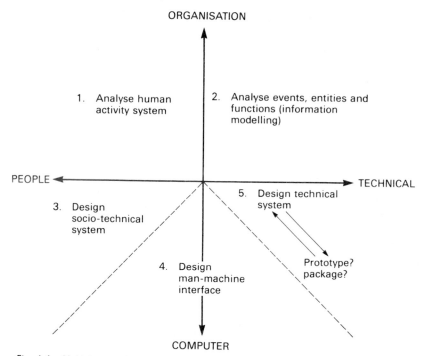

Fig. 4.6 Multiview: an integrated approach (adapted from Antill and Wood-Harper)[16]

One difficulty is that Multiview cannot utilise the strengths of different approaches and techniques without also taking on board some of their weaknesses. The following are just a few examples.

As in Checkland's 'soft' systems methodology, Multiview, in practice, fails to confront the very real possibility of fundamental clashes in material and economic interests in organisational life. In fact, user involvement in analysis may exacerbate such conflicts rather than reduce them.

The employment of traditional tools and techniques in Multiview may result in practice in the surrendering of the responsibility for analysis and design into the hands of the systems analyst once again. Moreover, where modern techniques like prototyping are proposed, it should be realised that not all computer systems can be designed incrementally. Furthermore, some problem situations may be easily and authoritatively defined. Here a more rigorous methodology, without a prototyping requirement, may lead to a more effective implementation.

Mumford's participative, socio-technical design approach tends to be applicable mainly to the computerisation of small organisations or small systems. Her case studies reveal the adoption of more indirect, less consensus type participation for the larger computer projects. A fall-off in the benefits of participation results. Multiview inherits this problem.

It is significant that the major published example of the application of Multiview is a small system in a mainly flat, non-hierarchically structured organisation—the distance learning unit in a polytechnic.[17] The major problems found in large applications—sheer number of people involved, the problems that participation brings, the intrusion of power and social factors, problems of control, timings and logistics—are largely absent from the Multiview case study.

Multiview also shares with the human-focussed design philosophies it seeks to embrace an inherent belief in the flexibility of computer technology. This is a proper emphasis. However, computer hardware and software do have determining effects on systems design to the extent that large manufacturers like Honeywell, IBM and ICL in fact create the technology. In this way, technical options are foreclosed in an organisation even before the systems analysis process begins. One possible way forward is indicated by the Swedish Utopia project.[18] Here the State and trade unions funded research and development of computer technology for the print industry. The twin criteria informing design were quality of product and quality of work life. Skilled print craftsmen participated in technological development. The resulting technology was sold to manufacturers and suppliers as viable, marketable products.

Multiview forms a useful starting point for the integration of different approaches to, and different tools and techniques for, the analysis, design and computerisation of information systems. But a further integration is necessary, between systems methodologies (whether participative or not) and the study of organisational behaviour. This implies changes in the training of systems analysts, but also the usefulness of including organisational specialists in design projects. Such an integration has several purposes:

(a) to understand and define the organisational context into which the system will be imbedded; this particularly applies to organisational structure, workflows, culture, politics and computer history

(b) to utilise types and levels of participation appropriate to *this* computerisation project

(c) to emphasise the need for, and perform, a full user analysis

(d) to ensure that results from (a) and (c) are used in information modelling; also to ensure that users assist in this modelling

(e) to restrict the design features to those that are organisationally, politically and culturally, as well as technically, feasible

(f) to manage the processes of participation over the period of systems development.

Many participative design methodologies are geared to a focus on human aspects within the project, but neglect human factors in the wider organisation. In fact, system acceptability in the wider organisation may impinge crucially on design success.

Participative methodologies also tend to underplay the role of politics within the project. This is partly because participation is itself often an attempt to bypass conflicts and emphasise co-operation and common goals in systems development. But, by definition, participation implies redistribution of power, however small. The management of participation politics needs behavioural skills.

Finally, participation in computer systems design creates expectations amongst users as to outcomes. These may easily be disappointed if the levels of participation are unrealistic. A related point here is that participants may decide upon, and help to design, aspects of the system which do not fit wider organisational requirements. For example, participants may prefer certain skill levels and responsibilities in their jobs. These may imply new gradings and higher pay levels. These would not be applied if they meant radical changes in the organisation's job evaluation and pay structure. The subsequent crisis in expectations amongst participants may not be helpful for systems development and acceptance.

CONCLUSIONS

The 'non-traditional' design approaches reviewed in this chapter share a concern for human-centredness and user participation in design practice. All have limitations and difficulties in practice, but all represent attempts to come to terms with the limitations of more traditional, hard design approaches. A path forward is to integrate the strengths of these approaches, while bringing to bear a new focus on organisational behaviour and the organisational context in which the system will be introduced.

As the computing world goes 'soft', radical changes in the role of the systems analyst are implied. The age of the loneliness of the long-distance systems designer may well be over. However, a question remains: will the power of the systems analyst be used to speed such developments, resist, or push them in other directions?

CHAPTER 5

Working with Computers— 1. Designing Jobs and Work Organisation

'I never feel enriched. I just feel knackered.'[1]
'The problem with American industry is too many idiot jobs, and not enough idiots to fill them.'[2]

INTRODUCTION

This chapter and the next focus on three areas—the work that users are expected to carry out within a computer-based system, the person–machine interface and the immediate environment in which work takes place. All these facets are important influences on the productivity of work life, but also the quality of work life (QWL), for people working with computers. Indeed, a cardinal point that many commentators make is that productivity and QWL are not exclusive but interrelated.

Job content, user-friendliness of computer equipment, software and work environment—all these can be easily neglected altogether. More commonly, design is informed by a narrow concern for technical efficiency, and a traditional view of the need to control workers closely wherever possible, due to assumptions about their motivations and attitudes and what makes for productivity. One example, from the 1960s, was the creation of the new job of data-processing operator. This involved the full-time keying into the computer of data from forms filled in by others. The major credit card companies batch-process millions of transactions a week and still maintain such posts. Clearly, improved ergonomics, software, screen layouts and rest pauses can only do so much here. The risk is that traditional principles of work organisation and job design will be carried over into computerisation projects.

However, there is nothing inherent in computer technology that demands less, or more, interesting jobs to be produced. The potential of computer technology can be harnessed to build upon users' existing skills and experience, and, indeed, to create new skills. Alternatively, work can be degraded or automated out of existence, with skills and decision-making designed out of jobs and into computer programs and systems. A more common practice has been to use technology to support existing structures, hierarchies and work systems, even where their growing inadequacy may have been a reason for bringing in computers in the first place. This chapter details a range of job design approaches and their implications.

JOB DESIGN

Job design has been usefully defined as 'the specification of the contents, methods and relationships of jobs in order to satisfy technological and organisational requirements as well as the social and personal requirements of the job holder'.[3]

A task has several dimensions. It may have a short or long cycle time, be precise and constraining or loose and discretionary, routine or non-routine, require few or many low-level or high-level skills. Job design refers to the way in which a task is made into, or various tasks are combined to form, a complete job. There is considerable scope for how this may be done and the resulting job may have a range of characteristics. Some of the possibilities are indicated in Figure 5.1. The examples here are highly selective but serve to indicate some of the job redesign tendencies already integral to many computer applications. The figure is not able to show the other frequent consequence of computerisation, namely the *elimination* of many jobs, whether routine and low-skilled or high-skilled.

With computerisation, jobs tend to fall into those that involve working full time with the technology, and those requiring only intermittent interface with the computer and VDUs. Job-holders in boxes 2 and 4 of Figure 5.1 will see the computer as a tool in their work, those in box 3 will have the enriched, full time, interesting 'new craft' jobs in computer systems, while the jobs that are left—computer-paced with low skill—fall into box 1.

It is difficult to establish patterns in the very complex picture that emerges from the job designs that have been produced by computer applications so far in the 1980s. However, one tendency has been for existing power structures to be maintained in organisations so far as possible. This means the more powerful interest groups getting their new jobs with computers in, or classified as in, boxes 3 and 4; some of the dependence on new 'computer specialists' is reduced by technological and software developments themselves (e.g. the routinisation of programming work); multi-task, low-skilled workers are created but usually to fit in with the requirements of technology-led development in flexible manufacturing and office systems. As discussed in chapter 3, the jobs that are left fall to those with the weakest organisational power or weakest positions in the labour market, frequently women.

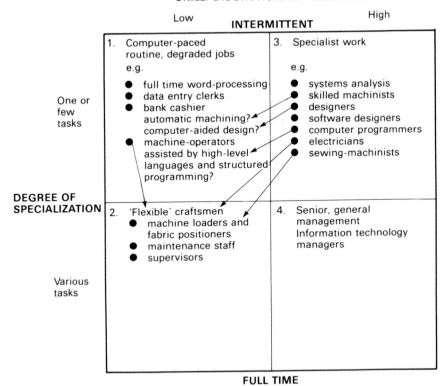

Fig. 5.1   Discretion, skill and specialisation in jobs

In fact, there are several different approaches that can be taken to job design and work organisation. These are reviewed below. Some approaches operate at the individual level, concerning themselves with the job needs of the worker in isolation. Others choose to recognise the social context in which work is performed. One surprising fact is that the job design principles on which any humanisation of work programme must be based have been known for many years, but have been rarely applied. One danger is that this pattern will continue with the application of computer-based systems to workplaces.

SCIENTIFIC MANAGEMENT-BASED APPROACHES

Scientific management-based approaches have been widely used not just with the older technologies, but also when computerising offices and factories. They have in common certain principles:

(a) They divide mental from manual labour. Job-planning and discretion is given to managers where possible.

(b) They maximise specialisation in skills.

(c) They minimise skill requirements.

(d) They minimise learning and training time.

(e) They achieve a full work load.

(f) They minimise the number and variety of tasks in a job.

(g) They create short-cycle jobs that are as repetitive as possible.

These principles may not always be fully applied, but the sorts of jobs that typically result even with partial application are indicated in box 1 of Fig. 5.1. Such jobs tend to be machine-paced, with a short cycle time. They allow little responsibility, and impose on the job-holder restricted mobility and social isolation.

Research into American manufacturing industry in 1978 found that such principles were widely used to achieve very limited objectives, namely the minimisation of production costs by reducing unit production time. Also, the major influences on job design were found to be first-line managers and design engineers; personnel managers were rarely involved.[4]

In fact, scientific management-based approaches create not one but at least two types of job. Where computers are to be introduced, planning, mental labour, discretion and skill will tend to be centralised in the hands of managers and a few experts. An example, drawn from the publishing industry, is shown in Figure 5.2. There is a question here for craft typesetters—will they be downgraded to data entry clerks, upgraded to take on editorial responsibilities, or replaced altogether?

But microelectrics permits a further development, with discretionary and skill elements being themselves computerised and removed from expert and managerial jobs. Research into 'expert systems' to replace financial and insurance advisers is only one of the more stark examples of the possibilities.

There are many examples of jobs at middle and particularly lower levels in organisations being degraded through, or at the same time as, the introduction of computers. In retailing, centralised information systems using electronic point-of-sale (EPOS) terminals take away departmental manager discretion in making price and stock-reorder decisions. Sales staff have become little more than cashiers at the terminals. Meanwhile, managerial control has increased. In banking, the post of bank teller has been subdivided into full-time cashier and lobby clerk. The former job is now very routine. For example, computer-based shared tills eradicate the need for each cashier to balance his/her transactions for the day. Lobby clerks can also find their responsibilities and discretion restricted by computerised procedures.

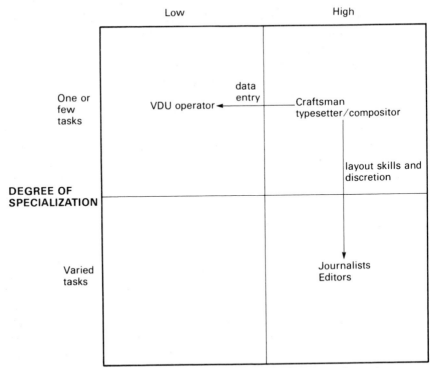

Fig. 5.2 *Computerised typesetting and job change in publishing*

In the factory, the skill and discretion to set up and operate machine tools has often passed to centralised program-writers who build these into their programs. Thus computer-numerically-controlled (CNC) systems have been used to reduce the role of skilled operator to machine-minder. One commentator on computer-aided design (CAD) concludes that it

'is likely to be accompanied by the subordination of the operator [designer] to the machine [computer] with the narrow specialisation of Taylorism [scientific management] leading to fragmentation and a loss of panoramic view of the design activity itself... CAD when introduced on the basis of so called efficiency, gives rise to a deskilling of the design function and a loss of job security.'[5]

In the clothing industry, the skilled male job of cutting has been largely computerised. At Hepworths, customer measurements are fed into a central computer, and the work is done by a much smaller number of less skilled women working at VDUs. Meanwhile, sewing machines can be automatically programmed for a range of tasks, and operators become loaders and fabric-positioners, needing much less training.

Such job degradation may arise almost accidentally, as a result of the failure to operate any conscious job redesign policy. It would be inaccurate to see it as a necessary consequence of the introduction of new technology. More properly, job degradation may be pursued due to perceptions and objectives of systems analysts and senior managers, competitive market pressures, labour market factors, or for reasons of organisation structure or trade union position. In other circumstances, and with other workers, quite different job design practices might be pursued.

Scientific management-based approaches can result in large increases in productivity and sometimes have helped to improve the ergonomic aspects of work performance. However, they create organisational rigidities and inflexibilities that can inhibit the potential of computer/microchip technologies. They undercharacterise human motivation and needs in jobs and the importance of social relationships in work. They also underutilise human capabilities and creativity at work, and are often seen as devices for management to increase control over their subordinates, with industrial relations problems developing as a consequence.

ALTERNATIVES

Several different job restructuring techniques have received limited organisational use in the past in attempts to offset the boredom and dissatisfaction engendered by the application of scientific management-based techniques. However, the introduction of new technology may act as a catalyst, speeding their adoption. For IT not only provides opportunities to change the contents of jobs; in many cases it also forces management to focus on the issue of content in new ways, and even for the first time. At such a juncture, managements may become open to the equating of computer system effectiveness with the conscious adoption of the more humanising job design strategies discussed below.

Job rotation
Job rotation permits a worker to switch jobs periodically with other workers doing work of similar skill level.

In one brewery, computerisation meant that operators lost many of the old manual skills needed to control the production process. Some manual tasks remained, but process control was computerised. VDU operators in a central control room responded to process information by keying in adjustments where necessary. However, the men were permitted to rotate jobs between control room and production floor. Interestingly, in this example, it was the foremen who became deskilled with the loss of their monitoring tasks to the computerised control system.[6] In a firm manufacturing lenses and spectacles, computer-controlled machinery reduced the skill and judgement required in the task of lens preparation. Job rotation was introduced to preserve job interest and content. Employees were trained in a range of functions. The staff supported this development, but it must not be seen in isolation. Wilkinson[7] points out how a multi-skilled workforce can have big pay-offs for management. Absence through sickness or holiday could be easily covered. As one manager commented:

> 'The staff are now reaching a point where I can move them around anywhere I want—and that is a wonderful thing for a production manager to say.'[7]

Job enlargement

Job enlargement involves increasing the variety of tasks making up a person's job by bringing together several tasks requiring similar skill levels.

As an example, CNC machinery does not require the skilled machinist to be degraded to machine-minder. Wilkinson[8] reports cases where the minder role was enlarged and traditional skills were preserved by adding responsibility for editing and adjusting programs. Interestingly, in some companies where machine programming was centralised away from the shopfloor, Wilkinson found machinists teaching themselves programming and making adjustments informally to maintain machining quality.[8]

In fact, some employers practice job enlargement as part of overall work restructuring schemes designed to enhance productivity. At Carrington Viyella in 1980 a highly automated spinning plant was introduced and, for their own reasons but also to fulfil the potential of the technology, both management and union agreed to new multi-skilled roles for operatives. However, such job enlargement can have knock-on effects. In one firm, the automation of the manufacturing assembly line meant the deskilling of insertion tasks. The task that remained was combined with test and inspection duties to form an enlarged job, but this was at the expense of specialist testing occupations—these jobs were eliminated.[9]

A final example of job enlargement is at Swansea Vehicle Licensing Centre. Here, the clerical work based around computer technology was fragmented into some nine job types. Some job enlargement was subsequently achieved by combining clerical and data-processing work. However, by 1986, after two years of operation, the novelty and variety of such jobs had lost their attraction. Job redesign also provoked long-running pay disputes because the new jobs were done by people from different pay grades.

As attempts to increase the morale and productivity of those working with computer technology, job rotation and enlargement by themselves tend to be of marginal importance. The variety they add to people's jobs are too often very small gestures made in workplaces where more scientific management-based approaches continue to be the norm. They are probably best used as parts of larger work reorganisation schemes, and where workers themselves actively demand their introduction.

Job enrichment

Job enrichment involves expanding a job vertically by adding together tasks requiring different skill levels until a meaningful job is created.

A job involves planning, doing and controlling tasks. Job enrichment is concerned with giving to the job-holder more of the planning, decision-making and control functions. These are more usually reserved for management through the design of the technology and the way work is organised.

Hackman[10] has produced a job characteristics model widely accepted as a guide to how to enrich jobs. According to this model, and much of the research done on job enrichment, a job must, firstly, allow the worker to use a variety of skills and talents at stretch over a number of differing activities.

Secondly, the job must be complete in the sense that there is a piece of work that has a beginning and an end, an identifiable product with which the worker can relate, and that the product has significance for, and an impact on, other workers or a customer. Skills must be used in a meaningful context; the job must make sense to the job-holder and those relying on the product of his/her work.

Thirdly, the job must allow discretion in giving the individual decision-making responsibility for how the work is planned, performed and controlled. Also the worker should have authority to act in unusual situations as well as those requiring the application of routine procedures.

Fourthly, the job must provide quick, clear, frequent and direct information to the job-holder on the effectiveness of his/her performance. This can reduce errors, underline the accomplishment of the job-holder and increase the meaningfulness of the work to that worker.

Hackman and many others have tested such job characteristics and show that higher job satisfaction and productivity frequently result. However, this picture needs to be qualified.

Some researchers build in three more psychological characteristics of enriched jobs, namely social interaction and recognition, continuous learning inherent in the job, and a desirable future as a result of job performance.[11] Herzberg would add that factors in **job context** (e.g. supervisory style, pay, working conditions) are as important as job content in their influence on worker motivation and satisfaction.

Job enrichment theories also contain several assumptions. A worker is assumed to want an enriched job. Where this is provided, job satisfaction should result, and the worker's motivation to work will result in higher productivity. This chain of reasoning can be questioned. Firstly, where a worker does not have high self-actualisation and status needs at work, job enrichment techniques will be misdirected and have little effect on behaviour, satisfaction or performance.

Next, there is no necessary link between job content and job satisfaction. A person's satisfaction can result as much from the people he/she works with, the pay, the conditions (e.g. holidays, hours per week, flexitime, the ease of getting to and from work) as from the actual work to be done.

Following from this, there is no automatic causal link between job satisfaction and motivation to work. In fact, a person may be highly satisfied with a job precisely because it does not require high motivation, effort and ability to accomplish it.

All this makes the desired connection between job enrichment and higher productivity more tenuous than is usually assumed. Furthermore, productivity is not determined by worker motivation alone. It also relies on such factors as worker skills and abilities, the adequacy of training received, the efficiency of technology employed, the nature of work organisation and the contribution of other workers. Thus, even where a job enrichment programme does highly motivate the job-holder, increased productivity is not always bound to result.

Trade unions, staff associations and many types of worker, whatever their skill level, resist job enrichment for its erosion of existing demarcations between skills and jobs on which may depend the employee's status, pay level and, indeed, continuing employment. The mid-1980s has seen a small but developing trend toward job flexibility influenced by many factors, not least the recession in the UK and the impact of computer technologies on work practices. Some trade unions have promoted this trend, but a majority still view the breakdown of existing job patterns with some suspicion.

Also, job enrichment may be resisted, or limited in its impact, by managers and supervisors where it is seen to reduce their own responsibility, discretion, control, and ability and right to manage.

In summary, systems designers need to be very discriminating and ensure that job enrichment is applied only in circumstances that merit and support its implementation and subsequent effectiveness.

One example of a successful job enrichment scheme occurred with the computerisation of customer records in one region of a nationalised service industry.[12] The old work organisation was ill-suited to the new computer system. Each department dealt with customer enquiries relating to its speciality; for example, equipment servicing, invoicing. A new consumer department was set up. Each clerk there became responsible for the accounts and records of, and all queries from, some 10 000 customers. A broader, inter-departmental role was being created. The scheme began as an attempt to match job design with computer and customer requirements, but as it developed, job enlargement became job enrichment. Clerks developed expertise in particular tasks, debt-collection and prepayment responsibilities were added, supervision became unnecessary and supervisory skills passed to the clerks. The gains, in terms of a halving of customer complaints, lower absenteeism and staff turnover, and increases in job satisfaction, were significant.

To be successful, job enrichment schemes need to pay particular attention not just to job content, but also to the provision of increased training, regrading and new payment schemes, and to the fit between jobs, and computer and product/service requirements. It is also important to establish precisely the job requirements of employees, and permit their influence in design.

In fact, recent research suggests that many employers are not pursuing a job design route that leads to deskilling and increased control over work. A 1983–85 survey of shop stewards in the UK frequently found technical change closely related to increases in skill levels, worker job control, and pay, but also increased effort.[13] It may be that trade unions are increasingly supporting the job design strategies discussed in this section as part of wider deals on pay and effort. Where this is so, then these job design approaches must be part of wider organisational development, with employment policies and management systems built less on the principle of *control* of work, and more on the principle of generating employee *commitment* to work. This notion is discussed further below.

SOCIO-TECHNICAL SYSTEMS APPROACHES

Once computer systems are operating, their use can expose the limitations of handling job design at the individual level; that is, taking a job-by-job approach. A learning process, a realisation of the further possibilities for higher productivity and job satisfaction, can move designers and users through several stages of job design. Thus, in the computerised records case cited above, work organisation eventually moved to a group working system.

Some design projects see the advantages of fitting new technology with group working systems from the start. In doing so they are usually adopting a socio-technical systems (STS) approach.

STS is a way of looking at organisations and a design philosophy rather than a specific design technique. However, its practitioners have tended to be identified with technical design, group working and worker participation in the design process as sources of satisfaction and productivity at work.

STS has been a meeting place for various currents. Originated by London Tavistock Institute practitioners as a procedure for managing the social problems of technical change in organisations, it also builds on most of the design principles of the job enrichment movement. Latterly, it has been found useful for the participative design and introduction of computer systems, with specific emphasis on the need for technology, job content and social and work organisation to complement each other. In fact, there are many STS approaches, but practitioners hold a certain view in common. This is summarised in Fig. 5.3.

STS approaches see an organisation as a system open to its environment. This means that it interacts, influences and is influenced by 'external' factors in

(a) its immediate **task** environment (e.g. competition, suppliers, customers, technological developments in its industry, sources of finance)

(b) its **general** environment (mainly political, economic, social, technological and legal factors).

Moreover, the organisation is viewed in terms of three major and interacting subsystems (Fig. 5.3). The crucial point is that these are interdependent. A change in one subsystem will have an impact on, and may require changes in, the other two. It is therefore crucial for the systems designer contemplating changes in the organisation's technological base to balance, and achieve a satisfactory fit between, the different elements of all three subsystems.

This is obviously more difficult than designing a computer system that is technically efficient in its own terms. But a technical system in itself is no guarantor of increased productivity and/or job satisfaction. According to STS practitioners, it is on this very point that systems designs still

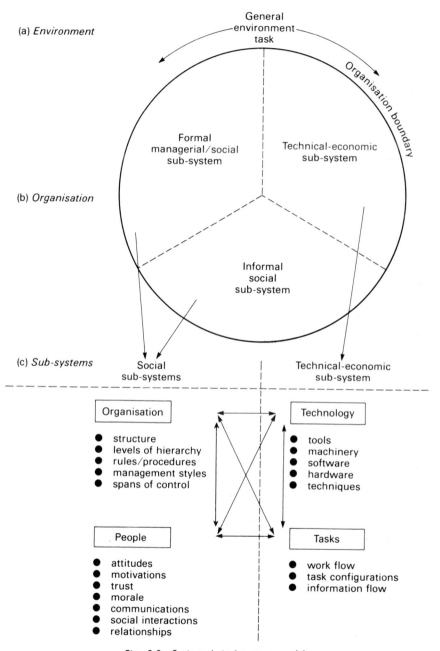

Fig. 5.3 Socio-technical systems model

stumble at the implementation stage and subsequently fail to achieve even their own limited technical objectives.

The systems designer should use the traditional STS approach with care, and with full consideration of choice, objectives, and cost and time.

The idea that a systems designer/manager can make **choices** about how these three subsystems are to fit together seriously underplays the organisational realities confronting any change initiative. Choices do not occur in a vacuum; there may be many influencing people and factors. The idea of 'choice' hides the fact that what is chosen is usually the outcome of the operation of a range of constraints, compromises, other people's perceptions, influence and power. The systems designer should be ready for many intervening factors that limit 'choice'.

Objectives are not arrived at unproblematically. For example, whose objectives is the designer seeking to achieve in aiming for 'an appropriate balance' between human, managerial, technological and economic factors? Is a satisfactory fit achieved by the design that produces the highest output? Traditional STS approaches have adopted an implicit managerial perspective on this issue, and this in itself may increase resistance amongst other interested parties against efficient running of the new system.

For socio-technical design, **cost and time** tend to be higher and longer than for traditional approaches. The process requires wider analysis, and therefore greater effort; user participation slows development and requires more resources; and conflicts and disagreements are given prominence—time is needed to resolve issues.

STS is a highly useful approach for organisational development and designing computer systems, but its proponents customarily are particularly concerned with its applicability to the design of jobs and work organisation. Buchanan and Boddy[14,15] have provided empirical underpinning for STS principles in designing work organisation and jobs in the computer age. Their research covers a wide range of industries and computer applications. It demonstrates that managements have considerable choice in how work is organised around computer technology. In particular, cumulative managerial decisions may 'distance' the employees from the task, severely limiting the contributions they make. Alternatively, decisions may deliberately bring about a high degree of 'complementarity' between employee and task. In the latter case the computer becomes not a **displacing** but an **enabling** technology, making full use of both technical capabilities and human skills.

STS approaches to job design also emphasise that the functioning of work systems frequently relies on group activity, and, where this is so, it is more logical to apply job design principles at this level. Furthermore, work in groups is more likely to satisfy human needs, develop responsibility and commitment and provide meaningful work. Thus STS design principles can serve as the umbrella in which the objectives of job rotation, enlargement and enrichment can be achieved.

WORK TEAMS

In the United Kingdom the idea of work groups taking over supervisory and managerial functions and becoming responsible for significant, discrete sections of the production process has frequently been met with alarm, and often dismissed as too radical. This has not been just in management circles either. However, the 1980s recession, more intense competition and the widening use of computer technologies may create sufficient pressure for the adoption of management and work systems that the Japanese have operated for many years without the spur of technology.

This section looks at two main options compatible with STS design principles and computerisation.

Integrated work teams

With integrated work teams, job enlargement and rotation are involved at the group rather than the individual level. A large number of tasks and jobs of similar skill level are assigned to a group with a supervisor. The job that each individual does can be left to the discretion of the group. It is possible to have a job rotation at such frequent intervals that in practice wide horizontal expansion of job experience occurs in the case of every individual in the group.

Such an approach removes some of the limitations of job rotation or enlargement at the individual level. It recognises the social needs that job-holders may have, while permitting less routine performance and more discretion and decision-making in the assigning and performing of tasks. The authors have seen it used successfully in a computerised office of some 15 employees, with word-processing, correspondence secretary, and mail, telephone and general secretarial tasks.

Hackman and Oldham[16] have pointed out that two factors additional to those mentioned in the discussion of job enrichment (see above) can crucially affect a worker's sense of involvement and satisfaction with the job. These are

(a) dealing with others—involvement with others, sense of teamwork

(b) Feedback from others—support and information on performance from supervisors and others.

Clearly, designs must rely on group settings to give jobs these additional characteristics.

Autonomous and semi-autonomous work groups

The design approach involving autonomous and semi-autonomous work groups operates job enrichment at the group level. This permits the advantages of vertical expansion of jobs, while allowing opportunities for job rotation and enlargement as well. There are many variants possible here. For example, it is possible for a group to be given a definite goal or output to achieve, and time limit, and then left to be **self-regulating**—free to plan, select members, decide allocation of tasks, set up inspection procedures and quality control, perform task, maintenance and supervisory roles, and evaluate performance and individual remuneration due.

In practice, even the classic case of STS design and autonomous work groups—at Volvo car assembly plant in Kalmar, Sweden—did not go so far.

Here, managers, union representatives and various experts participated in a joint effort to redesign the factory. The conventional assembly line was removed, and replaced by 30 workshops, each with up to 20 workers. Each team had considerable discretion over its organisation and speed of work. With this loosely coupled system, each team area needed terminals with access to the computerised production, process and quality control systems. These gave information on specification of car to be assembled, position and state of vehicles in the factory transport system, and error rates and requests to correct.

The computerised information system did give ultimate control to managers, but significantly they only received summary reports in hard copy. Only supervisors, work teams and quality control engineers had easy on-line access to terminals. Here, computer systems, along with the more traditional assembly-line technology, were decentralised, and designed around increased autonomy, responsibility, and discretion for work groups.

Such radical developments in Sweden, and also in Norway, have been compromised by context, history and culture when transplanted to the UK. Thus Mumford[17] describes her involvement in computerising a purchase invoicing system at Rolls Royce. Here, a representative design group found the autonomous work team concept too radical, and an individual job enrichment programme insufficient for overcoming problems with the existing work structure. The 60 clerks had been divided into four grades. The major problem seemed to be the very routine work and high labour turnover amongst the lowest-grade workers. However, the higher-grade clerks wished to retain their status and pay levels. A compromise was achieved with the creation of a main group, and a higher-status group looking after special activities and suppliers. These were serviced by a group of lower-grade clerks carrying out common, routine tasks.

Needham[18] studied a reorganisation of assembly work in an engineering factory. He found that autonomous work teams offered major benefits to individual workers and the company. But in order to sustain these in increasingly difficult trading conditions of the early 1980s:

> ' ... some of the more traditional management controls and functions would have to be retained to ensure that the benefits deriving from greater job satisfaction and greater flexibility were not obtained at the expense of efficiency and operating costs ... in the longer term, self-regulation, particularly when applied to work rate, quality and attendance, proved to be something of a myth.'

This indicates that designers need to have a broad picture of the factors affecting the effectiveness of what is eventually implemented. Needham indicates that recruitment difficulties, industrial relations problems in the context of relatively full employment, and worker demands for more say in matters affecting their immediate work environment all made the adoption of autonomous work teams a viable option. But when these factors disappeared, and other factors became important, the self-regulating work group approach had to be considerably revised.

In fact, the Volvo Kalmar plant itself indicates some of the problems with the autonomous work team solution to job design. The assembly line, though not visible, was still there. Company production quotas had to be met; buffer zones between teams were too small and were made smaller by the addition of new work stations for new models. Each work group became closely dependent on the surrounding teams. The discretion that work groups had over work pace and breaks proved minor. The quality control system was ended and left to foremen and engineers. Some team areas started their own division of labour, and failed to rotate jobs.

In terms of lower absenteeism and labour turnover, more satisfying jobs and higher productivity, Kalmar is a qualified success.[19] The crucial limiting factors turned out to be the re-emergence of the assembly line in another form; the maintenance of the existing power structure (e.g. the foreman role persisted with as much power as previously, and each was appointed by management); and that the changes in work organisation were not paralleled by revision of the piece-rate payment system based on the old assembly line. The lesson here is crucial for all job redesign initiatives—the success of the scheme will depend on adjustments in a range of contextual factors. If these are not forthcoming, the scheme will degenerate in order to fit existing structures.

CONTROL OR COMMITMENT?

In all the job design practices under review, there can be traced managerial attempts to solve a central organisational problem: how to organise and maintain control over work, without reducing the employee commitment necessary to achieve required productivity levels.

Traditional bureaucratic systems achieve outputs by a division of labour, promoting specialisation and close definition of tasks, and minimising the discretion in jobs wherever possible. Rules, procedures, a hierarchy of control, and technological design itself, as well as the payment system, are all meant to assist in keeping the employee on target. Where they have been used, the more humanising job redesign methods have been attempts to ameliorate the deleterious affects of these control devices on employee commitment to their jobs, and thus their productivity. They have also been used to reduce at different organisational levels the problems of co-ordinating and integrating activities divided by specialisation.

When computer technology is introduced it can be designed to fit in with, and perpetuate, these existing control patterns. But to reap the full benefits of something as sophisticated and costly as flexible manufacturing systems (FMSs) or computer-integrated manufacturing (CIM), work and production may need to be reorganised. With so much automated, the extent of information to hand, and so many operations able to be actioned from one work station, the traditional boundaries between functions like design, production planning, maintenance, manufacturing and quality control become blurred and crumble away. As they develop, the same becomes true for computer-aided design and computer-aided manufacturing (CAD/CAM) systems and office automation (OA).

In the 1980s, many US companies are seeing the advantages of both computerising and at the same time adopting organisational forms and work patterns dependent, according to several commentators, upon the **commitment** of workers rather than their **control**.[20,21] Methods of developing such commitment include establishing shared values and goals; vertical enrichment of jobs, with workers taking over more expert, supervisory, and even managerial work; personal development opportunities to attract those who can adapt to continual change in methods, job content, products and services; emphasising teamwork and rewarding relationships at work.

Such initiatives have immense job design applications. As one example, in mid-1986 General Motors had detailed plans to introduce both advanced technology and autonomous work teams at their Livonia plant in Michigan, and several of their Opel plants in Europe.

However, the idea of the 'commitment' organisation inducing a new, and happy, marriage between computer technology and the humanisation of work is not without its problems. Firstly, control never leaves the 'commitment' organisation, it merely takes new forms. Control becomes self-control, from the internalisation of values and attitudes by employees. It also comes from group pressure. But computer technology itself provides the technical means for monitoring employee performance closely. In this respect, traditional organisations identified control as over activity, precisely constraining how a job is to be done. Computer systems are being designed to achieve such control with many types of employees, but with the 'committed' worker it may well be sufficient to monitor *results* closely and reap the benefits of designing flexible work patterns surrounding computer systems.

Secondly, the 'commitment' organisation may be as much about passing the feeling of control, rather than its reality, to its workforce. Control over employee behaviour does not have to be visible, or even felt, to exist. Computer technology aids this illusion of freedom in burying the controls within software. Being 'in charge' of sophisticated machinery also communicates to the computer user feelings of power. These can assist the illusion.

Thirdly, the principles of the 'commitment' organisation will probably not apply to all employees. One developing trend in the UK is for job design promoting autonomy, responsibility, team-work and skill in harness with computer technology to be practised for a small primary core of an organisation's workforce. These would have long training, good working conditions, high pay and job security—all inducements to stay committed to the organisation. For more peripheral jobs, computer technology could be used to design out skill and discretion. The people filling such posts would need little training, have low pay and be easily substitutable.

Finally, computers and more participative, flexible workforces have sometimes unacceptable implications for managers and supervisors as well as unions. Thus team working tied in with the automation of the Metro production line at Longbridge did not fit well with the traditional production culture of local Leyland managers and was dropped. Vertical job restructuring eats into supervisory authority. At the same time, trade unions in Germany have sometimes resisted autonomous team working for fear of losing their own monopoly of representing worker interests.

CONCLUSIONS

The discussion in this chapter has several important implications for those responsible for design.

Firstly, workers want more responsibility and control over their work than systems design usually allows for.

Secondly, individual job design must be seen in the context of, and be consistent with, broader work group organisation.

Thirdly, there are benefits, and also costs in involving in its design those who will work in the newly designed work system.

Fourthly, a narrow focus on the design of job content will miss the importance of looking at possible large-scale changes at the level of work organisation. The designer needs to remember that it is not just the job a person does that influences behaviour, attitudes and performance; even more crucial is the *context* in which job performance takes place. In this respect it is also important to ensure that job redesign is matched with such items as work flows in the organisation, payment systems and the supervisory and management control systems.

Fifthly, computer systems *are* being utilised to deskill and marginalise, as well as displace many types of workers, including those at managerial levels. These are human choices and not inevitable. The principle of complementarity is more likely to be used in job design where human skill, personality, judgement and discretion is required and is (as yet) not programmable.

Sixthly, the more humanising job design strategies are seeing some use in the improvement of the quality of work life of small sections of the workforce. One purpose here is usually to promote some form of 'commitment' organisation.

Seventhly, in practice, these design approaches may see greater use as, not humanising, but primarily transitional devices for freeing up job demarcations throughout organisations and intensifying effort. Managements and designers may be turning to these because of the inadequacies of traditional approaches, but also the lack of alternative visions. In this way, traditional bureaucratic organisations can be moved towards less hierarchical, more flexible work patterns that facilitate the operation of highly integrated and sophisticated computer technologies being developed in the late-1980s.

CHAPTER 6

Working With Computers—
2. Environment and Workstation

'In its earliest days, the automobile looked much like the horse-drawn carriage that it was gradually to replace... The development of the visual display terminal parallels that of the automobile. Where VDT's are concerned, we have just left the era of the horseless carriage.'[1]

'Protecting the public from workplace and environmental hazards is not simply a medical or technical problem. It is also a political and economic problem, and the way to a hazard-free environment involves power and politics.'[2]

INTRODUCTION

This chapter investigates human aspects of the user/machine interface, software design and the immediate environment in which computer and user will function. The major focus will be on VDTs—now the main means by which people interact with computer systems at work. According to one research group, Pender Associates, there were in 1986 over two million VDUs in operation in Britain compared with 200 000 in 1975. But how should they fit with the people operating them? A key word is 'ergonomics'.

Ergonomics (literally 'the natural laws of work') studies the manner in which the anatomical, physical and psychological needs of workers relate to their immediate working environment. A major focus is the human/machine interface and how it can be designed to achieve worker satisfaction, health, safety and productivity. The limitations of traditional ergonomics in the face of computer-based technologies have led to additional concerns. These focus additionally on screen–user interaction and 'software psychology', the latter definable as the consideration of the important behavioural factors associated with software production from the point of view of the programmer and different types of user.

Traditionally, designers of workstations and their immediate environments have identified cost-effectiveness with 'cost of equipment' and 'technical merit' with little regard for significant factors that influence human comfort and efficient performance. Perhaps this approach is best revealed by the picture given of the 'end user' at the 'terminal'. The user is the last part of the design to be considered. The user is also frequently characterised as adaptable, flexible, even inexhaustible. Such systems, in operation, tend to be abused, partially used or even fall into disuse; they can have harmful effects on users; by no stretch of the imagination are they cost-effective. The remedy lies in putting users at the centre of design, not at its periphery.

Many systems designers still identify the consideration of human factors in systems design almost entirely with sound ergonomic practice. A major premise of this book is, simply, that this is mistaken. However, ergonomic considerations are still an important, and indeed necessary, part of any computer systems design. As this chapter reveals, that significance is only underlined by what happens when human-centred design practices are neglected.

JUST A BAD PRESS?

A casual observer of the workplace scene could be forgiven for believing that computer terminals and VDUs are so hazardous that, like packets of cigarettes, every one should display a government health warning. Manufacturers themselves attempt to dissipate this sense of alarm by promoting aggressively in sales literature the ergonomic soundness of their equipment. How has this picture of 'workplace hazard' developed?

Part of the reason lies with the high profile given to the health and safety issues amongst trade unions like ASTMS, AEU/TASS, NALGO, APEX, ACTSS and NUJ. Their white-collar members have been the ones most affected by, and most vociferous about, working with the VDUs installed in UK workplaces since the late 1970s. The several reviews of UK new technology agreements arrived at between employers and unions between 1977 and 1985[3-5] show that, after job security, health and safety issues received most attention. This is not surprising, given the relatively developed position of unions on health and safety in the 1970s, even before 'new technology' became an issue. This was underpinned by 1974 legislation and 1976 regulations laying down the need for union involvement in maintaining workplace safety standards, and encouraging information and training from, and consultation with, employers.

Health and safety matters have also received considerable promotion because, unlike, say, pay and job content, the issues tend to be much less contentious and easier for employers to make concessions on. Indeed, employers stand to gain in several ways from being concerned about health and safety matters. Firstly, many employers (though not all) do appreciate the relationship between worker productivity and healthy and safe workstations and environments. Secondly, health and safety concessions can be used as a cheap way of buying union agreement on more contentious issues. Thirdly, it is often useful to allow conflict on other issues surrounding computer technology, like job loss or status changes, to be displaced into the health and safety arena, where they become more manageable. Trade unions may encourage this focus because complaints on health and safety, backed as they are by legislation, are more likely to be seen as legitimate; furthermore, there is greater chance of convincing the employer of the need for action.

Behind all this there has also developed considerable evidence, from independent research and numerous surveys, to show that computer systems have been, and still are being, designed and operated in ways hazardous to their users. Why is this so? The important factors seem to be

(a) what manufacturers choose to make available

(b) buyer and user ignorance, or lack of concern, about the inappropriateness or poor design of equipment; cost considerations or pay increases may be considered more important

(c) misuse of equipment

(d) inadequate training

(e) a narrow focus on equipment quality and specification which neglects other crucial contributory factors such as work-pacing, shift-working, performance-monitoring, job and work organisation design, effort intensification through computerisation, and operator isolation.

The introduction of much of the computer technology in a period of recession, with a reduced Health and Safety inspectorate, an unsupportive government and declining union memberships has weakened the bargaining power of the main countervailing forces to employer policies in this area. Even where 'new technology' agreements were successfully negotiated, trade union policies, at least in the early 1980s, tended to be misdirected into laying down precise standards for items like screen glare, size of characters, rest pauses, colour brightness, noise and temperature. Not only are such quantitative standards often difficult to measure; suppliers are not always open about the design specifications of their equipment; moreover, standards are usually imported into agreements from trade union guidelines in a fairly random manner. The items in (e) above received little attention.

Beyond this, as on other workplace issues, there may be a considerable gulf between arriving at an agreement on VDUs, and securing its enforcement. Even more crucially, 'new technology' agreements have been pursued as general policy within the trade union movement only by a small number of white collar unions. Additionally, it should be remembered that a majority of the UK workforce are not in trade union membership and do not even receive the limited protection that a 'new technology' agreement could offer.

COMPUTER HAZARDS

The research findings on the health issues surrounding VDU work derive from a mixture of user questionnaires, controlled studies and scientific investigations into areas like radiation emissions, vision impacts and clusters of pregnancy problems. The more sober studies are invariably cautious in their conclusions and call for more research. The problem here is that a 'not proven' verdict can be too easily accepted as giving a clean bill of health to a diversity of equipment and uses. Caution is still required, but employers and manufacturers are often reluctant to respond in this way. Also, it is important to look very carefully at the relationship between survey and study results and who their commissioning agents are. Finally, user complaints are not always an ideal source from which to determine the reality of health hazards (such complaints may be made for reasons other than health and safety), but these have to be a starting point.

A review of user surveys and detailed studies[6-12] shows that complaints fall into six main areas, outlined below.

Visual dysfunctions have formed the area of major concern. They range from temporary effects like eye-ache, watering, redness, burning, double or blurred vision, seeing coloured fringes, headaches to chronic problems like glaucoma or cataracts. Many studies confirm that VDT operators wearing glasses or contact lenses have a greater frequency of complaints about vision. VDT operation may require different glasses and may also reveal the need for use of glasses for the first time. There is now overwhelming evidence that acute short-term eye disorders correlate with VDT operation, but are preventable. It is difficult to establish whether long term chronic visual dysfunction results from VDU viewing quite simply because there have been so few studies on this issue.

The second area of complaint concerns muscle and skeletal pains. These commonly take the form of problems with the neck, back, arms, shoulders, fingers, hands and occasionally the legs. Many different studies show that muscular–skeletal complaints vary with type of VDT work. However, complaints are greater amongst all VDT operators compared with people in related occupations.[13] Particular problems are repetitive strain injury (RSI), or tenosynovitis, caused by rapid repeated use of fingers, wrist and arm, and resulting in inflammation of tendons and tendon sheaths, pain, swelling and numbness; also carpal tunnel syndrome (CTS), from repeated wrist flexing and use of fingers, causing damage to the median nerve. Though little research has been undertaken to show chronic disorders resulting from VDT work, repeated keying, RSI and CTS are definitely linked. Furthermore, the most common complaint of low back injury can be related to VDT operators sitting in fixed positions for long periods of time.

The third area concerns psycho-social problems. These involve job stress that can contribute to chronic conditions such as stomach and intestinal disorders, heart and artery diseases, reduced resistance to disease, and emotional disturbances. Contributory factors seem to be fear of job loss, work pressure, supervision and job dissatisfaction. Job-related stress may be the most serious problem facing VDU operators. However, such stress is probably more related to other job, social and organisational changes surrounding computerisation, rather than arising from VDT work in itself. [14]

The fourth complaint area concerns skin rashes. These take the form of skin reddening on operators face, neck and upper chest. In some cases, rashes like first-degree burns have appeared on clothed parts of an operator's body. Reports from the USA, Canada, Norway and the UK have linked these effects to the build-up of static electricity around the VDU and its operator, and also to the emission of very low frequency radiation from the VDT. [15]

The fifth complaint area concerns emotional disturbances. These take the form of anxiety, anger, moodiness, depression, frustration and psychosomatic symptoms such as stomach disorders, sweating, heart palpitations and muscle tension. Complaints vary with type of VDT work, but tend to be more frequent amongst VDT operators than people in related occupations. Again, such disturbances probably arise from a mixture of stress-inducing causes rather than from the VDT equipment itself. However, in a review of research, DeMatteo[2] also suggests that VDT radiation and electromagnetic emissions can create stress and have harmful health effects.

The sixth area concerns pregnancy problems. A range of surveys and reports link clusters of pregnancy problems with VDT work. These clusters may arise as a statistical freak; unfortunately, there is not enough research evidence to support this as the necessarily correct explanation. Attempts to link reproductive hazards with high-frequency ionising radiation can be safely ignored, especially as the newer VDUs produce little such radiation. [16] Research is now switching to the health hazards of low-frequency non-ionising radiation emissions from VDTs. The results, up to late-1987, show no clear linkage. Stress induced by other factors, or anxiety about the possible reproductive hazards of

VDT work, can be alternative explanations for subsequent miscarriages, premature births and other difficulties.

A very complex and unclear picture of the health hazards of VDUs emerges. It is not always possible to separate out the health effects of VDUs from health problems arising from other causes. Indeed, many health difficulties may be related more to the environment and the work that is done—content, pace, operator isolation—than to VDU equipment itself. Survey and study results can be misleading because they generalise from examples and do not always answer the question, 'Is VDU work hazardous, given the specific equipment and specific circumstances and how they are used in this workplace?'

Caution should be the keynote in health and safety policy. Thus trade unions like SOGAT, APEX and NCU are surely right in their guidelines to suggest that, in the absence of reliable research, pregnant women should have the right to transfer to non-VDU work. The rest of this chapter investigates some of the ways in which computer work can be made healthier, safe and productive. As will emerge, the achievement of these aims is often as much to do with design of jobs, work organisation, workstation, environment, user training and even organisational design as with the design of equipment alone.

THE USER AND USER-FRIENDLINESS

It is all too easy for designers to overlook the different types of tasks performed at VDTs. A general distinction can be made between workstations for

(a) data enquiry

(b) data entry

(c) dialogue tasks

Most workstations fall into all three categories but with one type of task predominating.

Users performing different tasks will have different needs. A viable user–task relationship needs to be defined early in the design process. Designers can derive from this analysis an understanding of how the various factors influencing performance need to interrelate. An interactive model of major components is shown in Fig. 6.1. The basic components are task, tool, user, workstation and environment. This section puts the user at the centre of design and looks at the crucial issue of usability.

These days a computer system can have a large range of users with different needs and tasks to perform (Fig. 6.2). A user may well be

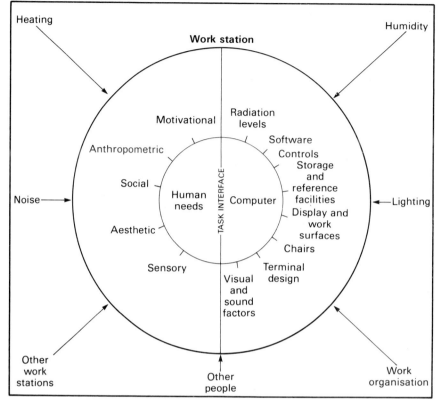

Fig. 6.1   Interactive model

experienced and knowledgeable about computers, highly motivated toward system use and not require much 'user-friendliness' built into the system. However, more typical, 'naive' users are not computer-centred. They have limited technical understanding, are not motivated by a technical interest in the system, expect the computer to minimise time and effort devoted to achieving their particular tasks and, in the face of non-delivery, will prefer to bypass rather than to correct the system.

Another distinction can be made between intermittent and full-time users, or, as Pierce[17] puts it, between those who work *with* VDUs (VDU as a tool) and those working *at* VDUs (VDU as a master?). A comprehensive 1982 survey of Canadian workers by the Canadian Labour Congress[18] found that operators working a full day at VDUs are more likely to experience health problems daily than those spending under two hours on VDU work. Furthermore, health problems are more likely the longer spent at a terminal without a rest pause.

117

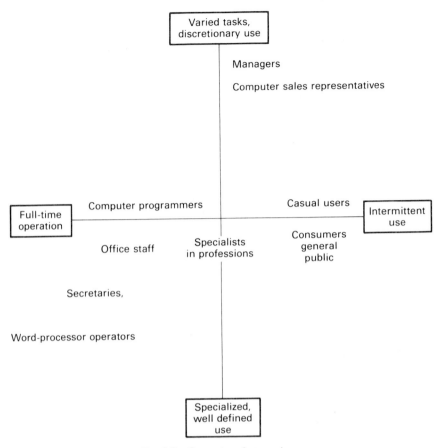

Fig. 6.2   Categories of use and user

Numerous studies support these findings and yet all too frequently user analysis is neglected and designers assume intermittent rather than full-time VDT use, thus creating health and safety hazards for full-time users. In itself, this can create pressure amongst users for the system to fall into disuse. More often a compromise position is reached, with the negotiation of rest pauses. This tends to be unsatisfactory, ignoring as it does the crucial health and safety issues and the need for redesign. Intermittent users may be less concerned with health hazards but nevertheless do have more discretion than full-time users to bypass the computer where 'user-friendliness' is only a feature of the sales literature.

A major problem in design occurs where the **utility** of computer equipment and system is equated with **usability**. A VDU terminal may have the capacity to fulfil a purpose technically (utility) without being

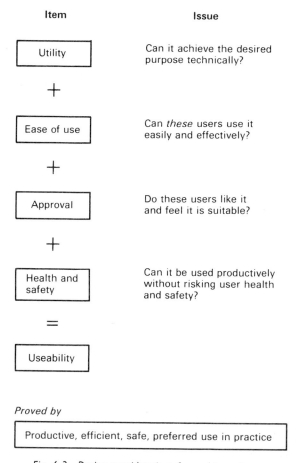

Fig. 6.3 *Design considerations for usable equipment*

easy to use, safe, liked, or actually used efficiently by some or all types of destined user. The main design considerations are shown in Fig. 6.3. The prime test of usability is whether the VDT is used effectively in practice. Of course, capital and running cost considerations can be, and are, used all too easily to justify cutting back on the usability of equipment and computer systems.

To summarise this section, it is useful to look at some of the work of the HUSAT (Human Sciences and Advanced Technology) Research Group at Loughborough University of Technology. Its members have written extensively on providing non-specialist users with usable systems. Eason[19] points to four main areas where design frequently fails. First, the system and user/computer interface may match badly with the actual organisational tasks of the user. Thus computer systems often force fixed sequence procedures on tasks that are more easily accomplished in other ways. Tasks may change or the user may outgrow the system. The task model held by the computer may be partial or not easily penetrated by the user.

Secondly, the fact that different types of user have different needs is ignored (see above). Thirdly, user support is kept to a minimum. A short training course, mainly on how to work the VDT, is considered sufficient. In fact, user-oriented manuals, on-line and human support are vital, especially for intermittent users.

Fourthly, contextual issues affecting system use are ignored, including personnel policies and changes in power, privacy, influence, levels of formalisation and job content and numbers.

The next two sections move on to look at design from the point of view of the user.

THE USER—BIOLOGICAL FACTORS

Design of the workstation and its physical and social environment should reflect the biological, physiological and psychological requirements of the human being(s) working there.

The main biological factors that need to be considered are as follows.

Body Dimensions and Physical Capabilities (anthropometric factors)
The relevant body dimensions and physical capabilities are standing and sitting heights, arm and leg reach, and angles permitting movement and viewing. All the components of the workstation and environment should permit economy of effort, and minimise fatigue and health and safety risks in the execution of tasks. The main areas to investigate here are potential problems with muscles, fingers, wrists and backs and their misuse or overuse, bad posture and poor circulation. While many guidelines on VDU workstation design have been produced, what would seem to be essential is the provision of chairs, desks, work and display surfaces, document holders, terminals, keyboards and VDUs that fit with general human dimensions and capabilities, but are also flexible and adjustable to take into account the physical differences between people.

Senses Including Sight and Hearing (sensory factors)

Sight.
Designers need to consider the limitations of human vision as well as its capabilities in the positioning and design of displays, control messages, VDU screens, warning lights.

The dangers of VDU working in terms of eye fatigue and distress and deterioration of eyesight have received much attention. Most trade unions now insist on defined rest periods away from continuous VDU working. Thus SOGAT (Society of Graphical & Allied Trades) requires a total of 15 minutes of informal breaks each 75 minutes of VDU work and the NCU demands a 15 minute break after each hour of continuous work on VDUs.

Some major points about VDU screens are

(a) the need for displays to consist of yellow or green characters on a dark green background

(b) the importance of avoiding character flicker on the screen

(c) the fact that the legibility of characters on the screen is crucial; the important factors are display size, character size and spacing and a concern for maintaining clear distinctions between characters likely to be confused (e.g. 2 and Z, I and 1, O and Q).

(d) the need for smooth scrolling of the text on the screen

(e) the requirement that brightness of the screen should approximate to that at which most people read a document in a normal office environment

(f) the need to minimise glare from other light sources being reflected from the display screen at the operator.

Environmental lighting should be flexible in positioning and adjustable in terms of intensity. The illumination level of the lighting and its positioning can have a marked effect on the extent of glare at work-stations. Colours in the environment, on surfaces like curtains, walls and ceilings, need to be carefully considered to avoid glare and sharp contrasts. Non-flickering, continuous lighting that approximates to natural sunlight is to be preferred. People tend to favour work environments with windows: VDUs should be parallel to these to avoid light being reflected on screen.

Hearing.
All working environments produce noise. Computer technology by itself tends to be, except for printers, a less noisy technology than many others. However, noise level is only one factor that must be considered in workstation design. Also, the computer environment may include many sound factors that can disrupt effective performance at the human/computer interface (e.g. people talking, telephones ringing, other machinery on a factory floor).

Among the main factors to consider, the first is noise level. Noise levels above 60 decibels can be highly distracting, but where a high level of concentration is required, noise levels should not exceed 55 decibels. However, different people have different hearing ability and noise tolerance.

The second factor is noise frequency. Constant, rhythmical sounds are preferable to irregular, sudden sounds, unless the noise has a particular warning purpose.

The third factor is noise variety. This helps to maintain operator interest and alertness. However, extremes in variety can be irritating and detract from efficiency.

The fourth factor is noise absence. While many see this as an ideal working condition, in practice the absence of sound can be disturbing and have adverse psychological effects. This is one reason why research is undertaken to establish a link between playing background/industrial music at work and productivity. Of course, one purpose of such music is to shut out more distracting and irritating sounds.

Comfort.
The temperature and humidity and degree of air movement at a workstation also affects worker satisfaction, health and productivity. Large departures from comfortable levels for these result in reduced performance. For offices, Peltu[20] suggests comfortable means of 21–23°C, 50–65% humidity, and 15 cm/s air movement. However, such levels depend on the amount and type of activity at the work-station, the clothing worn and the age, sex and even country of origin of the operator.

THE USER—PSYCHOLOGICAL AND OTHER FACTORS

The main psychological factors that need to be considered are as follows.

Attractive Surroundings (aesthetic)
The designer needs to be aware that people's tastes and definitions of what makes a work environment pleasant may vary considerably. Also, there is no necessary link between aesthetic surroundings and improved performance. There is the danger that if aesthetic criteria are dominant in design, efficiency criteria may be surrendered.

Interpersonal Relations (social)
The design must permit access to and interaction with other work group

members, clients and the like, both face to face and through communications hardware.

Individual Psychological Needs (motivational)

Much behaviourist research shows that human performance at work can be linked to the satisfaction or otherwise of a number of basic needs. These are not inevitably linked to the acquisition of money or material gain. Several of these needs are discussed in chapter 5. For present purposes it is sufficient to highlight

(a) a sense of status—resulting from the allocation of equipment, tasks, title and responsibilities in line with age, merit and experience

(b) a sense of privacy—this can result from giving operators personal space marked off as theirs and under their control

(c) a sense of individuality—this can be a product of permitting operators to put a personal stamp on how they work, use equipment, and interrelate with others.

There are many other factors that need to be considered when designing workstations and environments for their intended users. Human beings do vary enormously not just in terms of size, physical capabilities and psychological make-up and needs, but also in areas like intelligence, skill levels, previous training, capacity for and speed of learning, level of motivation to use computers, and memory. Human variability suggests the need for adaptive systems to permit access by different-level users, but also to allow for user learning.

The following sections discuss some of the issues raised so far, but in more depth.

TASK, INTERFACE AND DIALOGUE

The traditions of ergonomics have led to improvements in computer systems hardware, but software considerations have not received the same attention. Here, all too frequently, designers have been concerned with computing solutions rather than with their presentation. The results are found in highly detailed data entry procedures, intolerant error management, inconsistent procedures, crowded screens, and ambiguous instructions and messages.

The problem once again is the unbalanced attention paid to system capability rather than to user behaviour, characteristics, attitudes and preferences. Users' mental models of their organisational tasks (e.g. invoicing, controlling stock) are ignored in design, while the software model of the system is obscure—difficult to make sense of and use.

Software designers frequently use 'computer-centric' language, assuming that users either will share their specialist knowledge and experience, or will learn to adapt to it. In short, too many systems are designed from the inside out; this even *sounds* wrong!

This section looks at the software interface, where the objective is for the operator to interact in meaningful and productive communication with the computer system. A basic model of this process is shown in Fig. 6.4. Hardware considerations are left to the next section.

A crucial first step in getting software interface design right is user-profiling. This means establishing user levels of skill and knowledge, the types of tasks that users do and how these translate to computer work. The type of dialogue a user should have with the computer terminal must be determined by

(a) whether the task is mainly data entry, requests for information, or requiring more active dialogue

(b) the type of user (see Fig. 6.2)

A naive user just beginning with the computer system needs to be prompted for information and carefully led through an interaction using clear instructions and natural language where possible. 'Regular

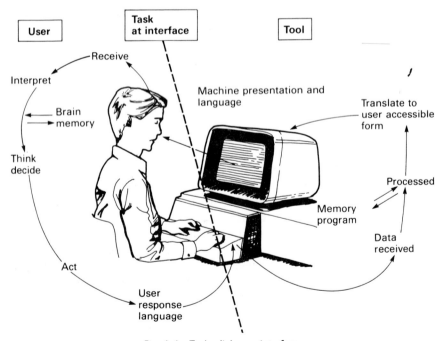

Fig. 6.4   Task; dialogue; interface

users' will tend to be more active and find 'naive user' assumptions in the software obstructive and possibly demotivating. 'Casual experts' will have a working knowledge of the system, but intermittent use will require system prompts and in some cases a full system-initiated dialogue. Experienced experts will know how the software works and how to operate it; as frequent users they will become excessively irritated by 'naive user' and 'casual expert' assumptions in the software.

Problems come when designers try to design a single system to satisfy a wide range of users and uses. They usually end up satisfying no-one. In fact, each application will have a range of user types from naive through to highly experienced. But the software must also allow for migration of users between these types, as knowledge, skill and motivation progress or regress. Clearly, flexible software is required to permit every user to adapt the system and its procedures to a specific task and user profile.

A key issue is the method used to implement dialogue. Figure 6.5 indicates the main options for dialogue procedures. The customary methods for naive and intermittent users should be form-filling, menu selection, question with very restricted answer, natural language or a combination of some or all of these. Strictly speaking, graphic interaction is not a form of dialogue, but as a design enhancement it may greatly assist naive users and is gaining in popularity. The user-initiated methods are more appropriate for regular, experienced users. The more complex and flexible user-initiated dialogue types are more suited to expert users.

For naive, inexperienced users the practical design problem is in keeping information load down to an acceptable level. A major objective should be simplicity. The skill in design is to achieve simple yet powerful interfaces for sophisticated systems. A major bottleneck in design frequently occurs at the point where users are or have become more experienced. To them, the simpler forms of dialogue appear more 'idiot-' than 'user-friendly'. Stewart[21] suggests permitting new users to start with menus or form-filling, while building into the software the option to override and enter information directly. Systems with a wide range of user types and tasks to perform need to have hybrid and parallel dialogue facilities.

The rest of this section concentrates on more detailed recommendations for user-centred interface and dialogue design. Within the design team it is useful to assign one person full responsibility for interface design, involve intended users and establish basic principles of a unified and consistent interface, marked by operational simplicity and clarity, with a user-friendly approach to error-handling. Good documentation is necessary, though it cannot substitute for suitable user machine interface design. Schneider and Thomas[22] describe the all-too-

Method	Initiated by	Detail
1. Form filling	System	Form displayed; blanks to be filled by user
2. Menu list	System	A set of options displayed user keys in choice; hierarchy of menus possible
3. Question and answer	System	Computer displays a range of questions; user responds with any answers
4. Question and restricted answer	System	Computer displays questions; restricted vocabulary available for answer
5. Question with three possible answers	System	As above but only "yes", "no", "don't know" available
6. Function keys	User/system	Input restricted to keys made available on keyboard; multi-function keys possible
7. Natural language	User/system	Dialogue conducted in user's natural language (in practice only restricted vocabularies available)
8. Command language	User	Well-defined limited number of commands available to user to initiate dialogue
9. Query languages	User	User request expressed in specified language, this may be 'keyword', 'natural', 'command', 'graphic'
10. Hybrid dialogues	User/system	Mix of dialogue styles available for different types of transactions on same machine
11. Parallel dialogues	User/system	Two or more dialogue styles available at user request e.g. menu selection or command language
12. Graphic interaction	System	Supplements the more conventional dialogue methods by conveying complex relationships and interactions graphically

Fig. 6.5 Methods of implementing dialogue

typical introduction of the naive user to the new interface:

'After I turned the terminal on, the following message appeared—
VERSION 3.3.3./10/81

ENTER LOGON/PASSWORD:
A "logon?" What was that? Noone had ever mentioned a
Logon. I could not even find it in the unabridged dictionary.
After spending 15 minutes searching through the manual I
realized a Logon was my account number.'

Clearly, the manual is partly at fault here. One solution is to ensure that
the user interface description is the first, not the last document written
for a system. It should describe what the system does rather than how it
works, and should address user knowledge levels and what the user
really needs to know to use the system productively.

But the on-screen messages are not immediately comprehensible.
'Logon' is obvious computer jargon; 'password' might give a clue to its
meaning but the form of the message does not indicate its status as a
command. A simple solution would be to show 'What is your account
number?' on screen.

Two helpful design principles are to 'maximise the routine intelligence
of the system' and 'maximise responsiveness'. The first one really means
get the computer to do the work, not the user. This will involve actions
like simplifying 'Logon' logistics, using 'what you see is what you get'
formatting on screen, and including a spelling checking facility for
word-processing. Maximising responsiveness can involve reducing lag
time between user action and computer presentation, but also the
provision of facilities like immediate acknowledgement of input, or
immediate status information on user demand.

The need for cognitive compatibility between user, software and
display cannot be emphasised enough. In simple terms, this means that a
major design objective should be matching the user's mental model of
machine behaviour and performance with the model of user behaviour
and characteristics and needs built into the software. Hammond et al.[23]
point to three main ways where user and software may not meet:
perceptual incompatibility refers to screen presentation not matching
user requirements; memory incompatibility occurs where the system
demand on user memory is not matched by user abilities; linguistic
incompatibility usually occurs as software messages and command
words move further away from natural language. As an example,
'DELETE P,S' may be understood by a naive user as 'DELETE P and
S'; in practice the program may have been written for it to mean
'DELETE P from S,' or to have some other meaning altogether.

Following the principle of maximising responsiveness, dialogue and
interface design should ensure that users are provided sufficient feedback to establish the state of the dialogue, the options now available,
and how each option can be operationalised. Users often need to know
the meaning of command words, the acceptability of their inputs,

detailed error messages and the *help!* facilities available. Feedback assists control over, and learning about, the system.

In fact, direct user control of the dialogue should be a primary objective of design. A logon procedure may require only one simple action but, notoriously, this is rarely the case in practice, and this is not always for good security reasons. The dialogue sequence should be flexible enough to permit the user discretion and guidance as required. Interrupt control should also be available to the user, whether this be to end the dialogue, cancel some aspect of it, seek *help!*, suspend the dialogue and enter another, or consult transaction and error details of the dialogue so far.

Users will always make errors. However, it is important to understand that the fault is more likely to be in the design than with the user. Norman[24] underlines this by deriving system design principles from investigations into classes of human error. There are many methods of reducing the possibilities of error, but a first objective is to provide the user with unmistakable error indicators. Thereafter, error tolerance without jeopardy to the system and its data should be built into software design. User-friendly programs select dynamically one of several error-handling procedures, depending on the error-handling capabilities of the current user. A major requirement for any user-friendly software design is that it protect users from the consequences of their errors, while providing the means for user-initiated corrective action.

This section has provided a basis for user-centred software and dialogue design. The focus now moves to hardware considerations.

WORKSTATION DESIGN

Ergonomic design of the workstation and basic VDT equipment is an important element in securing the health, comfort and productivity of VDT users. Despite the fact that these ergonomic principles are long-established and well known, user surveys continually reveal that they are usually only partially applied. As one example, a 1983 survey by APEX (Association of Professional Executive, Clerical and Computer Staff) found a majority of VDT users without foot rests, adjustable chairs and desks, new furniture for use with the new technology, sufficient depth on work surfaces, adjustable hoods on VDTs, and vertical and horizontal adjustments on screens. Should the assumption be made that employers and designers do not take ergonomic design of equipment seriously enough, it should be remarked that users themselves frequently do not do so either.

Figure 6.6 illustrates key considerations in equipment and workstation design. The major characteristics of a workstation should be that

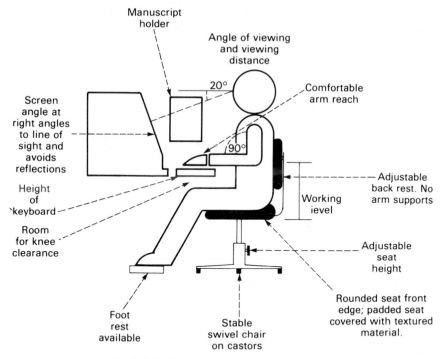

Fig. 6.6 VDU equipment and workstation design.

it is individually adjustable while still stimulating a dynamic pattern of movement. The adjustability should be built into the equipment to establish relationships as in Fig. 6.6. The stimulation of movement is important because maintaining a posture over a long period induces 'static' load which is more fatiguing, painful and dangerous than 'dynamic' sitting. In the latter case, loads on muscles and bones can be spread to different parts of the body. This can obviate some of the damaging effects where basic design has not catered for an individual user's requirements. The real problems come with equipment and furniture that forces the user into faulty postures and practices for long periods of time. Some of the ways this can be avoided (in addition to items shown in Figure 6.6) are as follows.

The chair should be a swivel chair, with height adjustable in the range 39–54 cm, and back support adjustable in the range 10–25 degrees from the vertical. The VDT operator should be able to make all adjustments seated in the chair in the normal posture, without excessive reaching or bending.

The desk's relationship with the chair should permit the user's elbows to be level with the work surface. Recommended height for writing should be adjustable in the range 67–79 cm, for keyboard in the range 52–67 cm. Desk thickness should not hinder leg and thigh movement for the seated user. Desk top space should be sufficient to allow for books and documents, document holder, and movement of VDU and keyboard to establish comfortable working distances. Storage space inside or under the desk is recommended by the Health and Safety Executive guide. Also surfaces should have a matt finish to avoid reflection or glare. Printers are best isolated from the working surface for reasons of noise and vibration; a separate table is one solution.

The document holder should be adjustable in height and direction so that the position of papers is the same height and viewing distance as the VDU. This avoids constant refocusing of eyes.

The VDU screen should have viewing distance adjustable to user comfort. The user should be able to adjust the angle of the VDU both vertically and horizontally. Larger screens and character sizes that can be clearly viewed from 0.7 metres are recommended. The luminance of the characters and background screen should be adjustable. (See also section above on the user-biological factors.)

The keyboard should be detachable and stable, with an angle of 5–15 degrees, and thickness of 30–50 mm. Wrist-rest slotting under the keyboard front should be provided where the board is in constant use. The keyboard should be matt finish to avoid glare and reflection. QWERTY is the internationally accepted keyboard layout. Special function keys should be distinct by colour, shape or position; normal alphanumeric function keys should be neutral in colour. Extra numeric keyboards should have normal telephone or calculator layout. In operation, the keys should provide feedback to user by touch and sound. Dimensions of the keyboard must avoid excessive size, so as to limit hand, neck, torso and eye movements by the user.

Other requirements are that cabling should be unobstructive and permit flexibility in positioning equipment. Storage space should be provided for manuals, documents and personal belongings. Waste disposal facilities should be provided.

The workstation should be designed to secure the comfort, health, safety and efficiency of the user. What becomes crucial is how all the design features listed interact with the user in actual task performance. Ideally, this interaction should permit the operator to sit correctly at the right working height, with equipment and documents designed to stimulate useful and healthy, and minimise uncomfortable and inefficient, movement.

ENVIRONMENT DESIGN

This section looks briefly at workplace layout for computerisation (immediate computer environment). A number of themes are then brought together by considering organisational factors that influence the productivity, health and safety of user performance at the user/machine interface.

Computer technology tends to require major changes in traditional workplace layouts, not least because of the computer requirements for clean, dust-free and tidy surroundings free from magnetic forces. However, these basic 'health and safety' requirements for computers are frequently not met, let alone those for human beings interfacing with the technology.

This is most likely to be the case in organisations where 'technology creep' is occurring; that is, where computers are coming in with minimal planning, in response to individual users' basic needs, with little management concern and with only slow growth in computer use. A user-friendly computer environment is most likely to result where computerisation is planned, where it involves large budgets, and where computers will become central to the organisation's operations and success. Between these two extremes a variety of practices will be found.

However, the introduction of computers does provide an excellent opportunity for concentrating minds on how to make radical improvements in work organisation, and factory or office layout. In manufacturing processes, computers can be kept centrally, away from the shop floor, or they can be designed as an integral part of shop-floor working. In offices, computer technology can be used in open office layouts with easy access for all staff members, or word-processing operations can be separated from other operations done by computer technology. Word-processing itself can be centralised or distributed throughout the organisation.

These different arrangements still need to observe common guidelines, however. The major factors in the immediate work environment that need to be considered and fitted together to achieve satisfactory human/computer interfaces are shown in Fig. 6.1 and have been discussed briefly already. A few additional points can be made.

The single most detrimental environmental factor for VDU users is glare. Placing VDT screens to avoid reflections from glare sources is one solution (e.g. parallel to windows and parallel to and between overhead lights). Minimising glare sources (e.g. no shiny surfaces, using curtains on windows, focussing lights in harmless directions) is another approach. Modifying the VDU screen is still another (e.g. fitting a screen hood, or using a filter over the screen).

Different VDT tasks need different lighting. General room illumination of 300 lux is useful where tasks involve mainly looking at the screen, but it needs to be higher (500–700 lux) where the primary task is reading hard copy.

Open-plan layouts or the provision of special word-processing rooms can help to reduce environmental hazards, not least because setting them up usually involves careful planning and encourages a focus on, and provides finance for, health and safety features. Ventilation is easier, adequate heating and lighting may be cheaper to install and run, but noise and distractions from visitors and other workstations may be greater, and privacy more difficult. Once again, managerial objectives need to be examined carefully. It is one thing to have open-plan layouts for health, safety and productivity reasons; quite another to aim to maximise control over users, cut office costs as much as possible, neglect health and safety features as 'expensive', and have little regard for the health consequences on users of pursuing such policies.

It becomes clear that if the aim of healthy, safe and productive work is to be met, a focus on the ergonomic design of interface, software, workstation and immediate computer environment cannot be divorced from wider organisational factors.

Thus the types of jobs that people are assigned have health and safety implications. Machine-pacing, work intensification, monitoring work performance by computer, highly repetitive, deskilled jobs with no opportunities for advancement can all raise stress and insecurity levels, and might induce unsafe practices, particularly where worker perception of workload and work pressure is very high. Incentive payment systems can attract people into cutting corners to achieve higher productivity levels. A failure to train users in safe ergonomic practices and make them aware of the ergonomic features of equipment will see the latter underused. Rigid task scheduling and shiftwork for full-time VDT operators will exacerbate fatigue, stress and other health problems. In short, job design, work organisation, work and personnel practices all have health and safety implications.

To control visual stress and muscular–skeletal hazards, it is not enough to redesign machine and workplace. Most authorities now recognise the need for a ten-minute rest-break after an hour of continual VDU work to arrest fatigue symptoms before they occur, only four hours a day of heavy work on VDTs, and a mix of VDT and non-VDT work. Also important are job variety and interest; worker control over work pace; no computer monitoring of rest breaks, arrival and departure times, error rates or VDT work speed; and no quotas for keystroke rates. But such issues inevitably bring in organisational politics.

In fact, it is difficult to divorce any health, safety and productivity issue at work from its political implications. The assumption of a consensus between employer and employees on health and safety is too often belied by the facts. From this point of view it is interesting to look at an example—the 1986 British Telecom code of practice covering VDU workers.[25] This was drawn up between BTUC (British Telecom Unions Council) and management representatives. Management—union agreement was particularly difficult to reach on three areas. Management resisted detailed provisions on the frequency and length of rest periods for VDT operators on grounds that national guidance was not appropriate to an organisation in which VDT usage varied enormously. The code agrees to eye screening for all first-time users of VDUs, but unions were unable to persuade management to accept that regular re-screenings should also be carried out. The code does not concede the right of pregnant employees to transfer away from the VDU work; local managers are encouraged to help such a transfer but no guarantee is made of suitable alternative work being available.

It would seem remarkable how much political activity and sheer negotiation was involved here, given the status of the document as a mere code of practice, and the issue at hand being the health and safety of employees working with computers. In fact, health and safety policy is routinely a contentious subject area in work organisations, not least because different interested parties variously perceive its control, cost and productivity implications. Once again, computer and political systems in organisations are found to be inextricably bound into one another.

CONCLUSIONS

The heralding of computers as a cleaner, healthier, and safer technology to work with is belied by the facts. There are hazards attached to the enchanted new workplace. These can be partially circumvented by better design of the equipment made available by manufacturers and suppliers. The application of ergonomic principles to equipment and software is important, but what remains crucial is the design of the interaction between user, task, tool and environment. However, design of the VDT workstation and immediate environment on ergonomic lines is a necessary but not sufficient condition for healthy, safe and productive work. Job design, work organisation, and work and personnel policies are also important determinants, and all factors cannot be divorced from the organisational politics inherent in computerisation.

CHAPTER 7

Computer Technology and Industrial Relations

'Technological change within the "advanced societies" has occurred within a framework described by the rule of the three R's: Rationalisation, Reorganisation and Redundancy.'[1]

'Trying to cope with technical changes via existing collective bargaining traditions is like fitting a six foot corpse into a five foot coffin!'[2]

'We have the bullets now.'[3]

INTRODUCTION

What is industrial relations *about*? It is common to identify the subject area as restricted to formal, collective relationships between employers and trade unions. However, as will emerge, there are many problems with such a limited approach. As one example, this definition implies that the non-unionised labour that makes up over half the British workforce does not experience 'industrial relations'. Therefore, a broader working definition is used here. This sees industrial relations (IR) as concerned with 'the regulation of and processes of control over people, their performance, working conditions and relationships at work'.

Traditionally in the UK the substance of industrial relations has taken the form of voluntary formal and informal consultation and bargaining, usually through agreed procedures. A range of issues may be covered, though the major topics are pay, working conditions, hours and job content. These issues will be handled on the one hand by management and their representatives, and on the other by employee representatives, whether the trade unions, staff associations or the employee as an individual. The 1970s and 1980s have seen the mainly *voluntarist* nature of industrial relations increasingly mediated by legislation relating to employment matters and trade unions.

In connection with microtechnological change, industrial relations in the UK is invariably perceived, not just by managers and systems analysts but by trade unionists themselves, as about the conflicts, negotiations, compromises and agreements that surround the *implementation* stage of a computerisation project.

Look again at Figure 1.2. In a 1982 review of computerisation in the brewing and several other industries, Davies[4] has shown that managers and computer specialists remained unquestionably in charge of the major choices and decisions up to and including the design completion stage. In fact, general UK practice, including in plants and organisations where trade unions are operating, is still to retain the traditional systems methodology. Part of this is managers and technologists attempting to retain their traditional hold over capital investment and technology decisions. But where trade unions are operating, it also stems from their insistence on using traditional mechanisms of collective bargaining through which new technology agreements can be arrived at just prior to implementation. By this stage, union and employee contributions and influence are severly limited, and much bargaining is about accepting the system and attempting to limit its negative affects. Of course, severe disputes may occur, and industrial action can delay implementation or disrupt the smooth running of a system once it has been implemented. Since this is not the fate that systems analysts and managers would usually reserve for their new computer system, what can be done to reduce the risk of this happening?

ATTITUDES, PERCEPTIONS AND PRACTICES OF SYSTEMS ANALYSTS

If systems designers take a narrow view of the content of industrial relations, they will dismiss it as nothing to do with them. They are specialists in computer systems analysis and design. Personnel practitioners are the industrial relations specialists. They deal with getting employee acceptance of any new system. Connected with this view is the idea that industrial relations 'problems' arise only in relationships between IR specialists and employees or their representatives.

Such problems include the use of procedures, the conduct of bargaining, the threatening and prevention of disruption. This view hides the fact that what the systems analyst does can itself create severe industrial relations problems. For example, a computer-aided design system can be designed with the effect of making traditional draughtsman skills redundant. At the implementation stage, the resulting job loss may create large-scale union resistance. Again, the failure to involve users in design of CNC or DNC machine tools and the surrounding work system may create unattractive work. This might create resentment and high absenteeism once the technology is operational, and at a later stage this could fuel grievances and disputes which seem to have little to do with their real cause.

A narrow view of industrial relations also supports the idea that not only have IR 'problems' got nothing to do with the work of the systems analyst but, furthermore, the solutions to those 'problems' are not in the hands of the systems analyst either. The solutions are the responsibility of the IR specialists and involve issues like improving procedures, different styles of negotiating, and making bargaining concessions. The notion of 'professional expertise' is often used by computer, as well as personnel, specialists to protect their jobs from other workers, but also to set a limit on the work they are required to do. Yet many of the solutions to, and, indeed, the prevention of, industrial relations problems may stem directly from the systems analysis and design practice adopted. Chapter 4 details why and how systems analysis and design of computer systems needs to become more human-focussed. A crucial part of this is for the systems analyst and designer to accept a broad definition of what constitutes the industrial relations field. From this must follow the understanding that analysis and design work is not remote from, but is essentially about, industrial relations.

MANAGERIAL OBJECTIVES

Systems designers are clearly constrained in their work by managerial aims for and attitudes toward new technology. One problem is that managerial objectives may vary in different circumstances, and indeed, as Willman[5] points out, at different managerial levels within the same organisation, but they invariably have industrial relations implications and ramifications. One scenario here is that for managers the consequences of computerisation may be difficult to predict, or just not properly recognised, at the planning stage of the computerisation scheme. The results of such oversights can sometimes be serious.

As one example, in 1982 the Department of Health and Social Security devised a 15 year 'operational strategy' to computerise the recording, assessment, calculation and payment of all UK social security and welfare benefits. There were many objectives, but a major one was £700 million savings on operating costs by 1995. However, this depended on 25,000 employees being displaced by computer technology in the same period.

The lack of industrial relations foresight and the adoption of a reactive confrontational style in the face of staff opposition in a highly unionised environment contributed to a seven-month strike at Newcastle computer centre in 1984. This delayed the computerisation project, soured the industrial relations climate and incurred costs of over £150 million.[6] By the beginning of 1987, in the face of increasing work loads, little benefit from the micros that had been installed, and little trust in management, employees were taking selective industrial action to press claims for *increases* in staff numbers.

A second scenario sees other managements quite clear about the implications of new technology; in fact, they seek to achieve their industrial relations objectives through computerisation. In this respect, computers may be used to achieve a wide variety of aims; for example, improved working conditions, higher-status jobs, a reduction in working hours or job security through improved competitiveness. Some managers have seen how computer systems can be designed to enhance their control over the workforce. For example, this can be achieved by deskilling work and programming the planning and decision-making aspects of a job. Alternatively, new distributed systems can lessen dependence on workers formerly strategically placed in a production process. This approach is perhaps best summarised by the managing director of Olivetti, when he said:

'Information technology is basically a technology of coordination and control of the labour force.'[7]

However, few managers would admit explicitly to such objectives, and it is difficult to establish how typical this comment is of managerial opinion.

Computer technology can also solve industrial relations problems at work not by improving management practice or developing personnel expertise but by simply exporting the problem; that is, replacing labour with computers. This seems to have been one of the objectives in the UK national newspaper industry in the late 1970s, when personnel practice had been notoriously poor, or non-existent, for many years.

Clearly, the industrial relations ramifications of managerial objectives over introducing new technology can be immense. It becomes especially important to identify these implications at a very early stage—when new technology policy is being formulated. These then need to fully inform systems design and managerial practice throughout the computerisation project. Beyond this, managements need to develop approaches toward handling the industrial relations issues that are likely to arise. This is crucial where those managerial objectives are likely to clash with employees who are affected by or who will operate the new technology.

MANAGEMENT: STYLES AND APPROACHES

The overall managerial approach to industrial relations in an organisation has an important influence on the manner in which new technology is received. While it is tempting to suggest 'one best way' for handling industrial relations and new technology, what marks UK practice in the 1980s is a diversity of approaches, and a complex picture of successes and failures, in an overall framework of employee acceptance of computer technology at work.

Brown and Sisson[8] and Purcell and Sisson[9] have pointed to a number of styles in IR management in the 1980s. An adapted summary is shown in Figure 7.1. These styles form a useful framework around which to structure discussion.

'Traditionalist' managers tend to be hostile to trade unions. A large number of small firms tend to be employer-dominated and are not unionised at all. The more overt forms of conflict that might surround new technology issues—strikes, go-slows and the like—are not apparent in this sector. However, where a firm is unionised or trade union action has interfered with the firm's operations, these employers have tended to take advantage of developments in employment legislation and the economic and anti-union climates of the 1980s to use the law in industrial relations.

Approach / Detail	Traditionalism	Sophisticated paternalism	Consultation	Constitutionalism	Reactive pragmatism or opportunism
View of technological change	Unitarist	Unitarist	Pluralist moving to unitarist	Pluralist or radical	Various
Rights of management	Managerial prerogative may be used in authoritarian ways	Management right to manage	Management right to manage	Managerial prerogative on major issues. Otherwise subject to formal agreement	Moves toward traditionalism and consultation in 1980's
Attitude to trade unions	Hostility to trade unions. Legal rights and protections use positively to exclude them	Unions not recognised for bargaining or an 'enterprise' union or staff association encouraged	Unions recognised but conflict played down. Consensus rather than conflict-based bargaining. Consultation preferred	Unions recognised and joint regulation through formal procedures encouraged	Unions often recognised for bargaining purposes but recession and their weakness in 1980s has encouraged tough and more unitary stances
Major personnel and IR trends	Direct relationship between employer and employee. Moral as well as legal contract stressed	Positive personnel policies used to satisfy individual aspirations and make collective representation unnecessary. Mutual loyalty. Open door policies. Attractive pay structures. Individual career development	Employee involvement stressed. Renewal of joint consultation procedures. Introduction of briefing groups, quality circles, job improvement committees. 'Solving problems' rather than 'settling disputes'	Regular negotiations on pay and conditions. Limits on what is negotiable codified in agreements. Consultative procedures encouraged. Moves toward more informal agreements in private sector	Less negotiating in 1980s. Short term view of recruitment and dismissal. Redundancies mainly reflect poor market conditions or government budgetary restraints
Examples	Small firms e.g. Messenger Group Newspaper dispute 1983	IBM, Nissan, Honda, Marks and Spencer, Mars, Citibank	Talbot motors, British Airways	Local Government, National Health service	Engineering industry, coal industry British Leyland

Fig. 7.1 *Management styles and approaches in industrial relations in the 1980s*

The most publicised case followed on from the dismissal of six National Graphical Association (NGA) members from Messenger Group Newspapers by the employer Eddie Shah in 1983. The union picketed the firm's Warrington site against court injunctions and eventually incurred massive legal fines. The less publicised aspect of this employer's confrontational style was the subsequent use of non-union labour to work newly introduced computer-based technology.

'Sophisticated paternalism' is most typical of very large firms, often foreign-owned, which tend to operate strategically on industrial relations as on other issues. Some, like Citibank and IBM, see themselves as 'non-union'. They create strong cultures and positive personnel policies to achieve job security and employee loyalty to render unions unnecessary. As one employee in a company in the USA remarked, on being interviewed as to why he was not a union member:

'What can they get for us ... another swimming pool?'

The case of IBM UK is instructive. Since foundation in 1951 it has experienced no lay-offs or strikes; average length of service by employees is 11.5 years. The industrial relations strategy behind such results has been designed to create a favourable environment for the reception of new technology in what are often 'high-tech' industries used to technical change anyway.

In fact 'sophisticated paternalism' is also typical of much smaller, often non-unionised, high-tech companies found in such places as Silicon Glen in Scotland and the M4 Corridor in South East England. These produce, mainly by computer-based technology, advanced components for similar technologies. Here, for example, software personnel are in much demand, command their own price, have a professional and personal interest in accepting, indeed developing, new technologies, find industrial action unnecessary and see little advantage in joining unions.

The 1980s has also seen the influx of Japanese firms which practice a unionised version of 'sophisticated paternalism'. Most typical is the agreement arrived at between Nissan the car-makers and the Amalgamated Union of Engineering Workers (AUEW) in April 1985. The main conditions included a single union; no industrial action; complete worker flexibility and mobility in present methods of production and in response to future changes in technology, production and processes; and common pay structure and working conditions for all staff. Similar deals have been reached with the Electrical and Plumbing Trade Union (EETPU); for example, at Toshiba in Plymouth, Sanyo's television factory at Lowestoft, Inmos microchip plant in Newport and Hitachi in South Wales.

The deals have tended to be in electronic-based industries, but have been invariably designed to favour the increasing adoption of computer systems in production processes and administration. Typically, these companies have built on new ('greenfield') sites, or taken over bankrupt firms, in areas of high unemployment. In a variant on the IBM and Japanese home-grown form of 'sophisticated paternalism', this has often enabled them to keep wages low, and not guarantee job security, but still gain acceptance of new technology and at the same time have few labour relations problems.

'Constitutionalism' as a managerial approach to industrial relations

> 'sees collective bargaining, and the explicit power relationship on which it is based, as the dominating feature of industrial government. Accordingly, great attention is given to procedural rectitude and written agreements, but little attempt is made to develop other links with the workforce.'[8]

A trend toward 'constitutionalism' was a notable feature of 1970s industrial relations. A number of studies recorded increased formalisation of procedures, more shop stewards and employer encouragement of their role, and greater recognition of trade unions for collective bargaining purposes.[10,11] More recent studies establish not the erosion but the stability of most collective bargaining systems in the 1980s.[12,13] Against this background it is unsurprising to find many employers and trade unions building upon existing bargaining machinery and handling the introduction of computer systems through the negotiation of new technology agreements (discussed in detail below).

'Constitutionalism' is a notable feature of the more highly unionised public sector in the UK and of large companies. A 1980s trend in both has been toward the decentralisation of collective bargaining. In the private sector, single-employer as opposed to multi-employer national bargaining has become more prevalent. In the public sector, the government has supported managements in decentralising bargaining in the coal industry and in privatisation candidates like British Telecom and British Leyland. After a major industrial dispute in the water industry, bargaining was moved from national to regional level. Such trends localise industrial relations and disputes and in the 1980s climate favour employers. For the introduction of computer systems, decentralisation of bargaining, consultation and information procedures significantly favours employers, because the extent to which employees and trade unions can make a strategic assessment of and response to the likely impact of the systems becomes severely limited. To extend this point, studies of new technology by Northcott and Fogarty[14,15] show that:

'Where it is introduced piecemeal, without immediately apparent threat to the jobs or other interests of current employees, it may be accepted with limited or no consultation, essentially through trade union inadvertence.'[14]

'PRAGMATISTS', 'OPPORTUNISTS' AND CONSULTATION

Despite this 'constitutionalist' spine that runs through much of managerial practice in unionised workplaces, Brown and Sisson[8] are probably right to see most employers, especially in the engineering industry, as reactive 'pragmatists' or 'opportunists.' The fact that a large number of British managers fail to be strategic in their approach to industrial relations may be symptomatic of a lack of strategic vision generally. Where it is merely a failure to integrate industrial relations considerations into wider business, company or organisational plans, this can still have serious results for how the human aspects of new technology issues are handled. However, as the authors concluded elsewhere:

'Even large UK organisations seem a long way from the "Holy Grail" of developing, let alone fulfilling, integrated and consistent business, industrial relations and Information Technology strategies.'[16]

'Pragmatic' and 'opportunistic' managers have responded to the favourable 1980s industrial relations climate, economic recession and the need for increased competitiveness in a variety of ways. A greater insistence on management's right to manage, collective bargaining in a lower key, and direct appeals to employees above the heads of their trade unions have established one style. In its more extreme manifestations at British Leyland and the National Coal Board, this came to be known as 'macho-management'. Ironically, in each case what began as a response to serious financial and market circumstances attained the level of strategy. In each case a highly confrontational style secured a package of changes that included the mass introduction of computer-based technology.

Between 1977 and 1981, British Leyland undertook a £200 million programme to modernise, and bring industrial robots and automated systems into, the Longbridge plant for production of the new Metro. In the face of a financial crisis derived from declining market share, low productivity, outmoded models and increasing dependence on government financial aid, the success of the Metro became essential for survival. The company sought to achieve changes in working practices, higher productivity and acceptance of new technology by abandoning participation and negotiation, undermining union power, and securing unchallenged managerial control over shop-floor labour.

In important respects the confrontation strategy was eminently successful. Winch and Willman[17] point out that a combination of changes in new technology, organisation and manning made the Longbridge Metro plant the most productive in Europe in 1983. Scarbrough[18] establishes the useful legitimating role that new technology had in the acceptance of autocratic management and the restructuring of production and work practices. BL trade unions had been insisting on new technology and massive investment for years; they could hardly resist these when they finally arrived. Moreover, managerial control over the design and introduction of new technology secured further gains in the technical control over future work practices and performance:

> 'There is little doubt that in the Longbridge case technological change provided a political juncture, a "window of opportunity" in which Taylorist forms of management control could be more firmly embedded in the production process.'[18]

The miners strike over pit closures and redundancies was the most publicised industrial relations event in the early 1980s. Again, the confrontational style of Ian Mcgregor was a response to government pressure, massive financial losses and poor market competitiveness. The National Coal Board pushed through 41,000 redundancies between 1981 and 1984, and intended to reduce the workforce from 190,000 to 70,000 between 1984 and 1988. Once again, technological change and a transformation of industrial relations through an assault on union power—that is, technical necessity and political expediency—became inseparable.

In fact, new technology was at the heart of a capital-intensive exploitation of the more easily mined central coalfields and the running-down of most of those in South Wales, Scotland, Kent and Durham. The Mine Operating System (MINOS) is a hierarchical, centralised computer system offering remote control and detailed monitoring of colliery activities. Its subsystems were introduced piecemeal into selected collieries from the early 1980s. It is this system that renders pits without it uneconomic.

It is doubtful if the 'no expense spared, no quarter given' approach to pushing through technological change in the coal industry could be adopted anywhere else but in the public sector with government financial backing. 'Macho-management' is rarely a good example to pursue without the backing of considerable resources and a strategic, planning dimension to new technology and related IR issues.

In any case, it has probably been an unfair epithet for many managers seizing the short-term initiative in desperate market conditions. Nor are employees always opposed to some versions of managerial decisiveness. Over many years, trade unions have frequently attributed industrial problems to managerial incompetence and lack of leadership. On this analysis, greater managerial confidence and determination could be, in some respects, a desirable change. Thus in 1984, faced with severe competition, management at Mobil Coryton oil refinery pushed through unilaterally a non-negotiable survival package that embraced voluntary redundancies, acceptance of new technology, reduced hours and increased job flexibility. Such positive action to break long-drawn-out negotiations during a crisis was not necessarily unwelcome.

But if managers have had the bullets in the 1980s, they have not always used them. In such favourable circumstances for the assertion of managerial prerogative, they have not always needed to. Another aspect is that many managers are constrained by fear of employee 'revenge psychology' in the event of an economic recovery. However, a more important consideration is the need to gain employee support for desired changes in technology and work practices, and retain employee co-operation in the day-to-day running of technology and operations.

This forms the background to moves toward a 'consultative' style in IR in the 1980s. One report puts the position starkly:

> 'Competing in design technology and production technology with the Japanese is not enough. To survive in the long term we must compete in the field of employee involvement.'[19]

In important respects, of course, new technology introduction and employee involvement are not separable, but go hand in hand. There is growing evidence of organisational shifts toward the consultative machinery and ethos shown in Figure 7.1.[12,20,21] However, the overall UK pattern is one of uneven development, with 'consultation' rarely reaching the level of IR strategy. A major problem is the cultural and historical industrial relations backdrop against which such initiatives are taken. Thus, many managers, wary of ceding power, circumscribe the degree and extent of consultation, while employees remain suspicious of managerial intentions.

Where new technology is concerned, a 1983 NEDO survey in the electronics industry[22] shows that NT introduction can be facilitated by employee involvement. A majority of firms confirmed that consultative procedures, and employee involvement, particularly at the planning or choice-of-equipment stage, increased shop-floor understanding of the issues, quickened the introduction of new technology, and generated commitment and readiness to adapt to redeployment.

The experience of Cadbury, the food company, in successfully managing a major reinvestment programme in new technology at its Somerdale factory underlines and extends these points. A long term practice of open and regular communication directly with employees and unions and through joint consultative committees had built trust and confidence in management prior to the new technology scheme. This foundation made an important difference in the painstaking, three year-long process of negotiating major changes through eight unions in a complex bargaining structure. Early and full information and consultation on all the implications of the investment programme for the workforce, including redundancies and changed working methods, also proved crucial, though

> 'A less constructive response from the workforce could have been expected if the company had only started talking when there was a problem (and Cadbury is of the opinion that UK management often makes this mistake in communication).'[23]

However, 1982 research into the brewing and other industries shows other, possibly more typical, managerial attitudes and approaches to new technology and industrial relations. Davies[24] found technological change regarded as 'non-negotiable', a (usually unwarranted) fear of union reaction to technological change, and extreme caution in passing information to the union side. Managers often advocated a 'softly, softly' approach. This meant playing down the importance of the new technology. One method was to introduce piecemeal and gradual technological changes, beginning with those least contentious in their manpower implications. This would reduce the perceived need for union information and involvement, while weakening union ability to resist future, less 'innocent' changes.

Many British managers are not forthcoming about information to employees nor about setting up consultative procedures to operate at an early stage (e.g. examining the feasibility of alternative computer systems). This may result from a desire to push through a scheme that has significant adverse impact on employees and trade unions. But a lot of fear of union reaction may be based less on unions' likely intentions and actions, and more on ingrained attitudes. These can create the very circumstances that are feared.

In summary, 'sophisticated paternalism and 'consultation' seem the most successful, if minority, modes for the introduction of new technology, at least where they attain the level of coherent strategy. 'Traditionalist' approaches may well secure employee compliance, but rarely their commitment. The management of industrial relations in the UK is notable both for its diversity of practice and its pragmatic, ad hoc approach. Though 'new' technology issues may force many managers into beginning to act more strategically on IR, this development has not always been assisted by the pro-management IR climate in the early and middle 1980s.

A 'constitutionalist' spine runs through most unionised organisations. Here, Fogarty and Brooks[15] are largely correct that case histories, studies and reports on microtechnological and other changes

> 'show again and again that firms have seen negotiation and consultation as essential to lasting success in the introduction of change; or if they do not, that neglect of joint procedures and direct involvement carry a sharp penalty.'

This applies as much to the highly unionised public sector. However, a key phrase is 'lasting success'. In the climate of the 1980s, short term success in introducing new technology has often been quite enough for management to be going on with, and, as discussed above, this frequently did not depend on consultation and negotiation. Moreover, the 'sharp penalty' may not always be forthcoming in less unionised organisations or in periods when trade unions are weak. However, trade union acceptance of new technology at work in the 1980s is not totally explicable in these terms, nor necessarily by managerial competence in implementing technical change. A more detailed assessment of trade union responses to new technology is required.

TRADE UNION RESPONSES

Trade unions represent nearly half the working UK labour force. They can significantly influence the success or otherwise of computer systems in a great number of organisations. It is important to understand their approaches and attitudes toward new technology and how their interests will be affected.

What do trade unions want from computer technology? The major concern is to make as much as possible the subject of negotiation. The 1979 Trades Union Congress report *Employment and technology* suggests that the major concern is with job losses. Heavy job losses are not seen as inevitable, but expected to result if new technology is introduced without union influence. Training and retraining commitments by companies and government agencies are regarded as vitally necessary. The report calls for a campaign to reduce working time, and the resistance of redundancies where possible. Organisations should be encouraged to grow and diversify into new markets and products, thus creating new jobs.

These concerns were backed by a 1979 TUC ten-point plan for new technology agreements:

1. No NT introduced by management alone. No change without prior agreement (status quo clause). Establish procedures for consultation.

2. Inter-union collaboration in negotiations.

3. Unions guaranteed access to information before decisions taken.

4. Aim to maintain and improve employment and living standards. No redundancies; alternatively, good redundancy payments. Any redeployment/relocation of staff to be planned and agreed

5. Provision for training and retraining. Use redundancy period for retraining.

6. Reduction of working hours and eventual elimination of systematic overtime.

7. Do not disrupt existing pay structures and set workers against each other. Share benefits of NT amongst all employees.

8. Unions have a say in systems design and reprogramming. No computer-gathered information to be used for monitoring work performance. Procedures to monitor personal data kept on workforce.

9. Stringent standards on health and safety, especially on use of VDUs.

10. Joint management–union team to monitor and review developments.

Though under TUC review at the time of writing, these points formed the basic bargaining agenda for the vast majority of unions in the 1980s.

However, economic conditions since 1979 have seriously weakened the bargaining positions of many unions and have facilitated management's introduction, and union acceptance, of technological change. Two examples illustrate how this can occur. The Banking, Insurance and Finance Union voted at its 1983 conference to promote resistance to automation where employers refused to sign new technology agreements aimed at protecting jobs. In practice, the union executive found little support for applying this across the board nationally. In the following 12 months it was asked to support only one attempt at local resistance— at Royal Liver Insurance. Allen Meadows, the union's vice-president, described the consequences:

> 'The members took action and the employer immediately sacked the lot of them. From the first day our battle was to get them reinstated.'[25]

Market pressures and product innovation can have significant impacts. In 1986, Courtaulds Spinning spent £4.5 million on the latest machinery (not computer-based) for its Maple textile mill in Oldham. Only such technology could produce the yarn packages to match the new technology operated by customers like Marks and Spencer. European competitors were also re-equipping. In a stagnant market, the technology was aimed at efficiency rather than output growth. It meant doubling labour productivity, and a reduction in labour from 250 to 150 workers.

The management view that it had little choice on new technology was shared by the unions, who had been pressing for technology investment for some time. In this context, the best deal involved no compulsory redundancies, some redeployment to low-tech mills, and, in a low paid industry, welcome wage rises for those who remained. The new working environment would also be quieter, cleaner and more efficient. A union representative commented that increased productivity 'will be very beneficial to the company and we want our share of it'.[26] But pay rises can hardly offset the long term, deeper repercussions of such deals, not just for those involved, but for the wider trade union movement.

Such contextual pressures as high unemployment, falling memberships and managerial initiatives to 'slim' organisations and working practices have influenced union behaviour in other ways. Distracted into the serious and urgent business of keeping up member numbers through inter-union competition or merger, negotiating redundancies and maintaining pay levels, union officials and shop stewards have been rarely in a position to give new technology issues specialist attention.

Additionally, new technology has rarely appeared in isolation, but as one part of a package of managerial proposals. This encourages trade unions to view, and treat, new technology in the same way as more traditional concerns and through the same bargaining machinery. These pressures partially explain why most union bargaining aims for new technology have been both limited and traditional. Demanning, productivity and pay have been the urgent issues of the day. Work-sharing, reducing working hours and systematic overtime, and a concern for influencing systems design have rarely received attention.

However, regardless of management strategy and economic context, trade unions have been ill-equipped to deal with new technology issues in the 1980s. Moore and Levie's findings[27] on trade unions at GEC, Midland Bank, Alfred Herbert and British Leyland prove their comment that new technology 'can reveal the inadequacy and inappropriateness of the conventional range, level, and time horizons of collective bargaining activity ... and it can expose the absence of reliable, relevant training, research and servicing back-up for workplace representatives'.

In researching new technology in the brewing industry, Davies[4] found a lack of co-ordination between union representatives in different companies of the same group, and no union organisation at central group level where the key investment decisions were made. Many managers commented on the lack of union expertise and preparation, while a trade unionist stated that 'his union had woken up five years too late, finding themselves in a hurricane of new technology with no planning for it'.[4]

From a trade union, but not a management, point of view, such findings have been unfortunate but all too typical. This is particularly significant in the light of evidence from a 1983–85 technical change survey embracing a wide range of unions and industries. Batstone and Gourlay[13] found that, in the context of employer strategy and the recession, the unions with strong workplace organisations integrated with the wider union were most able to negotiate actively and over a wide range of issues concerning new technology.

With few exceptions, individual unions have not effected a strategic approach to new technology, despite the widespread concern for doing so registered at TUC committees and conferences. Coherent policies have been most likely in single-industry and single-employer unions, or where the union represents a single occupation. Strategy has been most successful in long term results for the union when going with, not against, the grain of employer strategy and technological developments. However, possessing strategy has been no guarantee of success. In 1985, the head office of APEX (Association of Professional, Executive, Clerical & Computer Staff) pushed for job design to be included in its new technology agreements. The strategy was to reverse the normal bargaining process. The principles behind work reorganisation would be negotiated first; only then would the implications for pay, hours and working conditions be considered. Only one branch took a practical initiative in this direction in the first 18 months. The large engineering company involved stalled on the issue for a year, APEX registered a failure to agree through formal procedure, but several months later over 500 redundancies were declared, and local union priorities were immediately pushed into quite a different direction.

In fact, most trade unions have failed to take initiatives on new technology. The major approach has been reactive, defensive, and after the event, responding to management initiatives rather than creating their own. Much of this lack of strategic thinking is of long standing and is not restricted to, but rather passed on into, new technology issues. This picture is confirmed by British case studies of computer technology and trade unions in engineering, brewing, insurance and chemicals.[28] The trade union inheritance for handling new technology emerges as, and remains, a decentralised, conflict-based industrial relations based on a limited workplace-level focus. The major focus is on pay and conditions surrounding jobs, with each union tending to support current sectional interests of members against those of management and even against those of other unions. Over new technology, as in other IR issues, trade unions have been as much 'pragmatists' as, if less 'opportunistic' than, the managements with which they deal.

In this context, it is not surprising to find that points 5,6,7 and 8 in the TUC ten-point plan have rarely received emphasis in negotiating new technology. Not unnaturally, managements have rarely seen it in their interests to point this out to the unions they are dealing with.

How important is this lack of union strategy to both unions and employers? Wilkinson[29] studied a range of computer applications in manufacturing firms in the Midlands. He found that, even after implementation, with systems up and running, shop-floor workers still had considerable scope for modifying design and continuing negotiations. However, this must be seen as a very circumscribed form of influencing management.

More pertinent is the fact that union failure to influence system design and impacts at earlier stages may store up problems for all participants. As one example, in 1984 Vauxhall Motors introduced a new computer system to control automated guided vehicles on the assembly line for the new Vauxhall Astra. Eight months later, EETPU members began a strike in a demarcation dispute over white collar staff operating the system rather than electricians. This cost the company some 400 Astras a day, shortly after the car's launch. Similar examples can be found above. The essential point is that a lack of union strategy and limited influence in design and implementation can induce similar limitations in the managerial approach. In this way, future problems will be stored up; union failures may even work more against the interests of management than against those of union members.

The above indicates the general influences on and concerns of trade unions over new technology in the mid-1980s. Such matters may well have important bearing on the type of design approach selected and how it is used, and the type of implementation strategy adopted.

Those responsible for systems design and implementation need to bear in mind Manwaring's point[30] that a specific trade union's response to systems design and implementation depends mainly on

(a) the perceived likely effects of the new system on members' range of interests; this can be influenced by the extent of information disclosure by management, but also by the quality of union research departments and their links with the wider union organisation

(b) the relevance of members' skills and experience to operating the new computer-based system

(c) the bargaining power of the union members *before* the computer system begins operations.

'Inheritors' of the new technology like the electricians' union (EETPU) have tended to be flexible and accommodating in their acceptance of computer systems, often against other unions' interests. When News Corporation moved printing operations for its newspapers from Fleet Street to Wapping, it began a long dispute that saw the dismissal of over 4500 NGA and SOGAT 82 print workers. EETPU members agreed to operate the new computerised direct-input system. The EETPU has successfully marketed itself to employers as a pro-technology union, but has also developed internal technology retraining courses frequently utilised by employers themselves.

White collar unions like ASTMS, TASS and MATSA and APEX have been highly cautious about the increasing impact of word-processing and office automation on their memberships. All have been concerned to negotiate new technology agreements. However, faced with declining memberships and needing to get footholds in high-tech industries of the future, by the mid-1980s they have followed the EETPU in formulating their own new technology and IR packages to attract employers.

In print, the compositors' union (NGA) has taken a much harder line on the introduction of computerised photocomposition that renders obsolete the traditional typesetting skills of its members. This led to intractable disputes at the Portsmouth News and Wolverhampton Star throughout 1985. Here, direct-input technology allowed journalists, tele-ad staff and editors working on VDTs to make up pages for print themselves. Fearing job loss, NGA members claimed the right to 'follow the job'. At different times, this meant final input becoming an NGA responsibility, or NGA members taking on some editorial and journalist duties. The latter claim brought the NGA in dispute with the NUJ as much as the employers.

An interesting comparison is presented by the Post Office Engineering Union (POEU)—renamed the National Communications Union (NCU) in the mid-1980s—and the Union of Communication Workers (UCW). Both recruit in the Post Office and British Telecom. However, the POEU organises mainly blue collar technical staff on the telecommunications side, while the UCW represents a range of lower-grade occupations, including postal workers, telephonists, telegraphists and cleaners.

As an 'inheritor' union, the POEU has been strongly committed to new technology, while looking to protect its members' job prospects. However, British Telecom privatisation brought 60 000 jobs at risk from the introduction of new technology, increasing competition and organisational restructuring. Also faced with a more hard-headed stance from management, in 1985 the POEU developed what it termed the 'broad strategy'. This involved a range of measures. Jobs would be preserved by negotiating the elimination of overtime and the reduction in working time from 37.5 to 32 hours a week, in exchange for including Saturdays in the normal working week. Other measures included the negotiation of a national new technology agreement; the strengthening of its own local bargaining units to match the decentralisation of management decision-making structures; and the widening of its membership base by union mergers and by promoting the expansion of BT itself into new business activities.

New technology represents a great threat to the jobs of UCW members in both the Post Office and British Telecom. Together with the union's nature as a highly centralised, one-industry union with a strong research department, this job threat has meant strong resistance to new technology in recent years. Even so, a highly detailed new technology agreement was negotiated with the Post Office in 1985 as part of a broader demanning and productivity package deal.

In summary, there is much evidence to undermine the common belief that trade unions block computer-based technical change. The 1980s experience is that, for a variety of reasons, trade union 'resistance' has been patchy, to say the least. In fact, a 1984 large-scale survey of workplace industrial relations shows considerable worker and shop steward support for advanced technical change, but much resistance to changes in work practices not ushered in by computers, machinery or equipment.[31] In practice, then, far from being resisted, computer technology has frequently legitimated, in union eyes, associated changes in working practices, that by themselves would have received considerable opposition.

NEW TECHNOLOGY AGREEMENTS

The main vehicle used by trade unions for a *negotiated* introduction of computer systems has been the new technology agreement (NTA). It would be a mistake to identify union plans, intentions, fears and published statements on microtechnological change for the substance of new technology agreements in their final form, and for union and employee behaviour in practice. As an initial point, the 1979 TUC statement and subsequent individual union guides must be seen as opening, rather than final bargaining, positions.

More importantly, there are many variables that affect what will be the substance of an agreement, or indeed whether an agreement is drawn up at all. These have received considerable attention above, but, in summary, include the industry, the perceived impact of the technology, management and union objectives, bargaining power, attitudes and particular interests as well as the state of the economy and of general and local labour markets. What in practice has been the record on NTAs? And what can be learnt from this?

After an initial surge in NTAs occurred from 1978, followed by immense union concern and activity over new technology from 1979 to 1981, in fact, to the end of 1985, the overall rate at which NTAs were signed has declined. Reporting in 1982, Williams and Moseley[32] found that only 24 of the 146 TUC unions had reached any NTAs with employers. In a later review,[33] they found over 240 agreements arrived at between 1977 and 1983. However, as Labour Research Department evidence also shows,[34] the vast majority of such agreements cover white collar workers only. In fact, only four unions—APEX, ASTMS, AUEW/TASS and NALGO—account for over 80% of the total agreements. In practice, other unions, particularly those representing manual workers, have a poor record on making new technology the subject of collective bargaining. This lack of activity is particularly pertinent given that where agreements have been made, it has been through *unions*, rather than managements, taking the initiative.

Many unions seem to believe that they can win back rights and conditions after systems have been introduced, as they have done with previous changes. This can occur to an extent. However, it is also true that many trade unionists have failed to understand the potential depth of impact of computer-based technology on a series of issues that in fact they *do* perceive as crucial, not least the nature and extent of union organisation itself.

Where bargaining over NTAs has taken place, it has been frequently at the local level, with a union looking after its own workers on a particular site. TUC plans for multi-union negotiation of new technology have rarely been realised. In addition, NTAs have been mainly negotiated through existing bargaining structures that have not always been appropriate for the sort of issues raised by new technology. As a result, the 'big picture' impact of computer systems on employment and across unions and workplaces has mainly escaped attention in the actual detail of the NTAs.

What sort of issues interest trade unions? It is difficult to generalise about a very complicated picture. However, it can be said that unions have reserved their *main* concern in NTAs for job security, pay and conditions, the physical aspects of health and safety, and prevention of encroachment by other unions. Reduced working time, quality of work life and job design have received little attention.

Batstone[35] and his colleagues undertook a 1984 survey of shop stewards in a range of public and private sector industries and unions. They found that negotiations over equipment selected and investment strategy occurred only 'in a small minority of cases'.[35] However, in nearly all cases the introduction of new technology involved negotiation of some sort, most typically on pay and manning. Health and safety and training were also negotiated in over half the cases examined.

What have the unions achieved? The results still tend to support the conclusion of Manwaring's 1981 study,[30] that except in the area of health and safety, 'unions have been largely unsuccessful in securing a share of the benefits from new technology; the rhetoric of model agreements has not, in general, been translated into negotiated concessions in clauses of actual "new technology agreements"'.

Moreover, despite Batstone's sample findings, the experience is that in many even partly unionised workplaces much new technology continues to be introduced unilaterally by management and is not covered by NTAs at all. It should also be remembered that the majority of British workers are not in trade unions and are rarely allowed to negotiate the introduction of computer technology.

The overall picture that emerges is that even in the exceptional cases where NTAs have been arrived at, computer technology has still been introduced on terms heavily influenced by and largely favourable to management.

Two final points need to be borne in mind when considering the design and implementation of computer systems. Firstly, Batstone's 1984 survey cited above found major disagreements between managements and unions (mainly over manning and work-related issues) in over half the public sector and about two fifths the private sector cases investigated. Industrial action was used in about half these examples. Also, industrial relations problems played some role in a third of the cases where the introduction of new technology was delayed. The processes of design and implementation must be clearly thought out if serious industrial relations problems are not to arise.

Secondly, it is also important to point out what can be achieved, through negotiating technical change with employees and their representatives. Westland Helicopters' Milton Keynes plant was brought back from the brink of closure in 1982 by intensive and difficult negotiations with its two unions on a wide package of changes. By 1984 it achieved full utilisation of office technology, computerised time- and attendance-clocking for all employees, monthly payment and by direct credit transfer extended to all employees, a single-status canteen, three-shift working in the factory with multi-machine manning, maximum flexibility of labour, and the inspection of components and CNC programming by operators themselves rather than by white-collar staff away from the shop-floor.

The machine-shop saw significant increases in productivity as well as job satisfaction as a result of introducing CNC machines designed not to undermine traditional machining skills but to consolidate and extend them. These drastic changes were achieved with the closure of another Westland plant and some job loss, mainly amongst supervisors and administrators. Job loss was handled mainly through early retirement, retraining, transfer and voluntary rather than compulsory retirement.

Clearly, major changes involving computer-based technology can be introduced by negotiating with trade unions. The technology does not need to be designed to control the workforce through deskilling task performance. Moreover, technological change need not be viewed narrowly. It can be considered in the light of a whole range of possible changes and issues, not least the interests and wishes of the people involved and affected. But a final note of caution is needed. As the poor business records of both Westland and British Leyland show, introducing new technology and getting the IR right are necessary, but may not be sufficient conditions in themselves for high organisational performance in the late 1980s.

TOWARDS A NEW INDUSTRIAL RELATIONS?

In the 1980s, the 'old' attitudes of management and unions still underlie the introduction of most computer technology into organisations (see Fig. 7.2). Such attitudes are linked with confrontation bargaining, a conflict-based industrial relations and deep suspicion of the other side's motives and objectives.

While position A, representing 'new' attitudes, is probably the ideal position for all parties involved in the introduction of new technology, it is very difficult to achieve. Not only does it depend on the new technology being used to the perceived benefit of all stakeholders, it also relies on a high degree of trust amongst the interested parties and a considerable shift in attitudes amongst managers, trade unionists and employees. Also position A can be very fragile. If there is a reversal of attitude or a betrayal of trust, or if circumstances (for example, poor company performance) make one party unable to deliver, it is quite easy for position C or D to develop temporarily until position B is eventually restored.

Position A assumes co-operative bargaining based on full information and consultation to employees at the earliest stages of design and equipment selection, and greater power-sharing in decision-making on new technology. These seem unlikely as immediate, general developments in the UK, not least because managements perceive their interests as largely having been served by the existing pattern of collective bargaining arrangements for the reception of new technology.

The 'new' approach is consistent with the design and implementation practices supported throughout this book. Whether or not this approach

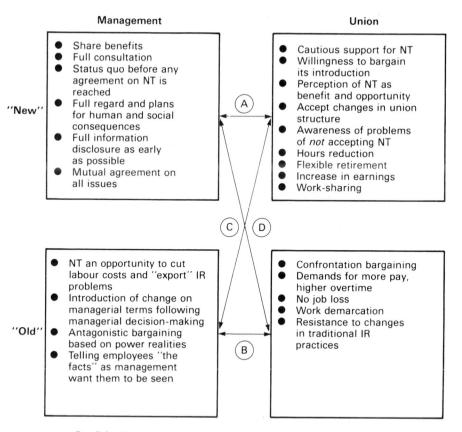

Fig. 7.2 Management–union attitudes to new technology in the UK

is followed by managers and trade unions, clearly it is crucial for those responsible for computerisation to understand management, union and employee attitudes and objectives on new technology and industrial relations, in order to attempt to work with if not reform them.

CONCLUSIONS

Organisations, employees and their representatives have rarely possessed a strategic perception of the interrelationship between industrial relations and the introduction of computer systems. A particularly pervasive view sees industrial relations issues arising only at the implementation stage of projects, and to be the preserve of personnel specialists.

The 1980s have seen widespread acceptance of new technology at work mainly on employers' terms, even where managers have adopted uncompromising approaches to gain employee acquiescence and co-operation. This cannot be explained only by the economic, legal and political climates and labour market conditions strengthening the hand of management and weakening the positions of employees and trade unions. In practice, employees have tended to support the legitimacy, and even inevitability, of technological change. Furthermore, trade unions have often been found wanting in their planning, internal organisation, awareness of and, as a result, responses to the long term implications of the new technologies. In particular, even where pursued, new technology agreements have tended to favour their managerial much more than their union signatories.

Computerisation may itself be the catalyst for a new industrial relations in many organisations, in particular concentrating minds on the usefulness of existing practices, procedures and relationships in the face of widespread technical changes. More often, new technology has been brought in through existing frameworks. Many of the problems of employee conflicts and sub-optimal systems running during or after implementation could be avoided by better human resource planning, more employee participation going back as far as the design stage, and deeper consideration of the industrial relations implications of decisions over systems design and how computer systems will be applied.

CHAPTER 8

Managing Implementation

'What needs to be emphasised here is in the close relationship
between all the stages of an innovation ... implementation cannot
be separated from all the other phases.'[1]
'The higher the organizational level at which managers define a
problem or need, the greater the probability of successful
implementation. At the same time, however, the closer the definition and solution of problems or needs are to end-users, the
greater the probability of success. Implementation managers must
draw up their ... plans [for computer systems] in light of this
apparent paradox.'[2]

INTRODUCTION

The implementation stage will reveal where prior analysis, design and
planning in the computerisation project have been inadequate.
Frequently what have been termed 'implementation problems' are in
fact the results of failures in these earlier activities. Implementation will
bring its own unpredictabilities that need to be handled. Not least of
these are human factors. In fact, in the usual implementation scenario it
is only at this stage, when changes become manifest and real, that
people seriously begin to question what is going to happen.

People become important for another reason. In a detailed analysis of
the economics of office work, Strassman[3] found that:

> 'Investments in human capital and in the other expenses of
> reorganisation will exceed the costs of any information
> technology over its lifetime. The largest cost of an infor-
> mation system comes from installing it, not designing it ...
> Insist on a comprehensive assessment of the expenses for
> training, for gaining user acceptance, for organisational
> learning, and for ongoing support before acquiring any
> technology. The technical choices should be determined by
> people costs rather than the other way round.'

The message is clear. It is in the interests of all organisations, even,
indeed especially, the most commercially driven, to assign much more

importance to people factors rather than technical issues when implementing computer-based information systems.

This is not the accepted view, and indeed at the root of many implementation problems is the overriding influence of traditional systems analysis and design practices. In particular, human and organisational issues are reduced merely to limiting resistance to change, the need to organise training, and the need to have enough staff of the right type available in the right place at the right time. In this way an over concentration on the technical can result in failure to deal with non-technical emerging issues. In turn, problems in these areas can begin to interfere with technical issues. Here the crux of the problem lies in the manner in which implementation is defined and conceptualised.

This chapter examines the proposition that implementation *is* organisational change, and points to the uses and limitations of organisation development (OD) approaches to handling technological change. Various implementation strategies are examined. Participation and its uses are discussed and various guidelines proposed for minimising implementation problems. Finally, a key focus of the book is developed into a political–cultural contingencies approach to systems implementation. This places at centre stage the **organisational context** in which computerisation occurs.

DEFINING IMPLEMENTATION

How people define implementation crucially influences the scope and method of its management. There are a number of ways in which the implementation of computer-based systems has been conceptualised.

In traditional systems analysis thinking, implementation is a discrete and late stage, the major tasks being

— managing the programming project; program, hardware, and system testing, system-fit testing
— management training
— site preparation
— procurement management
— staff preparation
— maintaining commitment and morale
— document preparation
— preparing test data
— operator training
— file conversion
— changeover management
— systems monitoring and maintenance.

Much of this is technical; even training and motivation are usually viewed in over-technical and mechanistic terms. Staff need to be motivated and solutions can be found in the traditional managerial kit-bag of motivating and leadership techniques. Training is seen as a highly organised and structured event.

Dickson and Wetherbe[4] take defining implementation a little further:

> 'When a system is truly implemented, it means that the installed system is used by the persons for whom it was intended, without significant problems ... a system is used when it is integrated in the work it was developed to assist.'

This points up that the very notion of implementation implies *successful* implementation. However, this still begs a crucial question, namely: *whose* definition of success will be the accepted guideline?

Alternative views are engendered when the system development life cycle approach is discarded. Participative and evolutionary systems development approaches, especially prototyping and the procedures recommended by the HUSAT group (see chapter 4), hasten this dissolution of the traditional divide between analysis, design and implementation; indeed, Eason sees the three as never-ending as long as the system continues to be used.

The participative and evolutionary approaches, together with Multi-view and Mumford's ETHICS (see chapter 4), are also anchored in the fundamental assumption that computer-based information systems can only be understood if viewed as part of larger organisational processes. Hirschheim[5] deepens our understanding of what this entails in the context of office automation:

> 'Offices are not "rational" and manifestly rule-following, they are social arenas where power, ritual and myth predominate. The set of rules or procedures followed in an office are not a simple empirical reality existing "out there" to be discovered by classical empiricist means; rather it exists in the minds of the social actors and is intersubjectively determined.'

Clearly, the 'empiricist means' of traditional systems analysis practice are of limited use in implementing computer systems into organisations where the very reality of rules and procedures is open to individual interpretation and indeed continual redefinition.

From these considerations it becomes necessary to reconceptualise implementation as a process or processes involving the introduction of changes connected with computer-based systems into social and political organisational areas where the acceptance and the very definition of the success of those changes tend to be continually renegotiated. In Keen's words:[6]

> 'Implementation is not just the installation of a technical system in an organisation but the institutionalization of its use in the ongoing context of jobs, formal and informal structures, and personal and group processes. Installation does not guarantee institutionalization. Implementation includes the technical process of installation and the behavioural process of managing change.'

Additionally, implementation must be seen as more than a limited number of once-and-for-all activities that amount to putting prior policy decisions into action. Braun's[1] description of manufacturing innovation applies to the introduction of computer-based systems as well: 'a complex phenomenon...[requiring]...a constellation of various circumstances to be propitious for the events to occur.'

The difficulties do not just relate to aspects such as space, capital, technical malfunctions and extensive reorganisation. There are also union negotiations on manning, pay and work practices; changes in power and social structures; and resistance from stakeholders—indeed sometimes resistance from the very managers commissioned to see the changes through.

Implementors of computer-based systems need to perceive implementation in all its complexity, and as a broad process involving a constellation of factors and changes processes, with human beings as integral initiators and experiencers of these changes. This conceptualisation will then inform, and thus aid, their subsequent practice.

THE SYSTEMS ANALYST AS CHANGE AGENT: AN OD APPROACH

One important activity in the implementation of a computer system is managing the *content* of the change. For the systems analyst this usually includes involvement in

- systems and program specification
- hardware selection
- testing
- deciding on and assisting changeover procedures.

But another critical activity is management of the *process* of change. This includes ensuring that

- change is well received

— people are working with the new system rather than against it

— the impact of system implementation and subsequent running is such that people support and use the system to achieve performance objectives.

This area has been neglected in traditional systems analysis practice. This has encouraged moves toward redressing the imbalance by integrating traditional systems analysis skills with the people-oriented 'change agent' role of an OD practitioner.

As established in chapter 2, organisational members are often unwilling to change long-established attitudes and patterns of behaviour. Furthermore, given the introduction of a computer system, people's behaviour and attitudes may not change at all, or may change for a short time before reverting back to older patterns. The ways of working that result influence the extent to which the new system is utilised as was originally designed, if at all. Lewin,[7] and later Schein,[7] addressed such problems by developing a model for intervening at the individual, group or organisational levels. Figure 8.1 shows this useful model and its development by Kolb and Frohman.[8]

From these models a crucial point emerges. As discussed, physical systems implementation may be treated as a late stage, but the implementation of the necessary *behaviour* change to support the emerging system must occur right from the beginning of the project. Failure to grasp the significance of this point for systems development can lead to the so-called 'people problems' frequently experienced at the implementation and subsequent operating stages.

Advantages of the models include the emphases on change as process rather than a 'one off', and the need for careful planning. The overall approach suggests the need in computer projects for

(a) establishing a felt need for computerisation

(b) establishing the support required to see the project through to satisfactory systems operation

(c) monitoring the progress of the project, and responding to resistance to the change process and the emerging system

(d) developing user commitment to the system.

Under item (b), establishing support may mean not only securing top management support but also making that visible to the organisation. Establishing change-agent credibility is crucial. User understanding and active acceptance of objectives and methods is also needed. A project champion who can make available required organisational resources is important throughout the project. Such methods are aimed at creating a 'critical mass' in favour of and actively supporting the computerisation process (see also Fig. 3.1 and chapter 3).

At the end of the project, commitment (item (d)) should be expressed as the users 'owning' the system, willing to use it and able to do so without the change agent's presence. In Lewin's terms, this means refreezing—locking the new behaviours into place so that they become the norm.

In practice, organisation development (OD) practitioners have concentrated on the 'people' element of organisation, in terms of motivation, beliefs, attitudes, interpersonal and intergroup relationships and organisational culture. Early OD writers and practitioners

Lewin/Schein approach	Kolb/Frohman approach	Systems development life cycle approach
1. *Unfreezing*	(a) *Scouting* Organization and change agent jointly explore mutual needs and abilities Entry point selected	1. *Definition* Proposal defined Feasibility assessment Information requirements analysis Conceptual design
	(b) *Entry* Problems, goals stated. Development of mutual contract and expectations Establish trust, commitment and felt need for change	
	(c) *Diagnosis* Collect data to define problems Detailed assessment of organization's and change agent's resources for change Establish feasible goals	2. *Development* Physical systems & database design Program development Procedure development
2. *Changing*	(d) *Planning* Define operational objectives Identify alternative solutions, action steps and possible resistance to change Develop action plan	
	(e) *Action* Putting into practice 'best' solution Keeping practice flexible in the face of unanticipated consequences	3. *Installation and operation* Conversion
	(f) *Stabilization and evaluation* Assess 'success' of change and need for further action or termination	4. *Maintenance*
3. *Refreezing*	(g) *Termination* Confirm new behaviour patterns Ensure handover of responsibility and ownership of system to client is complete Cease work on project	5. *Post-audit*

Fig. 8.1   *The systems analyst as change agent—some illustrative models of planned change*

subscribed to humanistic and democratic values, seeking to move 'immature', authoritarian, closed organisations towards openness, democratic leadership, 'maturity' and 'health'.[9] A link was implied between the extent to which an organisation supported responsible, high-trust, self-actualising behaviour (people given opportunities to fulfil their potential) and organisational effectiveness.

Desanctis and Courtney,[10] in an article entitled 'Toward friendly user MIS implementation', have made a strong case for using OD techniques in the implementation of management information systems (MISs). They stress that OD and MIS implementation have similar goals and theoretical foundations and address themselves to similar problems, namely overcoming resistance to change, gaining support of top management in the change effort, and developing techniques for the implementation of change. Thus, if information systems practitioners have previously neglected the 'people' element in computer system implementation, then a ready-made set of values and techniques to redress the balance exists in OD. The specific OD tools, and the behavioural problems in MIS implementation to which they can be applied, are shown in Figure 8.2. One can agree with Desanctis and Courtney that where an MIS is to be newly computerised or updated, OD techniques and tools are more likely to be needed

(a) the more extensive the MIS system change is going to be

(b) the more resistance there is to the existing MIS

(c) where organisation norms do not value the existing MIS or foster its frequent use

(d) the more conflict exists between the MIS area and other areas of the organisation

(e) the more dramatic the MIS change.

However, there are problems accepting their idea that an MIS consultant or systems analyst should be used for technical aspects of systems change, while a separate OD practitioner would carry out 'social system' tasks such as surveying user needs, assessing resistance and communication problems, assessing the impact of the system on attitudes and job satisfaction, and enabling human adjustments to structural changes.

Much of their reasoning here is an admission of defeat. There *is* strong, and published, evidence showing that all too often systems failures at the implementation stage are due to lack of attention to human variables, or failed attempts to involve users in systems planning and design, or lack of management involvement in MIS design.[11] Also, one accepts that, as technicians, systems analysts have rarely been

Behaviour problems	OD tools
Determining user attitudes toward the current system and assessing user information requirements	Survey feedback
	Group diagnostic meeting
Poor communication between systems analysts and users, particularly in the determination of user information requirements	Communications training a. Active listening b. Transaction analysis c. Role playing of assessment meetings
User resistance	
User ignorance regarding how the system works and how to use it	Defreezing techniques
Developing norms that encourage system use; positive climate toward MIS	Training sessions (taught by systems technicians; monitored and administered by the OD consultant)
Interpersonal, conflict resulting from changes in job content and power after MIS change	
Managing conflict between MIS personnel and general management	Laboratory training a. Stranger labs b. Cousin labs c. Family labs
	Role negotiation technique
	Organizational mirror technique

Fig. 8.2 OD tools for change problems (from Desanctis and Courtney)[10]

trained in other aspects of business enterprise, including human relations psychology. However, as computer systems are being moved into
the core of organisational communications, such training for systems
analysts becomes *more* crucial, not less.

In fact, the requirement is not for the involvement of more specialists
in systems implementation, but the development of more generalist
approaches amongst all parties involved in the implementation.
Desanctis and Courtney's suggestion permits systems analysts to maintain 'hard systems' thinking; the only contact with users will now be
their technical training. This will have impacts on the sort of system they
will come up with. Moreover, managers will also be able to avoid
responsibility for the people element in system implementation. It can be
handed over to OD consultants. Finally, the OD practitioners are not
required to learn about the technical system and project management.
One can question how useful and credible their contributions might be
in systems implementation.

Clearly, OD tools and techniques have definite applications in systems
implementation, but key users must be systems analysts who have had
appropriate training and have integrated OD methods with other more
traditional systems analysis skills. Survey feedback methods are useful
throughout the development and implementation of computer systems,
while team-building has particular relevance to the development of
design and project teams.

This merely hints at the type of job changes that can lead to more
effective systems implementation. At Citibank, for example, the move is
toward every user being a systems manager. The traditional communications chain is long and can create unnecessary difficulties. It involves
user, systems analyst, systems designer, programmer and operator. As
established in chapter 4, these have different viewpoints and interests,
but also tend to communicate in almost different languages. Citibank's
radical solution has been to abolish systems analysts. User do-it-yourself
(DIY) relies on the commitment of users to becoming their own systems
analysts, specifying requirements and managing their own projects
through to successful completion.[12] However, user DIY at Citibank
requires strong back-up. Firstly, contract programmers are hired to
work for users. Secondly, the firm's selection policy ensures that users
have the required intellectual qualities, personality and 'fit' for DIY and
the related organisational culture, Thirdly, Citibank has run hundreds
of 'managing technology' courses to provide users with the technical
skills necessary to get started.

As another example, Land[13] usefully distinguishes between traditional software engineering and information systems engineering. The
former has been primarily a technical task using formal methods and
tools. The latter is a developing, much broader role, definable as

assisting in the design and construction of information systems that enable an organisation to function more effectively. As such, information systems engineering relies on social processes, with communication skills, participative methods and judgement as essential features.

However, in such new job types, OD approaches and techniques must be used with caution. One weakness is their limited attention to, and limited ability to deal with, power relations in the organisational change process. A further impediment can be the attitudes and values traditionally adhering to OD, [14] though much OD practice (as opposed to academic work) has largely discounted a humanistic ideology that finds itself far out of touch with the social and economic conditions and organisational realities of the UK in the mid- and late 1980s. In a US context, Kochan and Dyer [15] suggest that OD techniques are rarely used with shop-floor workers because OD values, concepts and models of change fit poorly with the normal parameters that define management–union relations (see also chapter 7 for UK comparisons). Alderfer [16] finds OD being practised mainly in stable US suburban school systems without inner city unrest, and in relatively successful businesses, usually not unionised.

A further problem with OD approaches is that they focus on the processes of changing human behaviour, attitudes and culture, while downplaying the contexts in which these changes are to occur, and the relationship between these changes and other aspects of the organisation. Figure 8.3 suggests the interdependence of the main organisational elements. Thus change in one element is likely to impinge on all the other elements. In implementing computer systems it is necessary always to have in mind the extent to which any implementation can have wider organisational consequences. [17] These need to be consciously planned for if systems 'fit' and purposes are to be achieved.

PARTICIPATING IN CHANGE: STS, USER INVOLVEMENT AND IMPLEMENTATION

Socio-technical systems (STS), and Mumford's contribution, received attention as design philosophy and practice in chapter 4. Beer [18] has classified STS as an organisation development technique that gained in prominence and importance as interest in, and the credibility of, job enrichment programmes receded in the 1960s and 1970s. Miller [19] has established the impact of the UK Tavistock Institute of Human Relations on its evolution since the 1940s.

In fact, it is only since the 1970s that the potential of STS for the design and implementation of specifically computer systems has been applied. Despite the wide claims made for its usefulness and a large

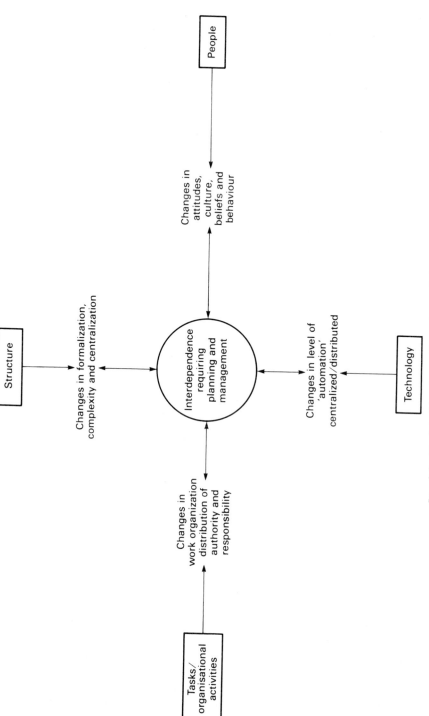

Fig. 8.3   The interdependence of organisational elements

literature on the subject,[20] it receives little attention in actual design and implementation practice. Thus, carefully devised STS procedures like Mumford's ETHICS are in fact used rarely. Many implementations pay lip service to the notion of participation; most permit a very restricted involvement in practice, with a paradoxical mixture of regard for the advantages of 'user involvement' coupled with a fear of losing control over the project's content and direction.

The major usefulness of STS and other participative approaches derives from their focus on otherwise easily neglected areas in computer system design and implementation, namely the relationships between systems design, job design, work and social organisation, job satisfaction of the users and systems effectiveness.

Beyond this, a strong case can be made for the benefits and rights of participation and user involvement. Firstly, although even participative approaches, except prototyping, still tend to categorise implementation as a discrete, late stage in a systems development life cycle, they do pre-empt many of the problems that are frequently experienced at implementation due to technically focussed designs and their consequences being unacceptable to systems users and those likely to lose out if the design is put into practice.

Secondly, there are likely to be organisational problems whatever new technology is being introduced. Tactically it may be better to allow conflicts of interest to emerge and be dealt with in design stages through participation rather than be left with a high-capital-outlay system which somehow has to be negotiated into use and may receive little support even when up and running. Keen[21] supports the idea that user involvement provides an arena for bargaining and conflict resolution at the design stage, thus promoting user acceptance at implementation. Participation may be particularly difficult where the new technology is advanced enough for present job-holders and future users to be unable to contribute to its design. Eason and Sell[22] found that here it is necessary to maintain user involvement by designing the new system with the maximum flexibility for operators to design their own jobs.

Thirdly, there is some evidence to support the notion that user involvement, user acceptance of the system and smooth implementation are related.[23] User involvement engenders system 'ownership' and commitment to its use, reduces user resistance and promotes realistic expectations of system capabilities, thus also preparing users to anticipate and deal with implementation problems. User involvement also aids technical system design in providing information and expertise on the organisation and its work not normally available in the computer services group. This can also aid better definition of user information requirements. These factors will feed into experiencing less implementation problems.

Fourthly, one major reason for resistance to systems implementation may not be the content or design of the system but the lack of control over its development and subsequent use. Participation provides a mechanism for retaining users' influence over and discretion in their work activities. However, what is crucial here is how much control users require, and how much influence computer staff, systems analysts and managers are willing to cede to other staff.

From these points arise major questions. What are the 'appropriate' types of participation? Who should be involved? How much influence should users have over different levels of decision-making and the process of change? The range of options has already been indicated in Figures 4.2 and 4.3. Mumford has suggested that participation in computer system design and implementation falls into three types: consultative, representative and consensus (see chapter 4). User influence over systems design rises in moving from consultative to consensus design. However, as was pointed out, in actual use Mumford-type methodologies tend to circumscribe the degree of participation allowed.

In particular, consensus participation is rarely used, not least because it tends to be time-consuming and a consensus is difficult to achieve. Indeed the authors' own experience of its use in automating an insurance company office was that it quickly turned into a negotiated type of involvement. Moreover, in practice the decisions arrived at were later 'adjusted' during implementation by those with real power—managers and systems professionals—to achieve their preferred results.

This point needs to be developed. There are inherent dangers in participative *design* methodologies where participants cease to have much influence over the change process once design is complete. Participation may raise expectations unduly; the outcomes of implementation may not be what was envisaged in the design. This can lead to user dissatisfaction and a less productive computer system may result. Prototyping and evolutionary systems development permit ongoing user participation and can avoid such traps.

Another aspect of this is revealed in Mumford's case of moving a bank's foreign exchange department from a batch to an on-line computer system.[24] Socio-technical system design was completed, but a post-implementation survey found that job satisfaction had decreased instead of increasing. This was found to be due to implementation rather than the organisation of work. Staff were doing more responsible jobs, but a delay in job evaluation and regrading caused morale problems.

Furthermore, while staff were learning to operate the new system, management were reducing departmental numbers from 61 to 53 in four months. Nor did the reorganisation reduce the internal promotion problems of the operating clerks. Clearly, participation in designing more interesting work is not the only, and sometimes not even the main, determinant of 'job satisfaction', and indeed this case serves to indicate the contextual factors that can limit the effectiveness of socio-technical approaches to the introduction of computer systems.

A final note of caution is offered. The advantages of participation and involvement of the target user groups in the design of computer-based information systems have been discussed, but the effectiveness of 'user involvement' in achieving a successful implementation can be questioned. Thus, in an extensive and convincing review of the research in this area, Ives and Olson[25] found the evidence too little and too unreliable a basis for establishing links between user involvement and system success.

Russell[26] points to another problem. In researching the implementation of new technology in the British chemical industry, he found user participation to be a mixed blessing. Designed to generate more trust and confidence in management, the disclosure to employees of information previously regarded as private to management could have the opposite effect. The difficulties of the managerial task were revealed, along with the uncertainties surrounding the technology and the business situation. Without careful handling, the result could be employee lack of confidence and poor morale.

Participation, even of the limited STS kind, can bring its own problems. The decisions as to who should participate, how and in what sort of areas and activities are difficult to get right, and depend on the circumstances which the system will become part of and transform. Increased participation can be time-consuming and eat into project schedules. Disagreements between participants can prove difficult to resolve; they may compromise design and lead on to implementation problems.

Participation in organisations has become like 'motherhood' and 'apple pie': managers cannot be against it, at least not in public. The problem here is that the managers may become all too willing to support the *idea* of participation, but little of its reality. As one example, the presence of a future word-processor operator in a system project group does not always mean *influence*. This can be easily circumscribed by other team members with higher status in the organisational hierarchy.

Users may become suspicious or unconvinced about the reasons for participation. Implementors must be particularly aware of the possibilities of, and employee sensitivities to, manipulation in participation schemes. This certainly seems to have had a role to play in the bank case discussed above. Here, management was experiencing difficulties attracting and retraining staff, and the introduction of a new computer system requiring less people was dressed up as an attempt to improve job satisfaction. Increased employee participation, and the language of participation, control and autonomy, need to be accompanied by increased *power* to participants to influence the ends to which their participation is put, if suspicions about manipulation are to be avoided. If these remain, then user involvement may become more of a hindrance than a help to systems implementation.

Full participative approaches are best used with prototyping techniques, evolutionary systems development, or where users can quickly contribute to systems design because the nature of the technology is relatively simple, or the users have been appropriately trained beforehand. It is also useful, for pragmatic reasons, to cut down on the numbers directly involved in design; following from this, consensus participative approaches are best used where the total number of users is small. What cannot be ignored is the politics of participation, and this is further discussed in the next section.

A POLITICAL–CULTURAL CONTINGENCIES APPROACH

This section outlines the basics of a political approach to systems implementation. Bringing a computer system into effective operation in an organisation is not solely about getting the politics right. However, getting the politics wrong has turned many a computer project into a long-term damage limitation exercise. How can this be avoided?

Organisational Politics

Systems analysts commonly see the planning, designing, organising and controlling of computerisation projects as rational behaviours. One theme of this book is that these activities are also essentially political. One must ask—whose plans, whose designs and whose objectives. Furthermore, organisations are inevitably political arenas with individuals, groups and coalitions attempting to influence others and events to protect and meet their own needs, interests and goals. An organisation where members' goals, perceptions or interests do not conflict is a rare one indeed. 'Playing politics' may not always be the primary activity, but it is an ever-present one to some degree. Two important considerations arise from this.

Firstly, the design and development of a computer system inevitably implies the ability to bring it into successful operation. However, while the expertise of the systems analyst may rarely be questioned in technical matters like analysis and design or hardware and software selection, such expertise and associated technical qualifications may form an insufficient power base for fulfilling the responsibility for seeing the project implemented. Unfortunately, computer professionals too often ascribe a rationality and a common sense to their projects that is not shared by those directly affected by implementation outcomes. As a

171

result, they fail to acquire and mobilise power and develop strategies to achieve objectives, and the system flounders at the implementation stage. Of course, faced with gathering signs of organisational hostility toward what they themselves regard as a technically high-quality product, computer professionals may well have fled from responsibility for project acceptance long before implementation.

Secondly, organisational politics breed in times of technological change. In studying cases of the purchase and application of computer equipment, Pettigrew[27] found that political energy was released not at the implementation stage, but mainly while decisions to go ahead with projects were being made. However, this cannot be taken as a general rule of thumb. The extent of political activity during systems implementation will depend on the extent to which power has been mobilised behind the project, and other options and paths of resistance are closed off *before* implementation. More correctly, then, political activity will become more obvious where there persist unclear goals and outcomes, different goals, the need to allocate limited resources, differing definitions of organisational problems and differences in information made available. Mangham's finding[28] is that:

'In circumstances in which people share power, differ about what must be done, and where these differences are of some consequence, decisions and actions will be the result of a political process.'[26]

The introduction of new technology will release political energy because of its anticipated and actual organisational and social impacts and the manner in which it is designed and implemented. A political approach may be more appropriate where the technological change impinges on core activities, will be pervasive and cut across departmental boundaries and will have numerous users. However, even in minor applications, the existing power structure will be disturbed in some way by new technology. It also represents a new organisational resource around which 'ownership' struggles will cluster. In this way, the implementation process will reproduce, but also amplify, existing strains in the organisation's political system.

In practice, political activity may well reach its highest throughout implementation as people's fears become realised. This can be a function of people avoiding facing up to the implications of computerisation at earlier stages. Also, failure to participate in change will be rational behaviour where the rewards for doing so do not seem commensurate with the efforts necessary, where there is a good chance of feeling manipulated and where the cultural norms of the organisation do not encourage trust and openness in interpersonal relations.[29] It also may be a function of the approach to implementation. Historically, computers have been implemented with the minimum of participation, the output of selective and reassuring information and little regard for the industrial relations implications. Such an approach is marked by highly political activity during implementation and subsequently.

Thus it is crucial to understand a particular organisation's political structure and how different types and levels of computerisation relate to political activity. Such understanding is the first step in planning and implementing a computer system. A political perspective implies the possibility of resistance and the need to gain organisational acceptance for computerisation. This is where contingency comes in; that is, being prepared to adapt the system to the political circumstances prevailing, while also being willing and able to operate in and change those circumstances. As Markus[30] puts it:

'If the implementor can divorce the need to see a system up and working from the need to achieve a particular result, several degrees of freedom exist.'

Power Revisited

This section extends the working definition of power and power bases established in chapter 1, and the role of organisational culture discussed in chapter 2.

Power is inherent in organisational relations. Its exercise both creates and arises from societal and organisational context. Matters such as how labour is divided, how the organisation is departmentalised, and how different categories of worker are rewarded are all the products of political activity. In turn, these results give for different people various degrees of control over information, decision-making, resources, punishments and the access of others to these. Power may also arise on an individual basis; for example, in terms of expertise, personal qualities and ability to be liked and persuade others. As a social relation within an organisation, power becomes expressed as people pursue aspirations through action to try to achieve outcomes. It is an interdependence relating to how skilfully people mobilise or deploy resources (power bases) and how important and scarce those resources are perceived or experienced to be by the parties in the relationship.

Power implies influence, control over resources and sanction. However, there is power in the threat of sanctions, in the potential of power. As Pettigrew[31] puts it:

'Control...may not be enough; there is also the issue of skilful use of resources. The most effective strategy may not always be to pull the trigger.'

As one example, because of their control over a strategically crucial resource, for many years the unionised workforce in the UK water industry needed only to threaten to strike to bring pay concessions from government. However, their bluff was called in the early 1980s and they went on to strike for the first time. The settlement was unfavourable to the water workers, and the overall outcome of the strike was a weakening of their position thereafter.

Power is exercised not only by those who are in the dominant coalition but also by, as well as through, lower-level stakeholders in an organisation. Participants in a power relationship are rarely on equal terms but always have some influence over each other, because power relationships imply some degree of mutual dependence for all parties. As far as computers are concerned, even low-level operators in computer systems can corrupt data, modify software in unrecognisable ways and damage the system in serious and costly ways.

But as computers become strategically important to an organisation, so they may hand over an important power resource to certain individuals and groups. One aspect of this is illustrated by the conduct of the UK Civil Service pay dispute in April 1987. Reluctant to undertake the risks and costs to members of a national strike, the civil service unions first encouraged short, selective strikes by the few members strategically placed in work at computer centres. The idea was to force government agreement to a pay deal by maximising costs to the Treasury through, to union members at least, 'cut-price' industrial action. As one example, trade union sources estimated that a week-long strike by 100 civil service staff at the Customs and Excise computer centre at Southend in mid-April 1987 cost the Treasury at least £3.5 million and potentially £15 million.

This example highlights only one issue—the importance of gaining the acceptance and support of key personnel once a computer system is up and running. It may also be wise to gain acceptance by those involved at and affected by the introduction stage of a computer project. How can these two objectives be achieved? An important power resource lies in the establishment of the **legitimacy** of change and subsequent operation. Establishing legitimacy is tied in with politics as the management of meaning.[32] This involves developing amongst employees shared norms and internalised values and beliefs that elicit their co-operation and commitment in system introduction and operation. Given the vulnerability of computer systems to low-level participant activity, it is not surprising to find hi-tech companies like Rank Xerox, IBM and Wang developing cultures based on high rewards, attractive personnel policies, encouragement of initiative and pleasant work conditions.In some hi-tech companies, computer technology for home-working and tele-working develops further this marriage between enhanced business performance through cost reductions, labour flexibility and 'putting people first' personnel policies. Examples in the UK include F International (a leading software house), IBM UK, Rank Xerox International and the American computer manufacturer Digital Equipment Company.[33] The development not just of power bases but also of an organisational culture that will support and sustain technological change lies at the heart of a political–cultural contingencies approach to introducing computer systems into organisations.

Change Agents

An argument can be made that systems specialists should not be involved in applying techniques like OD or user participation where political problems are likely to result; they lack the political skills needed to handle these.[34] A counter argument (discussed above) is that such skills are an important part of a computer professional's job if a computer application is to be successful. Additionally, the systems designer's intervention into an organisation is necessarily a political one for reasons already advanced. But further, political problems will inevitably develop, given the trepidation and ambivalence generated by the computer professionals' specialist culture, the trade language and the mystery of an expertise—needed but inaccessible to many organisational members.

In fact, it is a mistake to assume that systems designers have not had enough power in the past. The problem has more often been too much power applied in ways that distorted and harmed the very implementation they were promoting.

The culture of expertise and the identification of computer technology with 'improvement' and 'progress' are in fact hard to argue against, as Scarbrough and Moran[35] found with trade union acceptance of CNC systems robots and electronic supervision technologies into British Leyland's car plant. In fact, as discussed in chapter 7, trade unions are as much wedded as managements to the notion of new technology as 'an inherently progressive force in society.'[35]

Systems designers may well exploit this mystique of technology; managers will accept their legitimate claims and hand over responsibility for computerisation to computer specialists; the latter can then make policy decisions in management's absence almost without being aware of doing so. In chronicling such a development in one computer project, Hedley[36] found that:

> 'There was therefore the danger of long-term decisions being made in terms of their appropriateness to system design rather than in relation to more fundamental criteria. Thus real control tended to shift to systems designers.'

The difficult problem is for system designers to come to accept how dangerous such a narrow 'political' approach can be for the successful implementation of computer projects. What matters here is their understanding of, and acceptance of responsibility for, implementation 'success'. Our argument throughout is that, in neglecting human factors, traditional systems practice has too often not produced such success. At implementation, what becomes a crucial determinant of system success becomes system compatibility with, and its use and acceptance by, the emergent political and cultural structure. Computer professionals need to develop wider political skills and sensitivity to promote this outcome.

The Power Audit

A first step is analysing the existing political and cultural system of the organisation. This means establishing membership of the dominant coalition and the sources of their influence. It also requires close analysis of lower-level participants, their power bases and the manner in which they, as well as the dominant coalition, are likely to support or resist any level of computerisation, and how crucial such responses might be to system development and implementation.

A second step is establishing the likely power bases of the change agents in the context of the existing political and cultural systems; also, how these power bases can be modified in the course of computerisation.

The third step is to establish a range of possible computer options and their differing effects on the existing distribution of power. More radical shifts in power distribution will require different strategies and alliances, and a much more careful political approach.

The fourth step requires an assessment of the political and cultural problems likely to be engendered in the course of developing and implementing each of the computer options identified. A preliminary assessment of the political feasibility of each proposed system can then be made.

The fifth step is to develop strategies and tactics to support the more likely systems and make an assessment of how successful differing combinations of systems, tactics and strategies are likely to be.

The power audit assists the change agents in understanding the existing power structure and culture, who is influential, who will resist different types of system, who will be affected in what ways by different proposals, and how different change strategies will be affected when different individuals and groups mobilise their power. It will end with an understanding of the political complexity of computerisation but also a clearer idea of the political feasibility of different types of system, design methodology and change approaches.

Mobilising/Gaining Power

An overview of the influence management process is suggested by Mayes and Allen[37] and is outlined here. Political goals need to be formulated, and an ends–means analysis carried out (i.e. *what* do we wish to achieve, and *how* do we go about achieving it?). Targets to be influenced are then identified, and incentives desired by the targets determined. Implementation involves mobilising these incentives and monitoring the results.

The management of politics and culture must continue throughout the computerisation project. In organisational settings, a political approach is rarely just a matter of accumulating enough power at the beginning of a project to do what you like thereafter.

Various approaches to influencing the process of computerisation are possible. Keen[21] suggest that the Information function be headed by a senior-level fixer with resources and authority to negotiate with those affected by any new system. A steering committee including senior-level managers will become actively involved in highly political aspects of the computer project. Under this umbrella, systems staff can establish credibility and influence events tactically:

— Make sure you have a contract for change.
— Seek out resistance and treat it as a signal to be responded to.
— Rely on face-to-face contracts.
— Become an insider and work hard to build personal credibility.
— Co-opt users early.[21]

Other tactics might include presenting a non-threatening image, aligning with powerful others, developing liaisons, developing stature and credibility by attending to a client's immediate needs before gaining approval for a less well understood project, and diffusing opposition by open discussion and bringing out conflicts.[38] In research on internal consultancy by systems analysts, programmers and operations researchers, Pettigrew[39] found at least five power resources that can be mobilised. A crucial one is expertise. The change agent can increase client dependence by heightening uncertainties to which the application of their expertise would be a remedy. Internal consultant activities across departmental boundaries also gives privileged access to, and so control over, organisational information. Political sensitivity and establishing relations with those with power is also important, as is the gaining of 'assessed stature' by identifying and serving the interests of relevant others. Group support by departmental colleagues and related consultant groups is a further power source that needs to be developed.

Implementation Problems

There are three problem areas in implementation to which the political–cultural contingencies approach needs to be specifically addressed. One is resistance to change, another is the danger of the change process running out of control, and the third, and related, problem is how to maintain influence over the political dynamics of change. We need to reiterate that computerisation must be seen in the context of wider objectives than the limited goal of gaining acceptance for a specific system. This implies that system modifications may be necessary in the face of politico-cultural problems. But, anyway, implementation should serve as an important period for learning about system design imperfections at the technical level as well.

Techniques for reducing resistance to change have been suggested throughout this book. To these can be added the need to make visible any organisational dissatisfaction with *present* systems, addressing people's attention to the consequences of *not* computerising, building in rewards and reasons for people to support the transition and the future system, developing an appropriate degree, level, and type of participation for different affected parties, and giving people the opportunity and time to disengage from the present state.

Additionally, temporary structures need to be set up to maintain control over the project in the transition period. Keen's recommendations above are relevant here. Also, adequate planning and resources are needed to see the transition through. Beckhard and Harris[40] suggest the need also to develop and communicate clear images of the future to organisational members, and this may indeed reduce uncertainty and resistance while promoting change in relevant directions. Nadler and Tichy[41] also suggests the need for establishing multiple and consistent leverage points, aimed not just at individuals but also at social relations, task and structural changes. It is also important to build in feedback mechanisms to monitor developments as early as possible.

Keeping power on the side of the computerisation project and handling the power dynamics of change is crucial. Here one needs to ensure that leaders and key groups maintain active support for change, that a culture and climate of success is created, but also that enough stability remains, and the pace of change is judged, so that the changes remain acceptable to involved parties.

The selection and implementation of a strategic approach is also a crucial aspect.

Strategic Approach

'Contingency' implies retaining a flexible approach to computerisation and building in opportunities to modify design where it is seen to be deficient. A contingency approach also means adopting a **change**

strategy appropriate to the organisational circumstances in which those responsible for implementation find themselves. Such a strategy involves intervening in the technical, political and cultural systems of the organisation at one and the same time.[42]

Change strategies range from being **closed** to **open** (see Fig. 8.4). Closed strategies are marked by a minimum of communications and consultation, negligible participation in design and implementation by the vast majority of interested parties, and the development of systems by computer specialists to achieve managerial objectives which tend to be control- and finance-focussed. Closed strategies are linked closely with the introduction of centralised computer systems.

Closed strategies are often linked with confrontational industrial relations at implementation, though this is not a necessary relationship, and depends on the power realities pertaining. Often these mean that little confrontation is necessary and the system is introduced unilaterally by systems professionals and management. This may be a sensible approach where the system is technically sound, and designed to minimise dependence on user skills and co-operation, or where organisational culture supports authoritarian management styles.

An example of a closed 'confrontation' strategy is the development and highly publicised implementation of the computerised photocomposition and print systems by News International at their Wapping site in 1985–86, discussed in chapter 7. A feature of confrontation strategies is the need to secure co-operation of at least part of the workforce. At Wapping it was the journalists. The following account gives some of the flavour of closed systems implementation:

> 'For most it was the first time they had been in the heavily fortified compound ... the first journalists to reach the new newsroom were astounded. The entire floor had been laid out as an electronic newsroom with everything in place. A desk was ready for all of them with an ATEX terminal on each. Phones were in place, the switchboard had just been installed, and all around them were genial men and women, many of them American or Australian, who welcomed them to their new workplace and asked to call on them for any help they would need. The day which for all of them would normally be a day off was designated as a time to familiarise themselves with the new technology ... everywhere were new faces, many of them women, who knew how the system worked and keen to make it work in practice.'[43]

More open strategies stress participative design, communications, consultation, and willingness to modify technical systems, job design and

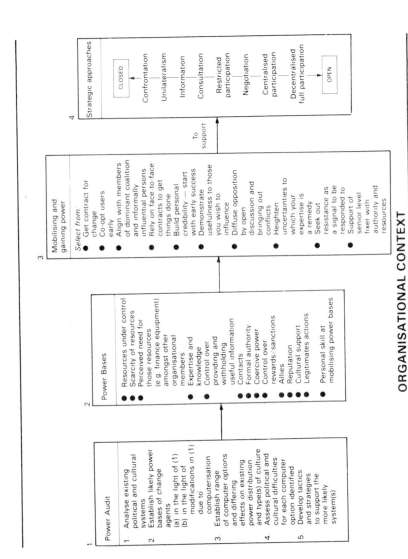

Fig. 8.4 *Power and culture in systems implementation*

ORGANISATIONAL CONTEXT

work organisation in the face of user feedback. Open strategies tend to be associated with negotiated change by agreement and consultative machinery in the formal industrial relations sphere. Some strategies are more 'open' than others. Prototyping and evolutionary systems development tend to be closely linked to open change strategies. Different types of participative approach are discussed in chapter 4. Wainwright and Francis[44] cite the example of a college of further education where an office system was successfully computerised using a decentralised, user-participative design approach. Socio-technical approaches tend to be less 'open' than this and often fall into the 'restricted participation' category in Figure 8.4.

An example of a variant on the participative approach is the successful introduction of new technology into the Norwegian Social Security system. Beginning in May 1984, the technical and training aspects were planned and designed centrally, local supervisors became responsible for new technology training and local users had considerable influence over designing their own work. In fact, new technology was seen as an OD vehicle to improve administrative and organisational competence of insurance offices, decrease specialisation, build up local autonomy, and improve working life and productivity through job reorganisation. All this implied high levels of participation at local levels to facilitate user influence, learning and commitment.

Clearly, one best change strategy for all circumstances cannot be advocated. Open strategies are more relevant where there is underlying support for the aims of computerisation, where there is a large number of affected parties, where there are differing views on how computerisation can be achieved, where power to resist introduction is widely distributed, and where user involvement will provide vital information for system development. Closed strategies will tend to be preferred where the benefits of participation are low, where there is widespread agreement and support for computerisation, where the promoters of the system are all powerful, or where the level of disagreement and hostility about the system is so high that participation is perceived to serve little purpose.

CONCLUSIONS

Where dependent on traditional systems design methodologies, systems project management has been technically oriented, with human issues perceived as mainly arising at the implementation stage. Furthermore, implementation itself has often been viewed as a discrete 'one-off', late event in a systems project. The failure to consider many human issues as significant until late in the project means that when they emerge there is often a reluctance amongst implementors to adapt, let alone abandon, the computer-based system in which so much time, money and labour has already been invested. People-management as an essential and primary implementation task can then become a self-fulfilling prophecy with a vengeance, with human issues and problems, and lack of user acceptance, persisting throughout the system's subsequent use.

A strong case can be made for changing the traditional role of the systems analyst, for systems professionals developing 'people' skills, and for the use of more 'people-centred' methodologies. Within their limitations, organisation development, socio-technical systems and participative approaches can assist in gaining acceptance for new technology.

A key task is to manage the people side of a computer project from its beginning. Particularly crucial is the management of the politics of computerisation. From a systems project management viewpoint, this means ensuring that the system becomes politically acceptable enough to be used effectively, and that a culture exists to sustain its continued use.

References and Guide to Further Reading

The guide to further reading for each chapter provides a highly selective introduction to sources that develop further, or in different ways, the main issues in the text.

CHAPTER 1. Systems design, people and politics—an overview
References

1. Advertisement in 'The city revolution', supplement to *Financial Times* 27 Oct. 1986, 12.
2. J. R. Oppenheimer on designing the hydrogen bomb.
3. Dr. Kenneth Wong speaking at the FT conference on electronic financial services—reported in the *Financial Times*, Oct. 1986.
4. Quoted in *Financial Times*, 12 Aug. 1986.
5. Eosys. *Top executives and information technology: disappointed expectations.* Eosys Consultants, 1986.
6. Checkland P. *Systems thinking, systems practice.* Wiley, 1981.
7. Taylor R. *The fifth estate.* Routledge & Kegan Paul, 1978.
8. Cyert R. and March J. *A behavioral theory of the firm.* Prentice-Hall, 1963.
9. Willcocks L. and Mason D. Computerising: lessons from the DHSS pensions strike. *Employee Relations*, 1987, **9**, No. 1.
10. Child J. Managerial strategies, new technology and the labour process. In *Job redesign* (eds Knight D., Willmott H. and Collinson D.). Gower, 1985.
11. See, for example, Porter M. and Millar V.—How information gives you competitive advantage. *Harvard Business Review*, 1985, **63**, No. 4 and Cash J. and Konsynski B.—IS redraws competitive boundaries. *Harvard Business Review*, 1985, **63**, No. 2.
12. See, for example, Buchanan D. and Boddy D. *Organisations in the Computer Age.* Gower, 1983.
13. Based on Dawson S. *Analysing organisations.* Macmillan, 1986—and Giddens A. *The Constitution of society.* Polity Press, 1984,
14. Bachrach P. and Baratz M. Two faces of power. *American Political Science Review*, 1962, **56**.
15. Schattschneider E. *The sovereign people.* Holt, Rhinehard and Winston, 1960.
16. Hickson D., Hinings C., Lee C., Schneck R. and Pennings J. A strategic contingencies theory of intra-organisational power. *Administrative Science Quarterly*, 1971, **16**.

17. Fischer P., Stratmann W., Lundsgaarde H. and Steele D. User reaction to PROMIS (presented at 4th symp. Computer Applications in Medical Care, Washington DC, 1980). *Computer Applications in Medical Care*, 1980, **3**, 1722–1730.

18. Child J. New technology and the service class. In *The changing experience of employment* (eds Purcell K., Wood S., Waton A. and Allen S.). Macmillan, 1986.

19. Reported in the *Daily Telegraph* and *The Times*, 29 May 1980.

20. Quoted in the *Observer*, 19 Oct. 1986.

Further Reading

General Introductions
Forester T. (ed.). *The information technology revolution*. Basil Blackwell, 1985. A very comprehensive guide; see especially parts 2 and 3.
Gill C. *Work, unemployment and the new technology*. Polity Press, 1985. Well written; includes many illustrative cases.

Introductions to Systems Analysis and Design Approaches
Dickson G. and Wetherbe J. *The management of information systems*. McGraw Hill, 1985.
Mason D. and Willcocks L. *Intermediate systems analysis*. Paradigm, 1987. Details standard system design practices.
Open University. *Technology: a third level course—Complexity, management and change: applying a systems approach* (T301 Block 4). Open University Press, 1983. Good descriptions of different systems perspectives.

Further Critiques of Technological Determinism
Jones B. *Sleepers wake! Technology and the future of work*. Wheatsheaf, 1982.
Ottoway R. (ed.). *Humanising the workplace*. Croom Helm, 1977. See particularly chapters 2, 3 and 4.

Managerial Objectives and Computer Technology
Buchanan D. Using the new technology: management objectives and organisational choices. *European Management Journal*, 1982, winter.
Child J. Managerial strategies, new technology and the labour process. In *Job redesign* (eds Knight D., Willmott H. and Collinson D.). Gower, 1985.
Piercy N. (ed.). *The management implications of new information technology*. UWIST/Croom Helm, 1984. Particularly parts 2 and 4.

Politics in Organisations
Dawson S. *Analysing organisations*. Macmillan, 1986. Especially chapters 2 and 7.
Lee R. and Lawrence P. *Organisational behaviour: politics at work*. Hutchinson, 1985.
Wilkinson B. *The shopfloor politics of new technology*. Heinemann, 1983.

CHAPTER 2. RESISTANCE TO CHANGE

References

1. Keen P. In *Visual display terminals* (eds Bennett J., Case D., Sandelin J. and Smith M.) Prentice Hall, 1984.
2. Lewin K. Reported in Sofer C. *Organisations in theory and practice.* Heinemann Educational, 1972.
3. Speaker at American Federation of Information Processing Societies, San Francisco, April 1982.
4. Fox A. *Man mismanagement*, 2nd ed. Hutchinson, 1985.
5. Markus M. Power, politics and MIS implementation. *Communications of the ACM*, 1983, **26**, No. 6, 438–441.
6. Dutton W. and Kraemer K. The automation of bias. In *High technology in American local governments* (eds Danziger J. and Dutton W.). Columbia University Press, 1982.
7. Rout L. Computer choler: many managers resist. *Wall Street Journal*, 1982, 4 June.
8. Paul L. Research on cyberphiliacs and cyberphobiacs reveals 30% of workers fear computers. *Computerworld*, 1982, 5 Apr.
9. Coli S. New category of phobics fear computers. *Akron Beacon Journal*, 1986, 6 Jan.
10. Howard G. and Smith R. Computer anxiety in management: myth or reality? *Communications of the ACM*, 1986, **29**, No. 7.
11. Thompson L. *New office technology—people, work structure and the process of change.* Work Research Unit, 1985, WRU occasional paper.
12. Galitz W. *Human factors in office automation.* LOMA, 1980.
13. Pettigrew A. Information control as a power resource. *Sociology*, 1972, **6**, May.
14. Keen P. Information systems and organisational change. *Communications of the ACM* 1981, **24**, No. 1.
15. Kanter R. *The change masters—corporate entrepreneurs at work.* Unwin, 1985. Quote from *Financial Times*, 1985, 29 May.
16. Strauss G. and Rosenstein E. Workers' participation: a critical view. *Industrial Relations*, 1970, Feb.
17. Robbins S. *Managing organizational conflict: a non-traditional approach.* Prentice Hall, 1974. (Also *Organization theory.* Prentice Hall, 1983.)
18. Littler C. and Salaman G. *Class at work.* Batsford Academic, 1984.
19. Swords-Isherwood W. and Senker P. Management resistance to the new technology. In *The microelectronics revolution* (ed. Forester T.) Blackwell, 1980.
20. Shaiken H. *Computer technology and the relations of power in the workplace.* International Institute for Comparative Social Research, Berlin, 1980.
21. Northcott J., Fogarty M. and Trevor M. *Chips and jobs: acceptance of new technology at work.* Policy Studies Institute, 1985, No. 648.
22. Cas E. and Zimmer F. (eds) *Man and work in society.* Van Nostrand Reinhold, 1975.

23. Asch J. *Social psychology*. Prentice Hall, 1952.
24. Sherif M. *Group conflict and cooperation*. Routledge & Kegan Paul, 1966.
25. Milgram S. *Obedience to authority: an experimental view*. Harper and Row, 1974.
26. Sayles L. *The behaviour of industrial work groups*. John Wiley and Sons, 1958.
27. Martin R. New technology increases management's right to manage. In *Microprocessors, manpower and Society* (ed. Warner M.). Gower, 1983.
28. Based on Willcocks L. *The dispute at Times Newspapers Ltd: a study of the issues of organisation, resistance and control in an industrial relations context*. MA thesis, 1981—also Willocks L. *Corporate strategy and Fleet Street industrial relations—the case of Times Newspapers*. Cranfield, 1985.
29. Crozier M. In *New office technology: human and organisational aspects* (eds Otway H. and Peltu M.). Frances Pinter, 1983.
30. Child J. and Tarbuck M. The introduction of new technologies: managerial initiative and union response in British banks. *Industrial Relations Journal*, 1985, Autumn.
31. Dickson G. *et al* Behavioral reactions to the introduction of a management information system into the US Post Office. In *Computers and management* (eds Sanders D.). McGraw Hill, 1974.
32. Rothwell S. Supervisors and new technology. *Employment Gazette*, 1984, Jan.
33. Dickson G. and Simmons J. The behavioural side of MIS. *Business Horizons*, 1970, **14**, No. 4.
34. See Purcell J. *Good industrial relations: theory and practice*. Macmillan, 1981—and Marchington M. *Managing industrial relations*. McGraw-Hill, 1981.
35. Handy C. *Understanding organisations*, 3rd ed. Penguin, 1985.
36. Burns T. and Stalker G. *The management of innovation*. Tavistock, 1961.
37. Randolph W. Matching technology and the design of organisational units. *California Management Review*, 1981, **23**, Summer.
38. Peters T. and Waterman R. *In search of excellence*. Harper and Row, 1982.
39. Child J. *Organisation—a guide to problems and practice*. Harper and Row, 1985.
40. Crozier M. *The bureaucratic phenomenon*. University of Chicago Press, 1964.
41. Hage J. and Aiken M. *Social change in complex organisations*. Random House, 1970.
42. Bonoma T. and Zaltman G. *Psychology for management*. Kent Publishing, 1981.
43. Tynan O. Change and the nature of work. *Robotica*, 1985, **3**, 173–180.
44. Handy C. *The future of work*. Blackwell, 1984.
45. Judkins P., West D. and Drew J. *Networking in organisations: The Rank Xerox experiment*. Gower, 1985.
46. Connor H. and Pearson R. *Information technology manpower: into the 1990's*. IMS, 1986, report 117.
47. Bardach E. *The implementation game: What happens after a Bill becomes law*. MIT Press, 1977.

Further Reading

Different Perspectives on Technological Change
Markus M. Power, politics and MIS implementation. *Communications of the ACM*, 1983, **26**, No. 6. Pinpoints several different viewpoints on computerisation and resistance; contains an excellent case study.
Pacey A. *The culture of technology*. Basil Blackwell, 1983. Argues against the values of technocratic consciousness and the 'culture of expertise'.

Computerphobia, Individuals, Groups and Resistance
Dickson G. *et al.* Behavioural reactions to the introduction of a management information system into the US Post Office. In *Computers and management* (ed. Sanders D.). McGraw Hill, 1974. An early and well researched study on resistance to computer technology.
Fearstein P. Fighting computer anxiety. *Personnel*, 1986, **63**, No. 1.
Howard G. and Smith R. Computer anxiety in management: myth or reality? *Communications of the ACM*, 1986, **29**, No. 7.
Keen P. Information systems and organisational change. *Communications of the ACM*, 1981, **24**, No. 1.
Mainiero L. and De Michiell R. Minimizing employee resistance to change. *Personnel*, 1986, **63**, No. 7.
Swords-Isherwood W. and Senker P. Management resistance to the new technology. In *The microelectronics revolution* (ed. Forester T.). Blackwell, 1980.
Thompson L. New office technology—people, work structure and the process of change. Work Research Unit, 1985, WRU occasional paper. Finds a range of factors that explain individual resistance; based on case studies; includes a list of recommendations about how to minimise resistance.

Organisations, Change and Culture
Child J. *Organisation—a guide to problems and practice*. Harper and Row, 1985.
Deal T. and Kennedy A. *Corporate cultures: the rites and rituals of corporate life*. Addison-Wesley, 1982, Strong on different cultures and their purposes.
Gustavsen B. and Hethy L. New forms of work organisation: a European overview. *Labour and Society*, 1986, **11**, No. 2.
Handy C. *Understanding organisations*, 3rd ed. Penguin, 1985.
Maccoby M. Using new technology. *Quality of Work Life*, 1985, **2**, Nos 3 and 4.
Walton R. and Vittori W. Information technology: organizational problem or opportunity? *Office: Technology and People*, 1983, No. 1.

The Environment of Technological Change
(*See the next section for sources on the British record for technology training.*)
Carnoy M. High technology and international labour markets. *International Labour Review*, 1985, **124**, No. 6.
Fogarty M. with Brooks D. *Trade unions and British industrial development*. Policy Studies Institute, 1986.

Handy C. *The future of work*. Basil Blackwell, 1984. See especially chapters 5 and 6. Argues strongly that British education and training need to change drastically to harness the new technologies and create a new world of work; offers a 'new agenda' and discusses the social choices available.

CHAPTER 3. HUMAN RESOURCE PLANNING FOR IT

References
1. Rothwell S. Integrating the elements of a company employment policy. *Personnel Management*, 1984, Nov.
2. Connor H. and Pearson R. IT manpower into the 1990's. *Employment Gazette*, 1986, Nov.
3. Rothwell S. Company employment policies and new technology. *Industrial Relations Journal*, 1985, Autumn.
4. Daniel W. *Workplace industrial relations and technical change*. Policy Studies Institute/Frances Pinter, 1987.
5. See, for example, Watson T. *The personnel managers*. Routledge & Kegan Paul, 1977—also Legge K. *Power, innovation and problem-solving in personnel management*. McGraw Hill, 1978—Cowans C. Personnel management in the 1980's. *Personnel Management*, 1980, Jan. and Manning K. The rise and fall of Personnel. *Management Today*, 1983, Mar.
6. See particularly Millward N. and Stevens M. *British workplace industrial relations 1980–84*. Gower, 1986.
7. Open University in Wales. *The application of new technology in the engineering industry in South Wales*. OU, 1986.
8. Clegg C. and Kemp N. Information technology—Personnel, where are you? *Personnel Review*, 1986, **15**, No. 1.
9. Evans A. and Wilkinson T. (eds). *How to introduce new technology*, especially chapters 2 and 3. Institute of Personnel Management, 1983.
10. Hendry C. and Pettigrew A. The practice of strategic human resource management. *Personnel Review*, 1986, **15**, No. 5.
11. Hall L. and Torrington D. 'Why not use the computer?' The use and lack of use of computers in Personnel. *Personnel Review*, 1986, **15**, No. 1.
12. Legge K. *Power, innovation and problem-solving in personnel management*. McGraw Hill, 1978.
13. Hepburn R. and Handy H. Switching on the City. *Management Today*, 1985, May.
14. McLoughlin I., Rose H. and Clark J. Managing the introduction of new technology. *Omega*, 1985, **13**, No. 4.
15. Rothwell S. and Davidson D. *Technological change, company personnel policies and skill deployment*. Manpower Services Commission, 1984.
16. Miller G. In 'Work', supplement to *Financial Times*, 1986, July 24.
17. See Knight K., Algie J., Dale A. and Fonda N. *Management of technology*. Part 1—Identifying management development needs; and Part 2 unit 8—Planning management development for information technology. Manpower Services Commission, 1986.
18. Butler Cox Consultancy. *Information technology: Value for money*. Butler Cox, 1986.

19. Eosys Consultants. *Top executives and information technology: disappointed expectations.* Eosys, 1986.
20. Knight K., Algie J., Dale A. and Fonda N. *Management of technology.* Part 1—Identifying management development needs. Manpower Services Commission, 1986.
21. Strassman P. *Information payoff: the transformation of work in the electronic age.* Free Press, 1985, p. 91.
22. Cross M. and Mitchell P. *Packaging efficiency—the training contribution.* Technical Change Centre, 1986.
23. Coopers and Lybrand. *A challenge to complacency.* For Manpower Services Commission and NEDO, 1986.
24. Rajan A. The technology training lag. *Management Today*, 1986, Sept.
25. Shepherd R. quoted in supplement to *Financial Times*, 1986, 24 July.
26. Atkinson J. The changing corporation. In *New patterns of work* (ed. D. Clutterbuck). Gower, 1985.
27. Zimmerman J. *Once upon the future.* Pandora, 1986.
28. Cockburn C. *Machinery of dominance.* Pluto, 1985.
29. Cockburn C. *Brothers—male dominance and technological change.* Pluto, 1983.
30. Huws U. *Your job in the eighties.* Pluto, 1982.
31. Werneke D. *Microelectronics and office jobs—the impact of the chip on women's employment.* International Labour Office, 1983.
32. Braun E. and Senker P. *New technology and employment.* Manpower Services Commission, 1982, July.
33. Webster J. Word processing and the secretarial labour process. In *The changing experience of employment* (ed. Purcell K. *et al*). Macmillan, 1986.
34. National Economic Development Office IT EDC and electronics EDC—*the impact of advanced information systems.* NEDO, 1983.
35. Earl M. Emerging trends in managing new information technologies. In *The management implications of new information technology* (ed. Piercy N.). Croom Helm, 1984.

Further Reading

At the time of writing there is still no one personnel management or systems analysis and design textbook that even begins to cover this subject area adequately.

Overviews

Daniel W. Four years of change for Personnel. *Personnel Management*, 1986, Dec. Summarises findings from the 1984 DE/ESRC/PSI/ACAS workplace industrial relations survey.

Evans A. and Wilkinson T. (eds.) *How to introduce new technology.* Institute of Personnel Management, 1983. Formulates guidelines from a personnel practitioner viewpoint; based on well researched case studies.

Gallagher M. *Computers and personnel management.* Heinemann, 1986. A refreshing attempt to inform personnel managers on computer systems, and indicate the potential for computers in personnel work.

The Role of Personnel

Clegg C. and Kemp N. Information technology—Personnel, where are you? *Personnel Review*, 1986, **15**, No. 1.

Legge K. *Power, innovation and problem-solving in personnel management.* McGraw Hill, 1978. A widely quoted and thought-provoking book.

Rothwell S. and Davidson D. *Technological change, company personnel policies and skill deployment.* Manpower Services Commission, 1984.

Watson T. *Management, organisation and employment strategy.* Routledge & Kegan Paul, 1986. Particularly the later chapters on employment strategy and the personnel role.

Computers in Personnel

Computers in Personnel have received considerable attention in the published literature. See, for example, the following.

Evans A. *Computerizing personnel systems—a basic guide.* Institute of Personnel Management, 1986. Written for the non-expert.

Page T. (ed.) Computers in Personnel—from potential to performance. Institute of Personnel Management and IMS, 1986. Contains the papers from the fifth national conference on computers in personnel; all conference papers have so far been published, and there are some very informative papers every year.

Individual Personnel Policies for New Technology

The following represent only a small sample of writings on individual personnel policies for new technology. There is no book that deals adequately with selection of staff or redundancy in relationship to computer technology.

Management development: Knight K., Algie J., Dale A. and Fonda N. *Management of technology—parts 1 and 2.* Manpower Services Commission, 1986.

Training: Cross M. and Mitchell P. *Packaging efficiency—the training contribution.* Technical Change Centre, 1986.

Rajan A. The technology training lag. *Management Today*, 1986, Sept.

Equal Opportunities: The Equal Opportunities Commission continually publishes up-to-date information on the subject. See also the following.

The Cabinet Office. *Be fair: an equal opportunities resource manual.* Institute of Personnel Management, in association with BACIE, 1987.

Stamp P. and Robarts S. *Positive action: changing the workplace for women.* National Council for Civil Liberties, 1986.

Developing Commitment: Walton R. and Susman B. People policies for the new machines. *Harvard Business Review*, 1987, Mar.–Apr. Surveys 24 US plants operating advanced manufacturing technology; finds some empirical evidence for the spread of new personnel policies that support the development of highly skilled, flexible, co-ordinated and committed workforces.

CHAPTER 4. DESIGN AND THE SYSTEMS ANALYST

References

1. Adapted from DeMarco T. *Structured systems specification.* Yourdon, 1979.
2. Hickson D., Hinings C., Lee C. *et al.* A strategic contingencies theory of interorganisational power. *Administrative Science Quarterly,* 1971, **16.**
3. Markus M. L. *Systems in organisations.* Pitman, 1984.
4. Keen P. and Bronsema G. *Cognitive style research: a perspective for integration.* Massachusetts Institute of Technology, Centre for Information Systems Research, 1981, working paper 82.
5. Checkland P. Systems theory and information systems. In *Beyond productivity: information systems development for organisational effectiveness* (ed. Bemelmans Th. M.). International Federation for Information Processing/North Holland, 1984.
6. See, for example, Jackson M. The nature of 'soft' systems thinking; the work of Churchman, Ackoff and Checkland. *Journal of Applied Systems Analysis,* 1982, **9**—also Mingers J. Subjectivism and soft systems methodology: a critique. *Journal of Applied Systems Analysis,* 1984, **11.**
7. Rosenhead J. Debating systems methodology: conflicting ideas about conflicts and ideas. *Journal of Applied Systems Analysis,* 1984, **11.**
8. Naughton J. *The Checkland methodology: a reader's guide,* 2nd ed. OU Systems Group, 1977.
9. Land F. Notes on participation. *Computer Journal,* 1982, **25,** No.2.
10. Mumford E. *Designing human systems.* Manchester Business School, 1983, pp. 24–30.
11. Wainwright J. and Francis A. *Office automation, organisation and the nature of work.* Gower, 1984.
12. Mumford E. and Weir M. *Computer systems in work design.* ABP, 1979. There are many variations on this methodology; e.g. those of Pava for both routine and non-routine office work. See Pava C. *Managing new office technology.* The Free Press, 1983.
13. Taylor J. Designing a computer-based personnel information system. *Personnel Management,* 1983, July.
14. Eason K. Managing technological change. In *Organisations: cases, issues, concepts* (ed. Paton R. *et al.*). Harper and Row, 1984.
15. Eason K. Tools for participation—how managers and users can influence design. *Participation in systems design: proceedings of conference held at London Business School, 7–8 April 1987* (ed. Land F.). (To be published.)
16. Antill L. and Wood-Harper A. *Systems analysis.* Heinemann, 1985, p. 108.
17. See Wood-Harper A., Antill L. and Avison D. *Information systems definition: the Multiview approach.* Blackwell Scientific, 1985.
18. See *Graffiti—the Utopia project: an alternative in text and images.* Swedish Centre for Working Life, The Royal Institute of Technology, Sweden, 1985.

Further Reading

Cross-Section of Views
Land F. (ed.). *Participation in systems design*: *procedures of conference held at London Business School, 7–8 April 1987*. (To be published.)

Critiques of Hard Systems Perspectives
Bjorn-Andersen N. (ed.). *The human side of information processing*. IAG North Holland, 1980.
Land F. (ed.) (as above).
Lucas H. C. *et al* (eds). *The information systems environment*. International Federation for Information Processing/North Holland.
Markus M. L. *Systems in organisations*. Pitman, 1984. A critical, sometimes caustic, look at the sins and omissions of traditional design approaches; an alternative is proposed.

Soft Systems and the Checkland Methodology
Checkland P. Techniques in 'soft' systems practice: part 1—Systems diagrams—some tentative guidelines; Part 2—Building conceptual models. *Journal of Applied Systems Analysis*, 1979, **6**.
Naughton J. Soft systems analysis: an introductory guide. *Technology—a third level course: Complexity, management and change—applying a systems approach*. The Open University Press, 1983, T301 Block 4. The clearest introductory guide available.
Wood-Harper A., Antill L. and Avison D. *Information systems definition*: *the Multiview approach*. Blackwell Scientific, 1985. Applies Checkland's approach to the development of computer-based information systems.

Detailed Critiques of Checkland
Detailed critiques of Checkland form part of a lively debate in the journal founded by him. Try the following.
Burrell G. Systems thinking, systems practice: a review. *Journal of Applied Systems Analysis*, 1983, **10**.
Jackson M. The nature of 'soft' systems thinking: the work of Churchman, Ackoff and Checkland. *Journal of Applied Systems Analysis*, 1982, **9**.
Jackson M. The nature of 'soft' systems thinking: comment on the three replies. *Journal of Applied Systems Analysis*, 1983, **10**.
Mingers J. Subjectivism and soft systems methodology: a critique. *Journal of Applied Systems Analysis*, 1984, **11**.

Proponents of Participative Systems Design
Hirschheim R. *Office automation*: *a social and organisational perspective*. John Wiley and Son, 1985.
Land F. and Hirschheim R. Participative systems design: rationale, tools and techniques. *Journal of Applied Systems Analysis*, 1983, **10**.
Mumford E. *Designing human systems*. Manchester Business School, 1983.

Technical Developments in Fourth-Generation Languages
Technical developments in fourth-generation languages (4GL) and prototyping are transforming the importance of, and the grounds of the debate on, participative systems design in the late 1980s. The following discuss these developments.

Alavi M. An assessment of the prototyping approach to systems development. *Communications of the ACM*, 1984, **27**, No. 6.

Eason K. *Information technology and organisational change.* Taylor and Francis, 1987.

Grindley K. *The Grindley report—4GLs: a study of best practice.* Institute of Data Processing Management, 1986.

Janson M. Applying a pilot system and prototyping approach to systems development and implementation. *Information and Management*, 1986, **10**, 209–216.

Law D. *Prototyping: a state of the art report.* National Computing Centre, Manchester, 1985.

Multiview
The most complete statement of Multiview is to be found in the following.

Wood-Harper A., Antill L. and Avison D. *Information systems definition: the Multiview approach.* Blackwell Scientific, 1986.

CHAPTER 5. WORKING WITH COMPUTERS—I. DESIGNING JOBS AND WORK ORGANISATION

References

1. Comment by a worker reported in Nichols T. and Beynon H. *Living with capitalism.* Routledge & Kegan Paul, 1977.
2. A manager quoted in Braverman H. *Labor and monopoly capital.* Monthly Review Press, 1974.
3. Davis L. The design of jobs. *Industrial Relations.* 1966, **6**.
4. Taylor J. In *Design of jobs* (eds Davis L. and Taylor J.). Goodyear, 1978.
5. Cooley M. *Architect or bee? The human price of technology.* Hogarth Press, 1987.
6. Case study discussed in Batstone E. and Gourlay S. *Unions, unemployment and innovation.* Basil Blackwell, 1986.
7. Wilkinson B. Managing with new technology. *Management Today*, 1982, Oct.
8. Wilkinson B. *The shopfloor politics of new technology.* Heinemann, 1983.
9. Rose M. and Jones B. Managerial strategy and trade union responses in work reorganisation schemes at establishment level. In *Job redesign* (eds Knights D., Willmot H. and Collinson D.) Gower, 1985.
10. Hackman J. Work design. In *Improving life at work* (eds. Hackman J. and Suttle J.). Foresman, 1977.
11. Discussed in Buchanan D. *The development of job design theories and techniques.* Saxon House, 1979. In fact, Hackman also sees social interac-

tion, recognition and feedback as key job characteristics, in Hackman J. and Oldham G. *Work redesign.* Addison-Wesley, 1980

12. A Work Research Unit study discussed by Association of Professional, Executive, Clerical & Computer Staff— *Job design and new technology.* APEX, 1985.

13. Batstone E. and Gourlay S. *Unions, unemployment and innovation.* Basil Blackwell, 1986.

14. Buchanan D. and Boddy D. *Organisations in the computer age.* Gower, 1983.

15. Buchanan D. and Boddy D. New technology with a human face. *Personnel Management,* 1985, Apr.

16. Hackman J. and Oldham G. *Work redesign.* Addison-Wesley, 1980.

17. Mumford E. *Working on quality of working life.* The Hague Nijhoff, 1979.

18. Needham P. The myth of the self-regulating work-group. *Personnel Management,* 1982, Aug.

19. For various opinions see Jonsson B. Corporate strategy for people at work—the Volvo experience (paper at The international Conference on the Quality of Working Life, Toronto, 1981)—also Blackler F. and Brown C. *Job redesign and management control.* Saxon House, 1978. Also *Financial Times,* 1985, 19 Apr.

20. Peters T. and Waterman R. *In search of excellence.* Harper and Row, 1982.

21. Maccoby M. *The leader: a new face for American management.* Simon and Schuster, 1981.

Further Reading

There is a vast literature on the subject of humanising work through redesigning jobs and work organisation. A useful bibliography can be found in Smith and Robertson (1985) below.

Computer Technology, Work Content and Organisation

Cooley M. *Architect or bee? The human price of technology.* Hogarth Press, 1987. Sees scientific management principles being utilised in the design of computer systems, particularly where office automation is concerned.

Thompson P. *The nature of work.* Macmillan, 1983. A well informed, clear and critical introduction to the debates on job and work organisation; chapters 4 and 5 are particularly useful.

Wood S. (ed.). *The degradation of work? Skill, deskilling and the labour process.* Several leading authorities assess and develop the 'Braverman thesis' that Taylorism in work design is still a fundamental form of managerial control.

Alternatives to Scientific-Management-Based Approaches

Bailey J. *Job design and work organisation.* Prentice-Hall, 1983. A sound, descriptive, if a little uncritical, review of the subject area; chapter 9 is specifically on new technology.

Buchanan D. and Boddy D. *Organisations in the computer age: technological imperatives and strategic choice.* Gower, 1983. Contains very interesting case studies on managerial objectives and the consequences for job design and work organisation.

Francis A. *New technology at work*. Oxford University Press, 1986.

Knights D., Willmott H. and Collinson D. *Job redesign—critical perspectives on the labour process*. Gower, 1985. An important collection of essays, many of which assess the relationship between computerisation and different approaches to job design and work organisation.

Robertson I. and Smith M. *Motivation and job design*. Institute of Personnel Management, 1985. A sound guide to the theories of motivation underlying job redesign practices.

Socio-Technical Systems Approaches

Buchanan D. and Boddy D. *Managing new technology*. Basil Blackwell, 1986. Develops a socio-technical systems perspective on designing and introducing computer-based systems; very clearly written; see particularly chapter 5.

Susman G. and Chase R. A socio-technical analysis of the integrated factory. *Journal of Applied Behavioral Science*, 1986, **22**, No. 3.

Taylor J. Long-term sociotechnical systems change in a computer operations department. *Journal of Applied Behavioral Science*, 1986, **22**, No. 3.

The Commitment Organisation and Moves to Flexibility

The following are useful starting points for looking at the commitment organisation and moves to 'flexibility'.

Gustavsen B. Evolving patterns of enterprise organisation: the move toward greater flexibility. *International Labour Review*, 1986, **125**, No. 4.

Peters T. and Waterman R. *In search of excellence*. Harper and Row, 1982.

Walton R. From control to commitment in the workplace. *Harvard Business Review*, 1985, Mar.–Apr.

Walton R. and Susman B. People policies for the new machines. *Harvard Business Review*, 1987, Mar.–Apr.

CHAPTER 6. WORKING WITH COMPUTERS—2. ENVIRONMENT AND WORKSTATION

References

1. Bennett J., Case D., Sandelin J. and Smith M. (eds). *Visual display terminals*. Prentice Hall, 1984.
2. DeMatteo B. *Terminal shock*. NC Press, 1986.
3. Manwaring T. The trade union response to new technology. *Industrial Relations Journal*, 1981, **12**, No. 4.
4. Williams R. and Steward F. Technology agreements in Great Britain: a survey 1977–1983. *Industrial Relations Journal*, 1985. Autumn.
5. Labour Research Department. Bargaining report no. 22.
6. Labour Research Department. *VDU's health and jobs*. 1985.
7. Association of Professional, Executive, Clerical & Computer Staff. *New technology—a health and safety report*. APEX, 1985.
8. Health and Safety Executive. *Visual display units*. HMSO, 1983.

9. International Labour Office. *Visual display units: job content and stress in office work*. ILO, 1986.
10. Smith M. Health issues in VDU work [review]. In *Visual display terminals* (ed. Bennett J.). Prentice Hall, 1984.
11. IBM. *Human factors of workstations and visual displays*. IBM, 1984.
12. National Communications Union. *The small screen with big problems*. NCU, 1986.
13. Arndt R. Working posture and musculoskeletal problems of VDT operators—review and reappraisal. *American Journal of Industrial Hygiene*, 1983, **44**.
14. See Cooper and Cox. Occupational stress among word processor operators. *Journal of Stress Medicine*, 1985.
15. Pierce B. (ed.). *Health hazards of VDTs?* John Wiley and Sons, 1984.
16. Report of London conference on allegations of reproductive hazards from VDUs. *Health and Safety Information Bulletin 109*, Jan. 1985.
17. Pierce B. VDUs—will the screen take the strain? *Personnel Management*, 1986, July.
18. Canadian Labour Congress. *Towards a more humanized technology*. Canadian Labour Congress, 1982.
19. Eason K. Human factors in information technology. *Phys. Technol.*, 1982, **13**.
20. Peltu M. *Successful management of office automation*. National Computing Centre, 1984.
21. Stewart T. Communicating with dialogues. *Ergonomics*, 1980, **23**, No. 9.
22. Schneider M. and Thomas J. The humanization of computer interfaces. *Communications of the ACM*, 1983, **26**, No. 4.
23. Hammond N., Long J., Morton J., Barnard P. and Clark A. *Documenting human–computer mismatch at the individual and organisational levels*. IBM Research Report HFO40. IBM, Hampshire, 1981.
24. Norman D. Design rules based on analyses of human error. *Communications of the ACM*, 1983, **26**, No. 4.
25. Reported in the *Health And Safety Information Bulletin 130*, Oct. 1986.

Further Reading

Ergonomics, Health and Safety Issues and VDU, Workstation and Environment Design
Bennett J., Case D., Sandelin J. and Smith M. (eds). *Visual display terminals*. Prentice Hall, 1984.
DeMatteo B. *Terminal shock*. NC Press, 1986. The title is true to its contents, but DeMatteo has very carefully researched the area of health hazards, and does not make his claims lightly.
Health and Safety Information Bulletin. An excellent source of up-to-date materials, published together with the *Industrial Relations Review and Report*; see, for example:

VDU round-up. *Health and Safety Information Bulletin 130*, Oct. 1986.
No evidence found for alleged VDU hazards. *Health and Safety Information Bulletin 109*, Jan. 1985.

Oborne D. *Computers at work: a behavioural approach*. John Wiley and Sons, 1985. A comprehensive, well researched technical review of workstation, dialogue and environmental design.

Health and Safety Issues

Association of Professional, Executive, Clerical & Computer Staff. *New technology—a health and safety report*. APEX, 1985.

Cox S. *Change and stress in the modern office*. Further Education Unit/ PICKUP, 1986, occasional paper.

International Labour Office. *Visual display units: job content and stress in office work*. ILO, 1986.

Pierce B. (ed.). *Health hazards of VDT's*. John Wiley and Sons, 1986.

Ergonomic Design and Computers

Grandjean E. (ed.). *Ergonomics and health in modern offices*. Taylor and Francis, 1984.

Sinclair M. Ergonomic aspects of the automated factory. *Ergonomics*, 1986, **29**, No. 12.

Stewart T. Ergonomics of the office. *Ergonomics*, 1985, **28**, Aug.

Dialogue Design

Dialogue design can seem a highly specialised area. The following are amongst the clearest general guides.

Cole I., Landsdale M. and Christie B. Dialogue design guidelines. In *Human factors of information technology in the office* (ed. Christie B.). John Wiley and Sons, 1985.

Norman D. Design rules based on analyses of human error. *Communications of the ACM*, 1987, **26**, No. 4.

Otway H. and Peltu M. *New office technology: human and organizational aspects*. Frances Pinter, 1983; particularly chapters 10 and 11.

CHAPTER 7. COMPUTER TECHNOLOGY AND INDUSTRIAL RELATIONS

References

1. Cooley M. Computers, politics and unemployment. In *Microchips with everything* (ed. Sieghart P.). Comedia ICA, 1982.
2. Trade unionist quoted by Moore R. and Levie H. In *The information technology revolution* (ed. Forester T.). Basil Blackwell, 1985.
3. Personnel manager quoted by Fogarty M. and Brooks D. *Trade unions and British industrial development*. Policy Studies Institute, 1986.
4. Davies A. The management–union relationship in the introduction of new technology. In *The management implications of new information technology* (ed. Piercy N.). Croom Helm, 1984.
5. Willman P. *New technology and industrial relations: a review of the literature*. Department of Employment, 1986, research paper 56.

6. Willcocks L. and Mason D. The DHSS operational strategy 1975–1986. Business case file in *Information Technology*. Van Nostrand Reinhold, 1986.
7. Quoted in *The Times*, 1981, Oct.
8. Brown W. and Sisson K. *Industrial relations in the future*. Routledge & Kegan Paul, 1984.
9. Purcell J. and Sisson K. Strategies and practice in the management of industrial relations. In *Industrial relations in Britain* (ed. Bain G.) Blackwell, 1983.
10. Brown W. (ed). *The changing contours of British industrial relations*. Blackwell, 1980.
11. Daniel W. and Millward N. *Workplace industrial relations*. Heinemann, 1983.
12. Batstone E. *Working order*. Blackwell, 1984.
13. Batstone E. and Gourlay S. *Unions, unemployment and innovation*. Blackwell, 1986.
14. Northcott J. and Fogarty M. *Acceptance of new technology*. Policy Studies Institute working papers, 1985.
15. Fogarty M. with Brooks, D. *Trade Unions and British industrial development*. PSI, 1986.
16. Willcocks L. and Mason D. Computerising: lessons from the DHSS pensions strike. *Employee Relations*, 1987, **9**, No. 1.
17. Willman P. and Winch G. The making of the Metro. In *The information technology revolution* (ed. Forester T.). Blackwell, 1985. The authors quote a survey in *Engineer*, 1984, 9 Feb.
18. Scarbrough H. The politics of technological change at British Leyland. In *Technological change, rationalisation and industrial relations* (eds Jacobi E., Jessop B., Kastendiek H. and Regini M.). Croom Helm, 1986.
19. Report of a joint management–union visit to Japan by Thorn/EMI Ferguson quoted in *Industrial Relations Review and Report*, 1984, June.
20. Daniel W. and Millward N. *Workplace industrial relations*. Heinemann, 1983.
21. British Institute of Management. *Employee participation*. BIM, 1981.
22. National Economic Development Office. *The introduction of new technology*. NEDO, 1983.
23. Cadbury Somerdale—the Management of Change. *Industrial Relations Review and Report 328*, 1984, 25 Sept.
24. Davies A. *Industrial relations and new technology*. University of Wales Institute of Science and Technology/Croom Helm, 1986.
25. Quoted in the *Financial Times*, 1984, 23 May.
26. Martin R. Quoted in the *Financial Times*, 1986, 13 Mar.
27. Moore R., and Levie H. New technology and the unions. In *The information technology revolution* (ed. Forester T.). Blackwell, 1985.
28. Ruskin College. *Workers and new technology: disclosure and use of company information—final and summary report*. Ruskin, 1984.
29. Wilkinson B. *The shopfloor politics of new technology*. Heinemann, 1983.
30. Manwaring T. The trade union response to new technology. *Industrial Relations Journal*, 1981, Autumn.

31. Daniel W. *Workplace industrial relations and technical change*. Policy Studies Institute/Frances Pinter, 1987.
32. Williams R. and Moseley R. Technology agreements: consensus, control and technical change in the workplace. In *Information society: for richer for poorer* (ed. Bjorn-Andersen N.). North Holland.
33. Williams R. and Moseley R. Technology agreements in Great Britain: a survey 1977–83. *New Technology, Employment and Skill*, 1985, Autumn.
34. Labour Research Department. Bargaining report 22, 1982.
35. Batstone E. The durability of the British shop steward. *Personnel Management*, 1985, Oct.

Further Reading
General Reviews

Daniel W. *Workplace industrial relations and technical change*. PSI/Francis Pinter, 1987.

Davies A. *Industrial relations and new technology*. Croom Helm, 1986. University of Wales Institute of Science and Technology. Part 1 provides a very useful overview; part 2 is concerned with detailed case studies.

Northcott J., Fogarty M. and Trevor M. *Chips and jobs: acceptance of new technology at work*. Policy Studies Institute, 1985, No. 648. A thorough review; the subheading summarises its main findings.

Willman P. *New technology and industrial relations: a review of the literature*. Department of Employment, 1986, Research paper 56. Provides an excellent bibliography; chapter 6 is a succinct and very useful sectoral analysis of industrial relations and technical change.

General managerial objectives

In addition to the sources cited above, see the following.

Buchanan D. Management objectives in technical change. In *Managing the labour process* (eds Knights D. and Willmott H.). Gower, 1986.

Purcell J. and Sisson K. Strategies and practice in the management of industrial relations. In *Industrial relations in Britain* (ed. Bain G.). Blackwell, 1983.

Storey J. The phoney war? New office technology: organisation and control. In *Managing the labour process* (eds Knights D. and Willmott H.). Gower, 1986. Finds managements in insurance firms have not fully exploited the control potential of the new technology; suggests they may well do so once a period of understandable tentativeness and experimentation ends.

Trade Union Responses

Association of Professional, Executive, Clerical and Computer Staff. *Job design and new technology*. Apex, 1985.

Batstone E. and Gourlay S. *Unions, unemployment and innovation*. Blackwell, 1986.

Corina J. Trade unions and technical change. In *The trouble with technology*, (eds MacDonald S., Lamberton D. and Mandeville T.). Frances Pinter, 1983.

Dodgson M. and Martin R. Trade union policies on new technology: facing the challenges of the 1980s. *New Technology, Work and Employment*, 1987, **2**, No. 1.

Manwaring T. The trade union response to new technology. *Industrial Relations Journal*, 1981, **12**, No. 1.

New Technology Agreements
Details of new technology agreements often appear in *Industrial Relations Review and Report*, which is published every fortnight. Broader reviews are provided in the following.
Hillage J., Meager N. and Rajan A. *Technology agreements in practice: the experience so far*. Institute of Manpower Studies, 1986, Report 113. Additional evidence supporting our conclusions.
Labour Research Department. *Survey of new technology*. 1982, Bargaining Report 22.
Williams R. and Moseley R. Technology agreements in Great Britain: a survey 1977–83. *Industrial Relations Journal*, 1985, **16**, No. 3.

Studies of Industrial Relations in Major Sectors
Child J. and Tarbuck M. The introduction of new technologies: managerial initiative and union response in British banks. *Industrial Relations Journal*, 1985, Autumn.
Lintner V., Pokorny M., Woods M. and Blinkhorn M. Trade unions and technological change in the UK mechanical engineering industry. *British Journal of Industrial Relations*, 1987, Mar. Supports the general picture put forward by Daniel and Fogharty of union acceptance of technical change in the 1980s.
Martin R. *New technology and industrial relations in Fleet Street*. Oxford: Clarendon Press, 1981. Covers the slow moves in national newspaper companies toward computer-based systems throughout the 1970s.
Norton J. *Management practices, new technology and industrial relations in the UK national newspaper industry—a study of the News International Initiative*. Thesis, London School of Economics, 1986. Updates Martin and provides a detailed analysis of the Wapping dispute.
Thompson P. and Bannon E. *Working the system: the shop floor and new technology*. Pluto Press, 1985. A study of the introduction of new technology at a Plessey plant.
Willcocks L. and Mason D. Computerising—lessons from the DHSS pensions strike. *Employee Relations*, 1987, **9**, No. 1.
Willman P. *Technological change, collective bargaining and industrial efficiency*. Oxford University Press, 1986. Includes research in the car industry and banking.
Winterton J. Computerised coal: new technology in the mines. In *Digging deeper—issues in the miners' strike*. Verso Publications, 1985.

CHAPTER 8. MANAGING IMPLEMENTATION

References
1. Braun E. Constellations for manufacturing innovation. In *Implementing new technologies* (eds Rhodes E. and Wield D.). Blackwell, 1985.

2. Leonard-Barton D. and Kraus W. Implementing new technology. *Harvard Business Review*, 1985, Nov.

3. Strassman P. *Information payoff*. Free Press, 1985, p. 237.

4. Dickson G. and Wetherbe J. *The management of information systems*. McGraw Hill, 1985.

5. Hirschheim R. *Office automation*. John Wiley, 1986, p. 279.

6. Keen P. VDT's as agents of change. In *Visual display terminals* (eds Bennett J., Case D., Sandelin, J. and Smith M.). Prentice Hall, 1984.

7. Lewin K. discussed in Schein E. *Organizational psychology*, Prentice Hall, 1980.

8. Kolb D. and Frohman A. An organizational development approach to consulting. *Sloan Management Review*, 1970, Autumn.

9. The terminology is from Argyris C.—*Intervention theory and method: a behavioral science view*. Addison-Wesley, 1970—but the ideas are representative of many OD writers.

10. Desanctis G. and Courtney J. Toward friendly user MIS implementation. *Communications of the ACM*, 1983, **26**, No. 10.

11. For example—Burack E. and Sorenson P. Management preparation for computer automation: emergent patterns and problems. *Academy of Management Journal*, 1979, **19**—Bostrom R. and Heinen S. MIS problems and failures: a socio-technical perspective—Part 1: The causes. *MIS Quarterly*, 1977, **1**, No. 2—Rothwell S. and Davidson D. *Technological change, company personnel policies and skill deployment*. Manpower Services Commission, 1984.

12. Waters S. A DIY approach to systems. *Participation in system design: proceedings of conference held at London Business School, April 1987* (ed. Land F.). (To be published.)

13. Land F. Social aspects of information systems. In *Management information systems: the technology challenge* (ed. Piercy N.). Croom Helm, 1987.

14. A full discussion of the limitations of OD techniques appears in McLean A.—Organisation development: a case of the Emperor's new clothes? *Personnel Review*, 1981, **10**, No. 1.

15. Kochan T. and Dyer L. A model of organizational change in the context of union–management relations. *Journal of Applied Science*, 1976, **12**.

16. Alderfer C. Organization development. *Annual Review of Psychology*, 1977, **28**.

17. A wider discussion appears in French W. and Bell C.—*Organizational development: behavioural science interventions for organizational improvement*. Prentice Hall, 1984.

18. Beer M. *Organizational change and development: a systems view*. Goodyear, 1980.

19. Miller E. Organizational development and industrial democracy. In *Organization development in the UK and USA: a joint evaluation* (ed. Cooper C.). Macmillan, 1977.

20. Major advocates include Bjorn-Anderson N. and Hedberg B.—Designing information systems in an organizational perspective. *TIMS Studies in Management Sciences*, 1977, **5**—Mumford E.—*Designing human systems*. (Manchester Business School, 1983—Land F. and Hirschheim R.—

Participative system design: rationale, tools and techniques. *Journal of Applied Systems Analysis*, 1983, **10**—Bostrom R. and Heinen S.—MIS problems and failures: socio-technical perspective—Part 1. The causes. *MIS Quarterly*, 1977, **1**, No. 2—Pava C.—*Managing new office technology: an organizational strategy*. Free Press, 1983.

21. Keen P. Information systems and organizational change. *Communications of the ACM*, 1981, **24**, No. 1.

22. Eason K. and Sell R. Case studies in job design for information processing tasks. In *Stress, work design and productivity* (eds Corlett E. and Richardson J.). Wiley, 1981.

23. For a sample only see Robey D. and Farrow D.—Information system development: a conflict model and empirical test. *Management Science*, 1982, **28**, No. 1—Lucas H.—*Towards creative systems design*. Columbia University Press, 1974—Gibson H.—Determining user involvement. *Journal of Systems Management*, 1977, Aug.—Lucas H.—*Information systems concepts for management*. McGraw Hill, 1982.

24. Mumford E. The participative design of clerical information systems. In *The human side of information processing* (ed. Bjorn-Andersen N.). North Holland, 1980.

25. Ives B. and Olson M. User involvement and MIS success: a review of research. *Management Science*, 1984, **30**, No. 5.

26. Russell J. The implementation of new technology: a question of attitudes. *Industrial and Commercial Training*, 1981, Mar.

27. Pettigrew A. *The politics of organisational decision-making*. Tavistock, 1983. Also Mumford E. and Pettigrew A. *Implementing strategic decisions*. Longman, 1975.

28. Mangham I. *The politics of organisational change*. Greenwood, 1979.

29. See Crozier M. *The bureaucratic phenomenon*. University of Chicago Press, 1964, p. 205.

30. Markus M. Power, politics and implementation. *Communications of the ACM*, 1983, **26**, No. 6.

31. Pettigrew A. Information control as a power resource. *Sociology*, 1972, **6**.

32. Pettigrew A. *The awakening giant: continuity and change in ICI*. Blackwell, 1985.

33. Details of these cases can be found in Curson C. *Flexible patterns of work*. Institute of Personnel Management, 1986.

34. Keen P. and Gerson E. The politics of software design. *Datamation*, 1977, Nov.

35. Scarbrough H. and Moran P. How new tech won at Longbridge. *New Statesman*, 1985, 7 Feb.

36. Hedley R. Organizational objectives and managerial controls: a study of computerisation. In *Industrial organisation—behaviour and control* (ed. Woodward J.). Oxford University Press, 1970.

37. Mayes B. and Allen R. Toward a definition of organizational politics. *Academy of Management Review*, 1977, **2**.

38. Suggested by Schein V. Organisational realities: the politics of change. *Training and Development Journal*, 1985, Feb.

39. Pettigrew A. Towards a political theory of organisational intervention.

Human Relations, 1975, **28**, No. 3.

40. Beckhard R. and Harris R. *Organizational transitions*. Addison-Wesley, 1977.
41. Nadler D. and Tichy N. In *Organisation development in health care organisations* (eds Margulies N. and Adams J.). Addison-Wesley, 1981.
42. This is close to the interactionist theory of Markus, [30] except that she sees the political–cultural approach as only one alternative amongst many. Our point is that given the nature of organisations, every approach to computerisation has to be a political–cultural one; i.e. all implementation approaches have to be sensitive to, deal with, organisational political and cultural circumstances.
43. Lloyd J. and Hague H. *Financial Times*, 1986, 27 Jan.
44. Wainwright J. and Francis A. *Office automation, organisation and the nature of work*, Gower 1984.

Further Reading
There is plenty of advice available on how to implement computer-based systems. Much of it runs into problems when attempting to convert specific experiences and observations into general rules applicable to all systems projects. A lot of the advice, it has to be admitted, deals in platitudes. The following sources are among the more considered and illuminating on the subject of managing implementation.

Overviews
Boddy D. and Buchanan D. *Managing new technology*. Basil Blackwell, 1986.
Rhodes E. and Wield D. (eds). *Implementing new technologies*. Blackwell, 1985. Mainly concerned with manufacturing industry, but contains many interesting articles by a range of authorities.
Strassman P. *Information payoff: the transformation of work in the electronic age*. Free Press, 1985. A major study of office automation in the USA; full of advice, mainly for managers.
Thompson L. *New office technology: people, work structure and the process of change*. Work Research Unit, 1985, WRU Occasional Paper 34. Useful review of case studies, with a list of recommendations on implementing change.

The Systems Analyst as Change Agent
The best article on the systems analyst as change agent is the following.
Desanctis G. and Courtney J. Toward friendly user MIS implementation. *Communications of the ACM*, 1983, **26**, No. 10. But see our critique.

Participative Implementation
Some sources on participative implementation appear under participative design (further reading chapter 4). Also see the following.
Bjorn-Anderson N. and Hedberg B. Designing information systems in an organizational perspective. *TIMS Studies in Management Sciences*, 1977, **5**.
Mumford E. The participative design of clerical information systems. In *The*

human side of information processing (ed. Bjorn-Andersen N.). North Holland, 1980.

Mumford E. *Using computers for business success.* Manchester Business School, 1986.

Pava C. *Managing new office technology: an organizational strategy.* Free Press, 1983. Develops an STS approach to office automation, relating the design of technology to different types of office task.

Taylor J. and Asadorian R. The implementation of excellence: STS management. *Industrial Management*, 1985, **27**, No. 4.

Management of Politics as an Implementation Task

Keen P. Information systems and organizational change. *Communications of the ACM*, 1981, **24**, No. 1.

Keen P. *Competing in time.* Harper and Row, 1987. An excellent overview of implementation strategies and securing competitive advantage using IT.

Mangham I. *The politics of organisational change.* Greenwood, 1979.

Markus M. Power, politics and implementation. *Communications of the ACM*, 1983, **26**, No. 6. Includes an illuminating case study on computerising accounting functions in a large company.

Mayes B. and Allen R. Toward a definition of organizational politics. *Academy of Management Review*, 1977, **2**.

Pettigrew A. Towards a political theory of organisational intervention. *Human relations*, 1975, **28**, No. 3.

Schein V. Organisational realities: the politics of change. *Training and Development Journal*. 1985. Feb.

Index